Some of my best friends are French

Colin Corder

Illustrations by Pete Boggon

Shelf Publishing

First published in Great Britain in 1992 by:

Shelf Publishing
6, St Albans Road
Codicote
Hitchin
Herts SG4 8UT
England
Tel: 0438 820059
Fax: 0438 821015

British Library Cataloguing in Publication Data

Corder, Colin

Some of my best friends are French

ISBN 0 9519205 0 2

Printed by Island Press Ltd, 0323 490222 UK

Some of my best friends are French

In 1973 Colin Corder wrote the first ever speech given at the European Parliament by a British member of the Socialist Group. It was a protest against French atmospheric nuclear testing. Despite this inauspicious start, his visit to Strasbourg inspired his now annual pilgrimage to France. Graduating by way of camping, caravanning and *gîtes,* in 1982 he bought a house in the Rhône valley, nestling between the Cevennes, Massif Central and Alps.

Now, when he drives into his tiny Ardechois village, he is acknowledged by Paulot, who spends his entire life leaning against a wall (one leg having been shot off in a hunting accident). This recognition takes the form of bending his non-supporting hand upwards from the wrist through forty-five degrees. To anyone but an expert, it is imperceptible. But to Mr Corder it means more than the *Légion d'Honneur* which this contribution to the *entente cordiale* will surely win him.

Foreword

Colin Corder, connu pour ses écrits et grand connaisseur des valeurs françaises, est certainement tombé amoureux de la France, pour entreprendre un tel ouvrage. Il essaye dans son livre 'Some of my best friends are French' de faire partager ses sentiments. Il me semble, qu'il ne se contente pas seulement d'éclaircir les vieilles querelles franco-anglaises, car son ouvrage me paraît bien plus symbolique. Je pense, d'une part, qu'il est appréciable, que ce soit un anglais, qui prenne l'initiative de se pencher sur le problème et, d'autre part, (c'est là que cet ouvrage prend toute sa dimension), que Colin Corder montre un exemple à suivre.
Il nous donne une leçon; se battre contre les préjugés que nous avons tous, sur les habitants des pays qui nous entourent, simplement parce qu'ils vivent et parlent différement de nous.
Mais le plus appréciable, est qu'il ne nous dicte pas de conduite à suivre mais au contraire, il met à notre disposition tous les éléments pour que nous puissions avoir notre propre avis.
Sans prétention, il apporte des éclaircissements sur notre façon de vivre et sur nos valeurs.
Il raconte de manière objective et réaliste ce que sont les Français et vous laisse ainsi le choix de nous apprécier.

Excellent idée encore, que l'utilisation du dictionnaire. Pourquoi? Parce qu'un dictionnaire apporte une réponse claire et fiable à une question et qu'il est consulté lorsqu'on ne comprend un terme et que l'on fait l'effort d'en connaître la signification.
Un dictionnaire de plus, est consulté à tout âge, parce que la culture est infinie et qu'on ne cesse jamais d'apprendre et de comprendre.

Ce qu'il faut tirer de ce dictionnaire, c'est qu'il en fait, un outil à la disposition des hommes pour comprendre les hommes et pour qu'ainsi, ils s'enrichissent.

Serge Blanco

For Colin Corder, a writer with a great feel for France, this book has obviously been a labour of love. In 'Some of my best friends are French' he shares this love of France with us.
For centuries there has been rivalry between our two countries. As an Englishman he touches on this problem but in such a way as to give us all an example which we can follow. A lesson in combatting the prejudices which we all feel towards the inhabitants of other countries simply because their language and lifestyle are different from our own. His book symbolises a fresh approach.
What I appreciated more than anything is that he does not lecture us on how to behave but contents himself with explaining and then leaving each of us to form our own opinion. Without being either pretentious or patronising, he throws light on what French people believe and how they live. He describes, in an objective and realistic way who we, the French, are, and leaves you the choice of whether or not to accept us.

Writing the book in the form af an A to Z is an excellent idea. Why? Because this format means that at any time you know where to go when you want to look up a term and gives you an answer that is both clear and relevant. A dictionary is something that you can consult whatever your age; culture knows no bounds and we never cease to learn and understand. By means of this book we can learn to know each other better and in so doing enrich ourselves.

Serge Blanco

Introduction

Thousands of books have been written about France. Travel guides, telling you where to go, what to eat and drink and what sights to see. Books aimed at an academic or business audience, full of detailed information about everything from literature to multinationals. Finally there is the latest sort - those written by English people living in France. The latter are often written from an outsider's viewpoint describing the inhabitants, at worst, as though they were animals in a zoo, at best, as quaint relics of a rural age that has long disappeared in Britain.

What I have tried to do in this book is to present the French (as opposed to France) from their own standpoint; to concentrate on their values and beliefs, to give an impression of how a French person views the world. It is not uncritical. The French are people of strong opinions and, every so often, violent actions. They themselves are scornful of many of their compatriots - Corsicans are lazy, Auvergnats are mean - and contemptuous of their politicians. Just as they are proud of their writers and their language.

To present the French in this way I have first concentrated on the language. The book can be read and, I hope, enjoyed by a non-French speaker. But if you really want to get to know the people you need to be able to communicate something beyond *deux bières, s'il vous plait.* So the initial chapter looks at the language; but in a way that puts motivation before everything. The French themselves will help you in this. The most halting attempt will elicit an encouraging response. And it will open the door to the innumerable *gentillesses* of the sort that I and my family have enjoyed at the hands of our French friends and neighbours.

I have spent a fair part of my life in Australia. There, there is no difficulty with the language (well, not once you have come to terms with the Order of the Raw Prawn). But there is still a tremendous problem if you are a 'whingeing Pom'; if you complain that the beer is fizzy, the flies awful and the pubs not as good as those at home. We need to take other countries on their own terms, not look upon them as England enhanced with sun, mountains and cheap wine. To do this we need to be *sympathique* to the country - to know something of its history, geography, traditions, personalities and so on. Travel only broadens a mind that is open.

So after the initial chapter, the main body of the book therefore sets out to give you what a London taxi-driver would call 'The Knowledge'. Who are the historical personalities - equivalent to Henry VIII and Cromwell - that are known to all French people? Who are the French counterparts of Terry Wogan, Cliff Richard, Graham Taylor, Charles Dickens, Bruce Forsythe and Paddy Ashdown? What are the differences in education, health, sport, sex and social customs?

Many more authoritative books have been written. But most of them run to over five hundred pages and are read only by students. This book is an attempt to make available in a readable form the information that such books contain (and a fair amount that they don't). To emphasise the difference from a conventional textbook, entries are mostly short and arranged in the form of an A to Z rather than into separate chapters on language, geography, history, entertainment and so on. Putting entries into alphabetical sequence makes for amusing bedfellows. Thus Michel Rocard has Rodin to thank for not being wedged between two revolutionaries, Robespierre and Rousseau. For historical entries chronological sequence is a casualty. Mitterrand comes before Napoleon who in turn precedes Vercingétorix.

The book is written in a light-hearted way not to trivialise the subject matter but to make it easy to read. But it has a serious intent - which is to make France, and above all French people, more accessible to the British. The suffix -ist, as in sexist, racist and disablist has somehow acquired the meaning of 'having prejudices based on...' There is a case to be made, therefore, for the adjective 'Frenchist' to describe people who write off all French people as unfortunate excrescences on an otherwise beautiful country. For people of that opinion this book is meant as a corrective blast.

You may find it instructive. If so, I hope it is as a by-product of your enjoyment of the book and not through any conscious effort at self-improvement. To that end, I have included original French words in the text. These are words which remain familiar from schooldays or which are readily understandable through being close to their equivalent English word in spelling. Well before the end you will be muttering inwardly: *'Ça, c'est evident'* or *'C'est normal'* and thinking of *l'Assemblée Nationale* rather than the National Assembly. Not through having set out to learn them for a vocabulary test but simply through having seen them a number of times in context. Where a word or expression is not obvious to a non-French speaker I have either translated it in situ or included it in the glossary at the back. Finally, I have resisted the frequent temptation to use "See also's" or "q.v's" judging that these interfere with the flow.

The book itself can serve as an example of how easy it is, given the right motivation, to make a little go a long way. I have, to my great regret, never lived in France, nor stayed there for more than six weeks at a time and then in the company of my English-speaking family. Yet by adopting the approach to the language described in the book my long-forgotten schoolboy French became more than adequate, and by interesting myself in what is going on around me I have learned a little about a fascinating country.So be encouraged. *Allez-y!*

This book could not have been written without a little help from my friends - or, less allusively but more accurately, a lot of help. Pride of place goes to Françoise Mason whose *farouche* defence of the French language, French writers, come to think of it of everything French, did much to keep the record straight in face of my attempts to be *humoristique.* Were this a Royal Commission she would probably have written a minority report to the effect that not all French people are hypochondriacs and not all writers were sex-crazed; as it is I have included the occasional dissenting footnote. Keeping the peace between us was her husband, Andrew, who also contributed many improvements.

Another Englishman with the good fortune to have a French wife is Rory Downham who found time, in between setting up a Franco-British club in Lyon, to suggest new entries and improve existing ones. To Gérard Mermet and Larousse I acknowledge my debt in allowing me to plunder the invaluable book *Francoscopie.* To Philip Jacobson of the Times I am indebted for putting their Paris office and archives at my disposal. I am also grateful to Richard Binns for encouraging me to self-publish when my study was littered with rejection slips. Finally my thanks to Janice at AMM for photocopying and binding successive drafts of the book. I write books the way other people paint walls - in a succession of coats each one of which covers up some of the deficiencies of its predecessor. I hope this did not need just one more coat....

What they didn't teach you in French class

Why are the British so reluctant to learn foreign languages? The answer - leaving aside the belief that everyone should speak English - is twofold. The effort involved - it takes ages to learn a language; and the perception that they were no good at languages at school.
To the first of these objections I cite a Frenchman's answer. Told that a particular project would take fifty years, General de Gaulle replied, 'Then the sooner we get started, the better'. But the second objection is the bigger obstacle. The notion that French is difficult. 'Ah, but I was never any use at languages', you say. Well, French five-year olds don't seem to have too many problems. No, your problem is that you learned your French at school. Most schoolteaching - French, Latin, Shakespeare, Geography, History - is an advanced form of aversion therapy. Your main satisfaction in leaving school is that never again will you have to learn irregular verbs, dates of battles, geological formations or speeches from Macbeth.

Think back to how you were taught French:

- *You dared not get anything wrong.* This led to a permanent disinclination to open your mouth in case you made a grammatical error. Errors were punished by 'doing corrections' or losing marks in exams.

- *The emphasis was on writing, not speaking.* In a precise reversal of the priorities when you are actually in the country, the oral part of a French exam accounted for only 10% of the total marks.

- *The method of teaching could have been expressly designed to destroy motivation.* What reward did you get for finally mastering the intricacies of the conditional tense? You progressed to the subjunctive!

- *Much of what you were taught is of little use in France and much of what is of most use is not taught.* For a start you can throw the past historic straight out of the window, rapidly followed by the subjunctive. Yet many people who, through years of rote learning, can still recite the future tense of an -ir verb, have never been taught the essential word *le truc'*. If there is one word that it is universally useful it is the word for a 'thingumajig'.

Let us see the difference that just that last piece of new knowledge can make. The battery light on your car dashboard is permanently on. Being a bit of a mechanic you suspect that it is the alternator that is the problem. Along with me, you haven't the foggiest notion of the French for 'alternator'. But you do know *'le truc'* and you have mastered another vital expression - 'isn't working'. Result, you go into the nearest garage, point at the alternator and explain *'ce truc ne marche pas'*. Simple isn't it? And you aren't now asked to write out and learn the French for alternator, you get your car fixed and the admiration of your offspring.

Put another way, you have *débrouillé* (sorted yourself out). I doubt whether you learned that at school either but it is one of the first expressions you need when you start to speak French in France. Your first nervous effort, full of grammatical howlers, will be greeted as the clearest evidence of incipient command of the language. *'Mais vous parlez bien français'*. What do you say to that? If you issue a modest disclaimer *'Non'* or more ambitiously *'un petit peu'*, this will merely cause your listeners to redouble their congratulations sensing that they have not been sufficiently eulogistic. No, the expression you need is *'Je me débrouille'* (I get by). Now you will immediately come face to face with another difference between school French and real French. Your listener will almost certainly repeat what you have said, adding a *'bien'* for emphasis and, of course, using the 'you' form rather than the 'I' form. *'Mais vous vous débrouillez bien'*, he says. You mutter a quick *'Merci'* and honour is satisfied. But in the exchange you have experienced that valuable learning process - reinforcement. Provided you are willing to have a go, speaking French is a lot simpler than ever you thought. Let us start by adopting an approach as far removed from learning French at school as canoeing down the Ardèche is from memorising the names of capital cities.

You reach your holiday destination late at night. In the morning your neighbours ask you when you arrived. Having racked your memory you construct the following reply: *'Nous avons arrivé hier soir'*, In written French this is *une catastrophe.* You have completely forgotten that *'arriver'* is one of those damned verbs that are conjugated with *'être'*. Moreover, this means that the past participle has to agree with the subject and have an 's' at the end. Go to the bottom of the class!

But not here. Here in St Maurice-sur-Cèze you are communicating. In spoken French you don't have to worry about putting 'e' and 's' on the end of things. Madame Martin would not know an auxiliary verb or past participle if she tripped over one. And, far from making you look silly, grammatical mistakes can be quite *charmantes.* After all, though we admire a French person who speaks perfect English, we warm to those who come out with quaint phrases like 'I am in London since six weeks'. Grammar is unimportant. You are no longer trying to get a good mark in your GCSE or A-level, you are trying to establish social contact with a fellow member of the human race. This gives us our first and most important rule:

Rule 1: ***You do not have to get things right.***

Let us go back to the *'Je me débrouille'* phrase. Every time you get into a conversation with a different French person you will be able to use this. Of course, you will have to have said something else first. But what is this likely to be? Well, if you have struck up an acquaintance with the people next to you on the campsite the odds are that they will ask you where you come from. *'Nous sommes de Cleckheaton. C'est dans le nord de l'Angleterre.'* Repeat that to every new person you meet and you will become fluent. 'Fluent' is probably not a word that you customarily use to describe your ability in foreign languages. But you will become fluent - here's the secret - in two sentences. You have taken the 'single step'.

Suppose there is a strike at Calais which forces you to go via Ostend. You then follow a different route through France from your usual one. Simple. Look up the French for 'on strike' *(en grève).* Your revised route consists mainly of placenames which are easy anyway. In no time you have constructed a mini conversation piece which you repeat at every occasion. At a more advanced level I once taught my teenage daughter the French for 'I'm annoyed that I speak French so badly' *(Ça m'embête de parler si mal le français).* This is a show-stopper. Every French male between the ages of sixteen and sixty (and a few beyond) immediately leapt in to deny the proposition and to assure her that, *au contraire,* she had made *'beaucoup de progrès'* .

For many years I made a good living on the international lecturing circuit by following the simple rule which sums up this approach. Apply it to languages and experience a *succès fou.*

Rule 2: ***It is easier to say the same thing to different people than to say different things to the same people.***

You are a lover of Chopin. You decide that you would like to master one party piece - the Revolutionary Etude is what you have in mind. Regrettably it is not possible to concentrate all your attention exclusively on one piece of music and thereby reach concert level. You cannot become proficient in selected areas - good at Chopin but useless at Brahms. Playing the piano is a seamless garment; you have to master scales, fingering and so on before you can play anything well. You would never get anywhere if you only had two or three weeks a year in which to practise. But learning a language is not like piano-playing. You can become proficent in specific areas. I speak French nowhere near fluently. But were you to listen to me talking about the Ardèche you might think I was fluent (a Frenchman wouldn't). Ask me to discuss basketball, racism or DIY and I flounder like anyone else.

Why did the Thames use to freeze over in the 19th century and not now? Not because winters were colder or the Thames flowed more slowly. It was because London Bridge had many arches. Ice could form around the base of these and finally join up. If you split any language into small areas of vocabulary you reduce the problem of communicatiing to manageable proportions. Ultimately your areas will join up.

Rule 3. ***Divide and conquer.***

School French always concentrated far too much on extending your vocabulary and far too little on how to make best use of what you already have. The most frequently used word colloquially to describe something that is particularly good is *'impeccable'*. Latch onto it and do away with *'formidable'*, *'exceptionnel'*, *'merveilleux'* and so on. Of course if your ultimate aim is to be elected to the *Académie Française* things are different, but for our immediate purposes one word for anything will suffice.
Along with this there are a number of everyday expressions that simplify things immensely. If your schooldays are sufficiently close, you may remember struggling with the irregular verb *'devoir'* 'to have to'. *Je dois, tu dois, il/elle doit, nous devons, vous devez, ils/ elles doivent* - and that's only the present tense! There's still the imperfect, *passé composé, passé simple,* future, conditional, pluperfect and subjunctive to go. Forget the whole lot. Get used to *'il faut'* as in *'il faut partir'* (we have to go) and you need never decline *'devoir'* again.

Rule 4: ***A little goes a long way.***

From the time that I left school I have never sat down to learn grammar or new vocabulary. I may have looked up a word that I was going to need, or that I did not understand in the paper, but always as a means to a specific, immediate end. Depending on your starting level, songs, crosswords, sport, television, Mills & Boon novels (called 'rosewater books') are excellent and painless ways to improve. Of course, the French, with their obsession with sex, insist that to learn properly *'il faut apprendre sur l'oreiller'* (the only place is in bed). Whilst the approach I am advocating is known in the training business as 'experiential learning' the latter application of it is, *je regrette,* outside the scope of this book. Nevertheless, the principle is unimpeachable - although this will not be accepted as mitigating evidence in your divorce. But what you can, and should, do is to take advantage of the well-known phenomenon that the quickest route to fluency is through liberal infusions of Mâcon Blanc.

Rule 5. ***Make learning a by-product of some other activity that you find enjoyable.***

From Theory to Practice...

The preceding rules form the basis of enjoyable learning. It remains to put them into practice. The key to learning a language is motivation and the willingness to 'have a go'. The greatest obstacle to most people is not grammar but confidence. Confidence comes from success, which is gained by a series of short steps each of which reinforces that which you have already learned. Learning a language is like a snowball that gets larger by gathering more snow as it rolls.

Les premiers pas

This book assumes that you have retained some vague knowledge of French from your schooldays. But in case your memory extends no further than *bonjour* and *merci,* let us start our confidence-building from the lowest possible base. What you have to do is learn a few words and then use them. For two reasons the first words to learn in any language are the numbers. The first reason is that these are the most widely useful. The second concerns the necessity to practise. If you mug up on the weather you will have difficulty in finding a local to practise on. The low level of your French makes conversation difficult with a stranger. But shop-keepers and barmen have to talk to you. So you start with the numbers and apply them to money. You learn to say *'seize francs, cinquante'*.

Take it gently. The simplest way is to go to a *supermarché,* restrict your purchases to pre-packaged items, then look at the till to see how much you owe. On your next visit you go to the *fromagerie* and buy fresh cheese. The additional amount of vocabulary is small. You now point at whichever sort of cheese you want and say 'this one' or 'that one' - *ça* will do for both. If there is a piece already cut of the right size then *'ce morceau'* is what you say. Failing this, the assistant will want to know how much to serve you. To do this he will position his knife on the cheese and wait to see whether he has suggested the right amount. Note that if panic sets in at this moment you can *vous débrouiller* by taking whatever is proffered. But all you need to know are the words for 'more' - *'plus'* and 'less' - *'moins'*. If in doubt, 'stop' is international. After wrapping each item the assistant will ask you whether you want anything else *'et avec ça?'*. Keep pointing until you have got all you want, then just say *'c'est tout'*. That's it - your first live French conversation after one hour's study!

Another advantage of learning numbers is the many different opportunities for practice. On the autoroute you spend hours looking at the number plates of cars in front. Mentally split the numbers into lots of two and say them in French to yourself. You are making progress when you can handle the numbers between seventy and a hundred. When you are fed up with that, you stop. Learning must not become a chore. When you are ready to start again, you can try deciphering the road signs. *Ralentissez* will do for a start. Since this is a rather important instruction it is likely that there will be a translation available. If not, you risk finding out what 'action learning' is all about.

Until you have tried to learn a language - Russian, Arabic, Chinese - with a different script or alphabet, you do not appreciate how incredibly useful it is to be able to recognise words. Make use of that fact. With minimal effort you will learn, or recall, *fermé, ouvert, sortie, péage*. For an encore try *Attachez vos ceintures.*

C'est parti...

We now jump on..... By an application of our five rules (particularly that involving Mâcon Blanc) you are gaining confidence. But in life you solve one problem, you create another. Now we come across one which any newcomer to a language experiences. Whilst you can control what you say and stick to things you know, you cannot control what the other person says. Another good reason for starting in shops is that responses there are more predictable. But once you switch to your neighbours on the campsite you are (metaphorically) on your own.

So how to cope? The first thing you need is to slow them down. *Doucement, doucement* is what you need (repeating words is always good). This may do the trick but there is bound to come a time when you have not understood what has been said. The actual expression you need is, of course, *Je n'ai pas compris.* On occasions, however, you will decide to bluff your way through. You cannot ask someone to repeat every single thing they say. The secret here is to identify key words in what is being said and to pay careful attention to any inflections or gestures that, if not giving away the sense, at least indicate whether a *oui, non* or *voilà* is the appropriate response. The context will often give you the sense even where the words do not. If your new-found friends show you their four-month old baby you do not need to be a linguistic genius to gather that an admiring comment would be in order. *'Qu'il est mignon'* (or *'Qu'elle est mignonne'* according to sex) you mutter, and more evidence will have been given as to your command of the language. If you go back to the same place next year and meet the same child, just say *'Il a bien grandi'*

Common expressions

What causes an expression to become colloquial is frequency of use. What makes for frequency of use is frequency of situation. Common situations are those in which we want to say things like 'Don't bother' or 'Don't worry about it', or 'It's getting better'.

Frequent use almost invariably brings about a shortening of the original phrase. This is certainly true of French. Below I have give both the full and successively shortened version of the first example, and for subsequent ones, just the shortened, colloquial form.

Ce n'est pas grave: shortened to *'C'est pas grave'* or even *'pas grave'*. The literal meaning is 'It's not serious'. You use it when your neighbour has just backed his car into your tent or spilt wine over your new dress.

Pas la peine - literal meaning - 'It's not worth the trouble', colloquial meaning 'Don't bother'.

C'est normal (accompanied *obligatoirement* by a shrug of the shoulders). To translate this ubiquitous phrase by its literal equivalent 'It's normal' completely understates the world view that is wrapped up in the expression. *'C'est normal'* is a statement about the perversities of life - about the way the world works rather than how it is supposed to work. It can express amusement when someone is beating the system, acceptance or resignation when the system is beating them.

C'est très gentil (that's very kind') should be your automatic response to any favour *(petit service)* that is done to you.

English is one of the few languages that does not have an automatic rejoinder to being thanked, although the Americans try to remedy this omission with 'You're welcome'. In French you should say either *'Je vous en prie'* or *'de rien'*. The latter is easier, because you don't have to remember whether to use *tu* or *vous;* the former is more polite.

All the above are responses. They assume that you are already in conversation. But sometimes it may be up to you to initiate one. Useful here is *'ça ne vous dérange pas?'* With its literal meaning of 'That doesn't put you out?', you use it when you plonk yourself in front of someone on the beach and completely obscure their view.

Another essential expression is 'Go away' - or its less polite alternatives. In ascending order of rudeness you can ask those annoying kids to *'Allez-vous en'*, *'Dégagez'* or *'Fichez-moi le camp'*. Incidentally anything that is getting you down, such as kids, can be described as *pénible*. This is a good example of a word which exists in English ('painful') but which is used in a much wider sense in French.

The equivalent of 'Cheers' is *'Santé'* ('your good health'), but this is often abbreviated to *'A la vôtre'* ('Here's to yours'). *'Chin'* is also used familiarly.

Two ways to express your discontent are *'Je m'en fous de...'* (I couldn't care a stuff about...) and *'J'en ai marre'* (I've had enough, I'm fed up).

Ça commence à venir...?

Now for some more good news. At school you were probably taught the expression *'Comment allez-vous?'* as a greeting. As such it is correct but about as common as its English equivalent 'How are you?' The normal form of greeting is '*ça va?*'.

You cannot survive long in France without discovering that for yourself. The reason I draw attention to it is that it is an example of a much wider use of expressions beginning with *ça* which make the spoken language a lot easier. Apart from *ça va* being shorter it is *invariable;* you don't have to worry about *tu* or *vous.* The heading of this paragraph means 'Are you getting there, making progress?'

I used to spend ages racking my brains for adjectives such as 'steep', 'slippery' or 'twisty'. No longer. All that is needed is *'ça monte', 'ça glisse'* or *'ça tourne'*. So addicted are the French to this construction that my neighbours once commented *'ça bouge, les Anglais'* (you English never stand still) as a commentary on my failure to adjust to the pace of life in the Midi.

As to the weather, instead of saying *'Il fait très, très chaud'*, you can merely say *'ça tape'* as a means of saying the the sun is beating down. At the other extreme *'ça gèle'** when the temperature dives below freezing and conversely, *'ca dégèle'* when it starts to thaw. The great beauty of this usage is that it replaces adjectives that are forced to agree with their nouns, or verb forms that have to decline, with a two-letter word followed by a verb in the third person, which is the easiest part of the verb to handle.

The same type of simplification is at work in the widespread use of the word *'on'*. The Princess Royal excepted, 'one' it is not much used in normal conversational English. Not so in French where *'On rentre chez nous'* to say 'We are going home', is an accepted construction. As with *ça* it has the great advantage of being in the third person. The latter is in all cases easier than the *'nous'* form which *on* commonly replaces. If you really set your mind to it you could virtually eliminate the use of *'nous'* as the subject of a verb.

Continuing in the 'make it easy for yourself' vein, consider the following sentence:

'Il est bizarre qu'elle n'était pas là.' (It's odd that she wasn't there)

For the life of me I can never remember whether such a sentence should start with *'il est..'* or *'c'est..'* I also have a vaguely uncomfortable feeling that a subjunctive could be in order somewhere along the line. The way to divide and conquer here is simply to split the sentence in two:

'Elle n'était pas là. C'est bizarre.'

I repeat, you are not going to win a literary prize, but thinking in short bursts is easier than labouring to construct sentences of which Flaubert or Proust would have been proud.

* *One of the things that made researching this book such fun is that French people hold strong opinions and are much less reticent to express them than your polite English person. Thus, when asked for their comments on drafts of the book, my conservative friends deleted any favourable references to the left and vice versa; Protestants made sure that religious problems were laid at the door of the Catholic Church and so on. Of course if an Englishman dares to attack a figure of the left, such as Sartre, then the most right-wing French person will rush to his defence. Nationalism is more powerful than ideology.*

My Parisian consultant, Françoise, jibbed at many of the expressions, describing 'ça gèle' *as ungrammatical (it should be* 'il gèle') *and* 'de rien' *as 'lower class'. You are therefore warned that I have learned my spoken French in a rural community in* la France profonde. *At a dinner party in the* seizième arrondissement *you may prefer to stick to* 'Je vous en prie' *and dispense altogether with* 'Santé' *and* 'Bon appetit'.

Short-cuts

French vocabulary is not as difficult as often thought. Obviously there are many words which are common to English and French - *table, nation* - and many which are almost identical - *organiser, projet, bleu.* In addition to these there are many words whose underlying similarity is hidden by minor linguistic differences. Knowing these often enables you to decipher an otherwise unknown word:

- the use of the acute accent or circonflex in place of 's' in English -

  étudiant (student), *étrange* (strange, foreign)
  mât (mast), *pâture* (pasture) *arrêt* (arrest)

- 'ch' in French sometimes being rendered as 'c' in English -*chat* (cat)
- 'au' in French translating to 'al' in English - *paume* (palm), *faux* (false)

The French word *'château'* incorporates all three of the above transformations. When we unwrap them it becomes 'casteal' which is more easily recognisable as 'castle'.

Rebonjour!

The French love prefixes. *'Encore une fois'* for 'again' is one of those complicated phrases they teach you at school. Far simpler just to stick *'re-'* on the front of whatever verb you are using. You already do it every time you say *au revoir.* Go further. You have proffered *'voilà le soleil'* as a comment on the weather; but now it has come out again after a period of *nuages.* Try expressing that using 'encore'. No, *'Revoilà le soleil'.*
'Dé' as a prefix gives the verb its opposite sense. Thus *'dégeler'* is to melt, or unfreeze; *'démonter'* is to take down (how often have you racked your brains for that simple word on your campsite?); the French not only *découragent* you from doing something, they will advise against it by *'déconseiller'.* We have already come across *débrouiller* in the sense of 'getting by' in the language. In fact it is a more generalised expression for sorting things out, getting yourself out of a mess (if it's a really bad mess then you *démerder* rather than *débrouiller).* When you shuffle a pack of cards you *brouiller* them; so *débrouiller* has the sense of unmixing things. If it is someone else who gets you out of trouble they will have *dépanné* you.

Vous partez?

There are three different ways in which we can form a question. The first is by starting with the phrase *Est-ce que..* or *Qu'est-ce que* - according to what we want to ask. Another way is to invert the verb and subject *Avez-vous un tire-bouchon, s'il vous plaît?* The simplest way is to keep the sentence in its original non-interrogative form and turn it into a question by simply raising the voice at the end.

Confetti Words

The French never have problems. They have either *'un petit problème'* or *'un gros problème'.* If they need help with their problem, they may ask for *un petit service* or *un grand service.* They won't be half an hour, they'll be *une petite demi-heure.* Journalists are taught to 'throw full stops' at their stories as a reminder to write short sentences. When speaking French you should aim to throw *'petit'* and *'bien'* at your sentences and possibly *'quoi'* at the end of them.

French is about emphasis. Don't say *'Jai l'intention..'* but *'J'ai bien l'intention'*. Don't tell someone that you got their letter but that you have *bien reçu* it. Forget all you were taught about *'n'est-ce pas'* and use *'quoi'* instead. It's a lot easier (although Françoise strongly disapproves). Remember to lift the voice. *'Il est intelligent, quoi?'*. Also it is *très courant* to repeat the personal pronoun at the end of a sentence, *'Tu as quel âge, toi?'*

Humpty-Dumpty Words

In Alice through the Looking-Glass, Humpty-Dumpty declares: 'When I use a word, it means just what I choose it to mean - neither more or less'. This is an excellent principle. My German teacher used to reckon that it was possible to travel round Germany saying only *'So'* with whatever inflection the context appeared to demand. *'Voilà'* iis similarly useful in France. At school you were taught that it means 'There is..' as in *'Voilà la plume de ma tante'*. But it can serve many other purposes. *'Voilà'* can mean 'That's it' and is a lot easier to say than *'Ça y est'*. It can mean 'I agree' or 'You're dead right there, Pierre' or even 'Well, that's just what you would expect of that lot...' It can be used to attract attention and compliments as - *'Voilà'* - you unveil your latest culinary creation.

Not quite in the same class, but still immensely useful is *'quand même'*. The nearest equivalent in English is 'well, all the same'. This expression should be used whenever the intonation of the speaker suggests that he has just related some injustice or slight. He may, for example, have complained about the people next door waking him up at two o'clock in the morning or about getting a parking ticket. In the latter case a sympathetic *'Quand même'* in reply would mean 'I agree totally that having left your car for four hours in the main street on market day across a sign saying *'Sortie de Camions'* you may have caused some slight problems, but the authorities should have overlooked it on account of the fact that you unexpectedly bumped into some old friends in a cafe.' This is what computer people refer to as a 'high-level language'.

Negatives.

At school you were taught (correctly) that the negative form is *'ne.....pas'*. In everyday speech you can dispense with the *'ne'* a lot of the time (as we saw with *'c'est pas grave'*)'. To use four syllables to say that you don't know is frankly *un peu dépassé,* colloquially. Practise shortening *'Je ne sais pas'* to *'shaypas'**.

* *Françoise, with her pride in the beauty of the French language, hit the roof at this, describing it as* 'petit nègre' *French.*

Although you should take care to swallow your *ne's*, you should make up for this by piling up any other negatives in the same sentence. The English language does not like double negatives. The French language, with its penchant for exaggeration, loves them. The more, the merrier. The French literal equivalent of 'I have never seen no-one, nowhere', is good grammar.

There are many occasions when the French use a negative in preference to a positive. Although *bon marché* is the correct translation of cheap, you will more often hear *'pas cher'*. And for the comparative 'cheaper', *moins cher* is a lot less of a mouthful than *'meilleur marché'*. Similarly 'quite a few' would colloquially be translated *'pas mal de...'* (not a bad number of...). And 'quite near' becomes 'not very distant' *(pas très loin).* Often the resulting expression is simpler grammatically. ' To remember' is an awkward reflexive verb. If you are like me, you will have problems composing the imperative form - there are too many *'vous'* for comfort. Far easier to tell someone not to forget *'N'oubliez pas...'*.

Exaggeration

The English are the masters of understatement. We understand that to describe something as 'not all that bad' is to confer high praise. It goes with the stiff upper lip and *sang froid.* But the French have Latin blood in their veins. So cast off your inhibitions and move up a gear in your choice of words. Earlier I recommended *'mignon'* as appropriate for describing babies; actually *'adorable '* is better for those under six months. If you get a puncture and are late for lunch it is not *un inconvénient*, it is *une catastrophe.* If the *boulangerie* is out of *croissants* by the time you get there on Sunday morning, it is *une tragédie.* Don't opine that the courier on your campsite 'could be a bit more helpful'; no, she is *'nulle'* (literally meaning 'nothing' i.e useless) or *zéro.* Never content yourself with one *très* in front of an adjective; at least three are required to impart any feeling of emphasis. Alternatively, you could just add *super* as a prefix as in *supercool* which is what you will then become.

As have already seen, if something is good, it is *impeccable;* conversely, something that has caused you a little irritation should be described as *infernal.* If the kids have left the room in a mess it is a *bordel;* and when French prop forwards are referred to as *barbares* it is describing their approach to scrummaging, not that they have been invited to play for a well-known wandering side. In like vein, look out for the opportunity to throw in some good strong adverbs - *énormement, infiniment* (as in *merci infiniment)* and, a favourite, *carrément,* as in *carrément à gauche* (right over to the left).

Once you are tuned in to this characteristic you will see it everywhere. Notice that nothing is ever 'the best in the world'. No, it is *dans le monde entier* - in the *whole* world. I always had trouble remembering the word *améliorer* when wishing to express the desire to improve my French. *'Ah, c'est pas le mot, Colin!'* You should say *perfectionner.'* To an Englishman the idea of explaining to someone, in broken French, that one is intending to perfect one's French, seems outrageously immodest. But in France one 'perfects' one's command of the language starting from any level; the connotation of adding the final gloss is not present in the French use of the word. I finally was prepared to accept this usage when a ski instructor, after an hour spent picking me up off the snow, said that I could come back for another lesson tomorrow if I wanted to *perfectionner* my ski-ing.

Finally, if someone recounts something mildly out of the ordinary, remember to say *'Ce n'est pas vrai!'* in a voice which indicates complete and utter disbelief on your part.

Gestures

Another way to impart emphasis is with the body. To speak French properly requires that you use your whole body. The best-known example is the Gallic shrug of the shoulders. Correctly used, this gives the impression of worldliness and *savoir-faire* when in reality it is covering up your lack of vocabulary.

Even more important is the wringing gesture whereby you shake your right hand as though it has just touched something exceedingly hot. This is immensely powerful. At a stroke you can dispense with verbs, adjectives, adverbs, prepositions - all the things that make communication so difficult. Suppose you discover that your neighbour on the campsite follows rugby - for instance, because his numberplate (33) shows him to be from the South-West. All you have to do is say 'Serge Blanco' at the same time wringing your hand vigorously and pursing your lips. This is short for: 'One of the many great French rugby players of recent years is Serge Blanco. I once saw him when France were playing England at Twickenham. There are many others I could name but in my opinion Blanco was in a class of his own'.

If you are ready for an advanced ploy add admiringly *'Quel phénomène!'* Technically it has the same meaning as the equivalent English word but it is used much more freely to express a generalised feeling of admiration.

You should also practise rubbing your thumb across your first two fingers *(très vulgaire - Françoise).* This action of counting money, indicates that the item under discussion is expensive. Once the art of body talk is mastered, you can have a fluent conversation without the need to say more than one or two words.

Thinking in French

Speaking a foreign language is not a sort of computerised table-look-up substituting an English word by its foreign equivalent. To master a foreign language you have ultimately to think in it. Don't get *découragé.* Thinking in French is not a switch that is suddenly thrown. It is a gradual process and also a question of attitude. Almost certainly you already think in French in some areas. What is the English for *'Appellation Controlee'?* You don't know. No translation exists. Where are the Elysian Fields? When you greet someone with a *'Bonjour, ça va?',* you don't start by thinking to yourself 'What's the French for 'Good Morning, how are you?' No, it is perfectly possible to begin to think in French from an early stage. The reason you don't do it is for the reasons already explained - you are accustomed to putting accuracy before expression and don't believe in your own ability.

'Divide and Conquer'. Practise in defined areas. Listen to songs without mentally translating them into English. Turn you car radio onto RTL and listen to what is being said. You won't understand a lot of it, but you will notice certain words and expressions which recur. You'll know you have cracked it when you start dreaming in French.

A TO Z

A Guide to Entries

'You should always leave the table hungry.'

Such was my grandmother's favourite admonition. It is a principle that is relevant to this book as a whole. Just as I hope the introductory chapter has left you wanting to try your French out, so what follows is meant to be a taster that will leave you keen to find out more for yourself about the country and its people. This book is not a comprehensive reference; it is a selection of things that French people know about.

There are a few guidelines which I have followed in compiling entries, an understanding of which will help you to know why particular entries have been chosen and not others, and why they are written in the way that they are.

The first principle is that in writing a particular entry I have tried to avoid the obvious. This has not always proved easy, particularly when writing about the geography of the country. But the absence, for example, of an entry for the *Arc de Triomphe* is because I could find nothing to say about it that had not already been said in a hundred guide books. If any reader can come up with an interesting snippet of information similar to that on 'catacombs' then it can take its place between Aquitaine and Argot*.

For the same reason I have only exceptionally used adjectives such as 'great'. General de Gaulle and Victor Hugo will survive without my explicit approbation. Praise is always boring. If, through this, I have occasionally trivialised a subject, or reinforced British prejudices or feelings of superiority, then I am *désolé.* My love of French culture and its people, my respect for its political and economic renaissance since the war, is second to none.

Secondly, the length of the entry is not a function of its importance but more of how much the average French person is likely to know about it. Thus television personalities are likely to get as much written about them as a king such as Clovis who tripled French territory. By the same token, when including photographs and illustrations I have in the main chosen those of contemporary personalities - it is more *branché* to be able to recognise Anne Sinclair than Descartes.

Thirdly, whilst every effort has been made to be accurate and precise, this is difficult when dealing with statistics. Up-to-date often means data collected in the late eighties. Such figures are not static. In preference to qualifying every such entry with 'approximately' or 'around', I have in most cases rounded figures up or down. Thus where the precise 1990/91 figure for the population of Brittany is 2,795,638, I have represented this, without qualification, as 2.8 million.

* Ce n'est pas une blague' - *This is not a joke. Any book that attempts to deal with contemporary events and personalities is bound to date. For this reason the initial print run is relatively small. I would be delighted to receive contributions to the next edition and look forward to a continuing improvement in terms of quantity and quality of entries.*

Two other considerations arise from the alphabetic sequence. The first is that a topic such as the history of France benefits from an overview which helps to make sense of the individual events and people listed. There is such an entry - but it is under 'H'. Long before you get to that you will have come across Clovis, François 1er and the Massacre of St Bartholemew. Logically you should read the entries for Cinema, History, Republic and Region on the first occasion that you come across an individual entry that falls within one of those classifications.

Secondly, there is an element of overlap and occasionally duplication. Thus the fact that Catherine Deneuve has been one of the models for Marianne is recorded under both entries. However, since repetition is one of the major techniques for learning, and as readers are presumed not to be going to read the book at one sitting, this is an advantage. An index is at first sight superfluous in a book that is written in alphabetical sequence. However there are many instances of people or places who get a mention without having a separate entry devoted to them. So if you want to know the claim to fame of Roger Vadim (and he has claim that most men would envy) you must seek him under 'Cinema'. 'Constitution' seemed such an intrinsically boring heading that I have buried an explanation of the Fifth Republic under the more interesting-sounding 'Cohabitation'.

The choice of when to use French rather than English is not quite as arbitrary as it may appear. Mostly it is to get you familiar with the language, a start on the process of thinking in French. Sometimes, as with *Bourgogne,* I just preferred the sound of the French word or, as with *région,* to show a specific use of the word. Sometimes I use the English version where previously I have used the French, simply because of a surfeit of italics in a particular paragraph.

Finally a word about the style. For a long time I worried about the inconsistency of the style in which different entries are written - some chatty, some pseudo-intellectual, some a bluffer's guide, some factual, others propagandist. I ultimately decided that the search for stylistic consistency was futile given the breadth of both topic and intended audience. If there is a common denominator it is, if I have succeeded, that they are all interesting in some way. However, you cannot interest all the people all of the time. I trust my more sensitive readers will forgive my lapses of taste, the serious-minded, my penchant for trivia, the casual holiday browser, my platitudes and the precise, my inaccuracies.

A

Abbé Pierre (b. 1912)

Catholic worker-priest who concerned himself with the lot of the down-and-out. His first attempt to help was by getting himself elected as a *député*. Finding little legislative influence he turned to direct involvement with the poor. His unique contribution has been to get the poor to help themselves by setting them up in hostels which must then become self-sufficient. This is achieved by means of collecting rags and junk and turning them to use or resale. His people thus became known as les *chiffonniers* (the rag collectors). The movement, creating the Emmaüs hostels, started in Paris and now has groups worldwide. He also collaborated with Coluche in setting up the *Restaurants du Coeur*.

In opinion polls he has competed with Jacques Cousteau, for the accolade of the most popular person in France although he is likely to have the last laugh. He must ultimately be a strong candidate for canonisation.

Abbreviations

If you were a foreigner hoping to appear street-credible in England, you would expect to know what BBC, MCC and TUC stand for. The reverse is also true. To gauge your current level of France-awareness, write down what the following abbreviations stand for, and what they mean:

RER	RPR	HLM	TGV
IVG	IGF	l'OM	VDQS
MLF	ONU	ENA	PCV
EV	CRS	EDF	CGT
PPDA	BCBG	BNP	SIDA
TVA	SMIC	PMU	SGDG

and finally, for your first trans-lingual joke, a French version of VSOP. The answers are on page 140.

Aboville, Gérard d' (b. 1945)

Person whose idea of a good time is to row single-handed across the world's major oceans. Maintaining Bretons' reputation as sailors, d'Aboville left Choshi, east of Tokyo on July 11th, 1991 and arrived at Washington State, on the west coast of America, 134 days later, having rowed 10,5000 Km and capsized 36 times. This trip across the Pacific was a follow-up to his conquest of the Atlantic in 1980. After a joyful reunion his wife is now said to be encouraging him to take on the Indian Ocean.

Académie Française

Canute-like body, originally set up by Richelieu in 1635 dedicated to the perfection of the French language. Now it has lost this role to the *commission de termonologie* set up to protect the language against the depredations of *franglais*, although it did recently bring its influence to bear in defence of the *circonflexe*. It is also guardian of a number of literary prizes. In general, however, its role has diminished as its prestige has increased.

A self-perpetuating clique of forty members, entry is by election to fill dead men's (or since 1980 dead women's) shoes. They dress up in white tie, long black coat embroidered in yellow or green silk for their meeting, carrying a sword. New *académiciens* are received with similar Gallic formality with the addition of vine leaves and a pointed hat.

All *académiciens* have to be French. When Marguerite Yourcenar was proposed for election in 1980 she had to hastily renounce the American nationality that she had adopted in 1945.

They are known as the *'Immortels'* but, as one academician pointed out, they are only immortal during their lifetime. All but about thirty of the more than 500 academicians since its inception have been totally forgotten. This could partly be because the right people do not get in. Among famous people who, for reasons other than being female, have not been members are Descartes, Pascal, Diderot, Molière, Balzac, Stendhal, Mirabeau, Flaubert, Zola, Proust and Sartre.

Accents

France has about half a dozen regional accents but without the degree of difference that there is, for example, between a Glaswegian, a Scouse and a Devonian.

Nevertheless, the similarity between understanding a middle-class Parisian, speaking slowly and choosing his words, and a Provençal peasant in full flood is like windsurfing on the sea in a force-8 after learning on an inland lake in a gentle breeze.

The most noticeable accent is that of the Midi, or south. This flattens vowels and adds a strange clanging noise on the end of an 'n'. Thus the word for 'mill *(moulin)* comes out as *'mouleng'*. This makes life difficult. It is slightly compensated for by the clearer articulation of individual syllables whereby words like *'êtes'* and *'trente'* becomes bisyllabic.

Although France has fewer different accents than Britain, it has many more dialects. This stems from the fact that the French language only became that of all the country at the time of the Revolution.

Adjani, Isabelle (b. 1955)

Highly talented second-generation Arab actress. She came top of her class at the *Comédie Française* and went on to appear in numerous films, in the process winning a number of *Césars* (French oscars) and a prize at the Cannes film festival. She came first in a poll (with 29%, just ahead of Emmanuelle Béart) as the woman with whom French men would most like to have *une aventure de vacances.*

Affairisme

The word for sundry financial scandals surrounding mainly the Socialist Party. A consultancy company, Urba-Gracco, is suspected of having taken bribes in return for planning permissions and public works contracts and using them to help finance the Mitterrand Presidential campaign in 1988 to the extent of 25 million francs. A previous investigation into the affairs of the company was closed down by the Minister of Justice (who just happened to have been Mitterrand's campaign treasurer). However the affair refuses to go away and early in 1992 the headquarters of the Socialist Party were raided by an investigating magistrate in search of incriminating evidence.

The main opposition parties tend to make less mileage out of this than one would expect, possibly because they too have the odd skeleton in the cupboard. Indeed one of the few things that the parties were able to agree on was to vote in 1990 for an amnesty for past offences (though this excludes corruption). The overall effect is to reinforce, dangerously, the apathy and cynicism with which politicians and the political system are viewed by the electorate.

Air France

One of the world's leading airlines with 117 passenger planes. In 1990 it flew 15.7 million passenger miles to 182 destinations in 74 countries clocking up 445,000 flight hours in the process. With Bocuse to advise them, in-flight food ought to be, and generally is, better than most other airlines.

Each year light-fingered passengers relieve the airline, *inter alia,* of 250,000 table napkins and 500,000 headsets even though the latter are incompatible with standard walkmen. In 1990 the total cost of disappearing items was £60 million from 35 million passengers.

SNCF, the French railways, lose even more esoteric things. In 1990 they lost 22,000 hammers (for breaking the glass in an emergency), 140,000 pillow slips and 800 bunk ladders.

Alcoholism

Alcoholism is a long-standing problem in a country where a generation ago tap water was not trusted and *vin ordinaire* was dirt cheap. There are an estimated four million excessive drinkers and one in three hospital admissions is alcohol-related. As long ago as 1954 a campaign was launched by the milk-drinking President, Mendès-France. Whereas alcoholism in England appears to be a middle-class problem, in France it is most prevalent among the rural poor (for the same reason that vodka-drinking is a problem in Russia). You do not tend to see many drunks and the idea of consuming large quantities of alcohol at a sitting, as happens in English pubs, strikes the French as odd.

The problem is gradually diminishing. Alcohol-related deaths have decreased from twenty thousand in 1975 to thirteen thousand in 1988. Over the last twenty years the consumption of cheap wine has halved - from 96 litres per person in 1970 to 53 in 1989 while that of better quality wines has almost tripled (from 8 litres to 21). Nevertheless, the French still hold the world record for alcohol consumption. At the same time they are the world's greatest consumers of mineral waters. This odd coincidence could be connected with their abiding concern for their livers.

Algerian War (1954-1962)
The French colonies of Tunisia and Morocco (which together with Algeria, Libya and Mauritius are known collectively as the 'Maghreb'), were granted independence in 1956. But Algeria proved a different kettle of fish. The local *colons* (French settlers) were violently opposed to independence and obstructed moves towards it. For eight years the Algerian nationalist movement, the FLN, fought a French army twenty times its size. Fearing a sell-out, the *colons* revolted and at one stage paratroopers invaded Corsica. On the mainland motorists tapped their hooters to the sound of *Al-gér-ie fran-çaise*. The *colons* looked to De Gaulle to head their movement and he declared himself 'ready to serve the nation' in this crisis, should it summon him. It did. De Gaulle ruled by decree for six months with the *colons* confident that he was on their side. It therefore came as a nasty surprise to them when in 1959 he announced a policy of Home Rule for Algeria. The *colons* regarded this as nothing less than treachery and attempted a coup. However when the officers revolted, the troops refused to follow. Algeria got its independence. The OAS *(Organisation de l'Armée Secrète)*, was formed by disgruntled officers, and was behind several unsuccessful attempts to assassinate De Gaulle, of which one is chronicled in 'The Day of the Jackal'. 800,000 disgruntled French Algerians *(pieds noirs)* poured back into France.
With the benefit of hindsight *France Métropole* can be grateful for De Gaulle's decision. Had Algeria stayed French, France would now have an additional 25 million Muslim citizens to add to its current concern with immigrants and, to judge by the first round of the elections in Algeria in December 1991, a large block of fundamentalist Islamic *députés* in the Assembly.

Alsace
Région of eastern France comprising the *départements* of Haut-Rhin(67) and Bas-Rhin (68). *Chef-lieu:* Strasbourg. Fertile, wooded countryside but also, with its 1.6 million inhabitants, many densely populated areas. It used to be a nesting place for migrating storks but modern technology, in the form of high-tension cables and pesticides, has virtually eliminated them. There is now a *Centre de Réintroduction des Cigognes* which is attempting, with some success, to restock their numbers.

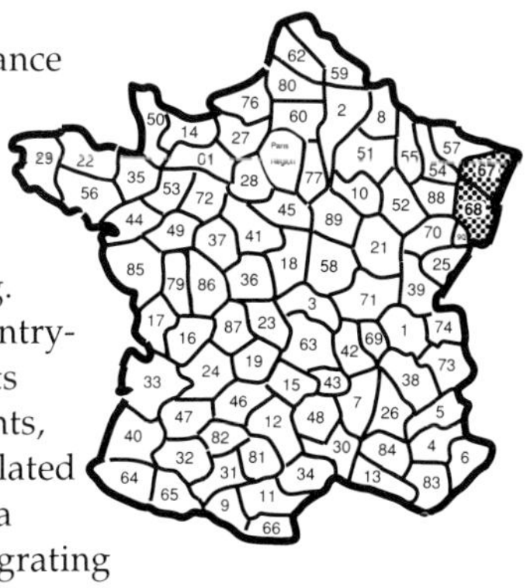

The region produces excellent white wine and most of France's beer. Bordering on Germany, it did not become part of France until 1678. In 1871 it was annexed by Prussia after the Franco-Prussian War but was restored to France in 1918.

Ancien Régime
Name given to the absolutist monarchical regime that predated the Revolution. Under this the *premier Etat* was the clergy, the *deuxième* was the *noblesse* and the *tiers* was the commoners. According to a French triplet, it was the:

- *nobles qui battaient* (went to war)
- *clergé qui priait* (prayed)
- *peuple qui travaillait* (worked)

Animals
There is a widespread belief that the English are a nation of animal-lovers in general and dog-lovers in particular. Compared to the French we are second division. In France there are 10 million dogs and 36% of the population are dog-owners. In the UK there are just over seven million dogs among 28% of the population. Paris has more dogs than children. No dog licence is required but care of dogs is a £2 billion industry. Nevertheless, every year fifty thousand dogs are abandoned by their owners immediately before the *grandes vacances*. This is despite the *Déclaration Universelle des Droits de l'Animal*, proclaimed in Paris in 1978.

Anouilh, Jean (1910-1987)
Dramatist, born in Bordeaux, author of a wide variety of different plays, comic, satirical and tragic. In the latter genre *Becket*, based on Henry II's turbulent priest, opened in London in 1991 to critical acclaim. Two other plays in each of which the heroine prefers death to dishonour are *Antigone* and *L'Alouette*, the latter based on the life of Joan of Arc.

Apéritifs
The simplest way to get to know French people is to invite them for an *apéritif*, colloquially shortened to *apéro*. These can be at any time but most usually at *midi* (lunchtime) or early evening. Pastis is universal in France so that providing for the men is no problem.

What the women will drink varies according to region, class and personal preference. Mme Martin, of peasant stock, mostly drinks water; one social class up, Mme Duplan contents herself with Kir. A chic Parisienne might take white wine or champagne.

The next problem for the *débutant(e)* French speaker is what to talk about. Topics are dictated not by mutual interest but by vocabulary. Discussing places one has visited in France is a good bet. Particularly if you can pull out a map and pore over it. This gives maximum communication with minimum vocabulary.

Much depends on whom you are having *apéros* with. There is a world of difference between local *agriculteurs* and middle-class acquaintances. The latter, probably without your noticing, will slow down their speech, eliminate slang expressions and generally make life easier. M. and Mme Martin make no such concessions. They are completely oblivious to any difficulty that you are experiencing. Every so often you hear a word that you understand. Hang onto it as you would the neck of a bolting horse and try to piece the rest of the sentence together.

Aquitaine

Extensive south-western *région* comprising the *départements* of Dordogne (24), Gironde (33), Landes (40), Pyrénées - Atlantiques (64) and Lot-et-Garonne (47), *Chef-lieu:* Bordeaux; population 2.8 million. Deservedly famous for its wines and armagnac, the southern part of the region comprises the Atlantic beaches and pine forests of the Landes stretching from Bordeaux to Biarritz. The town of Agen, the prune capital of France on the banks of the Garonne, was judged to be the happiest city in the country.

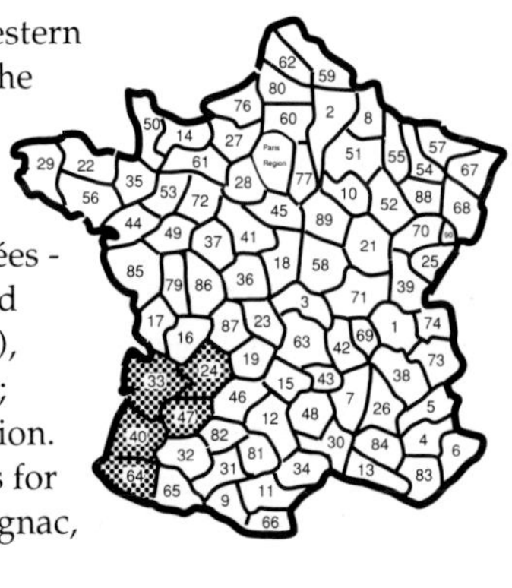

Historically Aquitaine for centuries had close ties with Great Britain through commerce, marriage and conquest but after the death of Henry II of England it was gradually brought under the control of the French monarchy.

Argot

There is a difference between colloquial speech and slang *(argot)*. The word *boulot* for *travail* (work) is colloquial and widely-used. Slang is often confined to certain groups - e.g. the young - and changes frequently. In general you are advised not to use it yourself unless you are virtually fluent. It can appear pretentious and you risk using the wrong expression in the wrong place. Do not, for instance, tell the *Maître D* at Maxim's that you have *'bien bouffé'*. Roughly translated, this means that you have had a good blow-out.

Asterix

Hero of comic strips *(bandes dessinées)*, a form of humour very popular in France. Having started in 1959 by 1991 it had sold over 220 million editions in forty languages, including Latin. Asterix, a Gaul, like his real-life predecessor, Vercingétorix, fights the Romans. Helping him to run rings round them are his friend, Obélix, a great lover of *sangliers* (wild boar), Assurancetourix, the village bard and Abraracourcix, the chief of the tribe. Of further assistance is Panoramix, the venerable druid of the village, who mixes a potion which has the same effect as spinach has on Popeye. Although the stories are always set in Roman times, the story line reflects more current *moeurs*. In the 1991 edition the tribe falls prey to *le feminisme.* A female bard from Paris incites the Gallic wives to drive their men out of the vil-

© 1992 LES ÉDITIONS ALBERT RENÉ/ GOSCINNY-UDERZO

lage. Meanwhile a female legion sets sail from Rome. However, when the two female forces meet they forget to fight as Asterix persuades the female bard to arrange a fashion show and shopping expedition for both sets of female warriors.

Autoroutes

The *autoroute* system covers more than 7000 Kilometers and has over 500 *péages*. Because of their propensity to take to the roads at the same time the French designate the days on which it is inadvisable to travel. This is a principle that can bear being extended to the roads themselves. Particularly since it often seems that vast stretches of the system have been built for one's personal use. Below is a map of the current network with the figures for traffic density. The left-hand figure is the average density excluding July/August; the right-hand figure is for July/August. The latter figure more than doubles on the peak weekends at the beginning and end of these months for roads between Paris and the coast. There is one major difference between *autoroutes* and motorways. For some unexplained reason French roads appear to require approximately one tenth of the maintenance of English. You will be unlucky to be held up by *travaux*. However you may run foul of farmers, lorry-drivers or any other group of protesters that has decided to block the roads as a way of exerting pressure on the government.

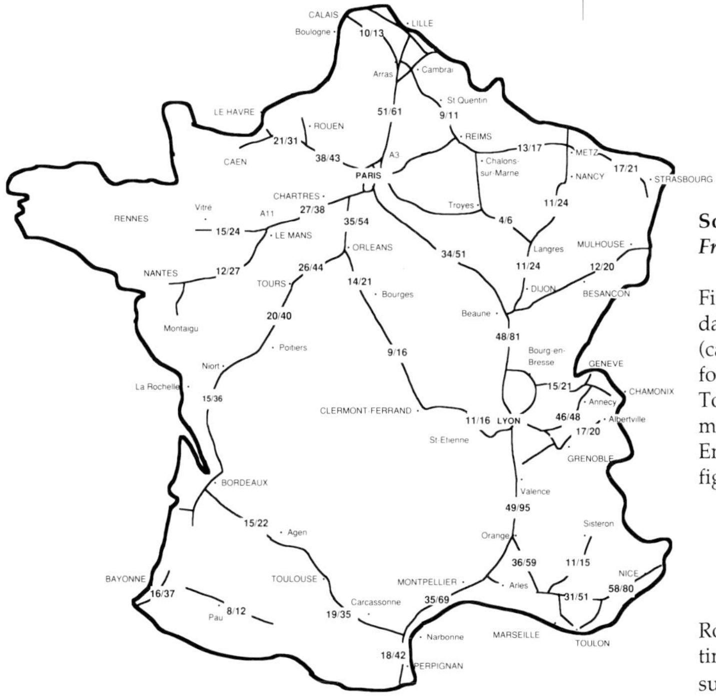

Auvergne

Région embracing a large part of the Massif Central, comprising the *départements* of Allier (03), Cantal (15), Haute-Loire (43) and Puy-de-Dome (63). *Chef-lieu:* Clermont-Ferrand Now accessible directly by autoroute, this region, apart from the heavily-industrialised Clermont, is an area of great natural beauty, particularly the area of *volcans*. However, life has always been hard in the Auvergne, which may account for its 1.3 million inhabitants having the reputation of being *économes*.

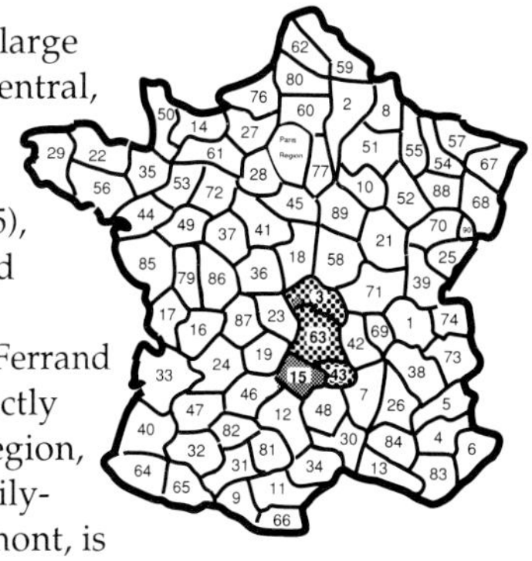

Aznavour, Charles (b. 1924)

Singer of Armenian extraction, who lived under Piaf's roof for six years, without, somewhat exceptionally, being her lover. He did, however, write songs for her in return for which she bought him a new nose. He later turned to acting and in 1959 won the *Grand Prix de l'Académie du Cinéma.*

Source: ***Association des Sociétés Françaises d'Autoroute, 1990***

Figures are for cars per minute during daytime. All figures are approximate (calculated by dividing ASFA's figures for cars per day by 15).
To give an idea of what the figures mean in relation to traffic density on English motorways, the comparative figures are:

M1 Junctions 9/10:	136
M6 Junctions 14/15:	88
M25 Junctions 5/6:	103

Roads with no figures were not open at time of writing but can safely be assumed to have a low density.

B

Baccalauréat

'Is there such a thing as a science of the unconscious?'

'Can self-knowledge ever be truly sincere?'

These are the sort of questions with which French students are confronted in the *baccalauréat,* universally referred to as *le bac.* Established by Napoleon in 1808, it is the examination that students take at the age of eighteen. Gaining the *bac* confers the automatic right to enter university and the middle-classes are obsessed by the need for their children to pass it. Roughly equivalent to English A-level, it is more broadly-based with an emphasis on rhetorical and deductive skills.
Students do not pass or fail individual subjects, but the examination as a whole. To do this they need an average of ten out of twenty. If you get twelve, fourteen or sixteen, you obtain respectively *la mention assez bien, bien and très bien.*
Philosophy still forms an important (though declining) part of the course. The *bac* entrant studies eight options combining many different subjects from one of a number of groupings *(séries). Série A, Philosophie-Lettres* used to have pride of place but in the modern world *(hélas!)* has been ousted by the more vocational Option C, *Mathématiques et sciences physiques.*

Balzac, Honoré de (1799-1850)

As an author he was as prolific as Barbara Cartland (though more talented) with 350 titles having up to a hundred characters each. He was forced to keep writing at a level of ten to fourteen hours a day in order to keep his many creditors at bay. His extravagance was legendary. He once bought sixty pairs of gloves in a month. Not surprisingly he was perpetually insolvent and a consistent theme of his novels, such as *Eugénie Grandet,* and *La Cousine Bette,* is the importance of money. In the words of one of his most famous characters, Père Goriot, *'l'argent, c'est la vie. Monnaie fait tout.'*
He is considered as the founder of the realist school of French novelists. His ninety-odd novels (grouped together into *La Comédie Humaine,* to rival Danté's Divine comedy) is a brilliant chronicle of French society during the first half of the nineteenth century.

Banks

London may be the financial centre of Europe but France still boasts four of the top international banks. Don't be fooled by the rural-sounding *Crédit Agricole;* it's the fifth largest bank in the world. Most banks are state-owned; all have their head offices in Paris, even *Crédit Lyonnais.* Foreign owners of *résidences secondaires* are allowed to set up a bank account in France, complete with *carte bancaire.* What you must not do is go overdrawn - which is not difficult with a couple of *prélèvements* (direct debits) and the slowness of transfer of funds in this electronic age. If a cheque bounces you receive a warning letter from the bank's computer. On the second occasion the right to issue cheques is withdrawn for a year. The bank will not refuse to honour any subsequent cheques for which funds are available; but they will not issue you another cheque book when you run out. So it is advisable always to have a spare book. Failing that, your local branch will help you to subvert the system.

Banlieues

The literal translation is 'suburb' and in some instances it retains the connotation of the leafy middle-class outskirts of a city (e.g as in Neuilly-Auteil-Passy, the chic suburbs of Paris in which to live). Increasingly, however, the expression is taken to refer to the deprived areas of low-cost housing, surrounded by waste ground and industrial zones, and populated overwhelmingly by the young, unemployed, single-parent families and foreigners. Thus *le problème des banlieues* is shorthand for the troubles that arise from such social deprivation.

Bardot, Brigitte (b. 1934)

The original sex symbol, star of *'Et Dieu Créa la Femme',* directed by Roger Vadim, whom she then married. Two husbands and three divorces later, she now lives a semi-reclusive life near St Tropez, devoting herself to wild-life rather than the wild life. Her total commitment to this cause is enshrined in a

Foundation she has set up and to which she has recently donated her £2 million St Tropez house. Should you wish to ingratiate yourself with France's most famous ex-film star you are advised to make a large donation to:
Fondation Brigitte Bardot, 4, rue Franklin, 75016 Paris.

Barre, Raymond (b. 1924)

Politician of great weight in the centre. Appointed Prime Minister by Giscard d'Estaing in 1976, he was not a career politician but a widely-respected economist. He introduced a classic austerity programme together with freeing the many price and other controls which were shackling the French economy. As happens with such programmes, its long-term economic success was matched only by its immediate electoral unpopularity. The latter was not eased by his neglect of, amounting almost to contempt for, the political arts. Consequently his government was defeated by the Socialists in the 1981 elections. He ran for President in 1988 but was eliminated in the first ballot having disregarded the fundamental law of French politics which is to form a party around oneself.

Barthes, Roland (1915-1980)
A *philosophe,* writer and critic who inherited the mantle of Sartre as left-bank intellectual. He developed so-called 'semiological' analysis. This examines products such as films, adverts and cars for the implicit messages or 'signs' contained in them. The simplest explanation is to say that just as human beings communicate as much with body language as in the actual words they use, so the way in which products are packaged and advertised - smoking is manly, fast cars are sexy - reveals a lot about the manufacturers' view of potential buyers. He became professor of literary semiology at the *Collège de France.*

Bartholemew, Massacre of St,
Massacre of French protestants (Huguenots) in Paris and other large cities on 23/24 August 1572 during the period of the Religious Wars. Ordered by Charles IX (who was only twelve at the time), it was instigated by his mother, Catherine de Medici and the duc de Guise. It was highly approved of throughout Catholic Europe and Philip II of Spain is reputed to have laughed for the first time in his life on hearing of it. The number of victims varies from 2,000 to 100,000 according to which side you believe.

Basque
An area which straddles the border between the extreme south-west of France and north-east of Spain. There are seven Basque provinces of which three (comprising about 20% of the total area) are in France - Labourd, Soule and Basse Navarre. The latter was the birthplace of Henry IV. Whereas the Spanish side is riven by Basque nationalism, the French are mostly happy to remain part of France.
The Basque language, 'euskara' is unique. Experts place it among the pre-indo-European languages languages which means that it is one of the oldest, if not the oldest, of European languages.
The Basques, like the Bretons, have a great maritime history. The first navigator to circumnavigate the globe, with Magellan, was a Basque. They were also the first whalers in Europe.

Bastille
Originally the prison whose storming on July 14th provided the symbolic start of the Revolution. Its importance as a symbol, then and now, was out of all proportion to its contents. When it finally surrendered it contained only seven prisoners (one of whom was the Marquis de Sade). Possibly in frustration at this lack of return for their efforts, the mob chopped off the heads of the governor and Swiss guards and paraded them round Paris stuck on poles. In political terms it marked the emergence of the Paris mob the - *sans culottes* - as the driving force behind the Revolution.

Baudelaire, Charles (1821-1867)
Dandyish poet who died from syphilis in his mid-forties. Some of his poems, of which the best-known collection is his *Fleurs du Mal,* were originally the object

of prosecution as being harmful to public morality. Baudelaire is his own best apologist for his failure to conform to contemporary society. His poem *'L'Albatros'* describes the majesty of that bird soaring high above the earth, concluding:

Le poète est semblable au prince des nuées
Qui hante la tempête et se rit de l'archer
Isolé sur la terre, au milieu des huées
Ses ailes de géant l'empêchent de marcher.

The poet's like the monarch of the clouds
Who haunts the tempest, scorns the bows and slings
Exiled on earth amid the shouting crowds
He cannot walk, for he has giant's wings

Posterity has accorded him greater worth than did his contemporaries. In 1989 a record £45,000 was paid for a letter written by Baudelaire to Mme Sabatier in 1857.

Bayeux Tapestry
Large piece of collective sewing commemorating, in 58 scenes, the last successful invasion of England - by *Guillaume le Conquérant* - in 1066. Its 70 metre length can be seen wound round the walls of a museum in the town of Bayeux in Normandy. On June 8, 1944 Bayeux became the first town to be liberated after the D-Day landings.

Béart, Emmanuelle (b. 1963)
Startingly beautiful actress, the daughter of Guy Béart, a well-known song-writer. Second only to Isabelle Adjani as a hearthrob, she was seen by British audiences in the title role of Pagnol's *Manon des Sources.*

Beaujolais
Southernmost part of Burgundy north-east of Lyon. From the A6 you catch a glimpse of the yellow brick that characterises many of its buildings. In the fifties Beaujolais accounted for a tiny percentage of all wine drunk in France and had no export trade. They then imported some expert *vignerons* to help them improve the quality of the wine and launched a brilliantly successful marketing campaign, not least in persuading people to race to get Beaujolais Nouveau on their table at an exorbitant price. Signs declaring that *'Le Beaujolais Nouveau est arrivé'* can be seen all over the world. As a result 165 million bottles are produced every year of which a third are quickly drunk as *'primeur'*.
Local wisdom says that Beaujolais from the northern vineyards - Moulin à Vent, Fleurie - is to be tasted, that from the centre, drunk, and that from the south of the region, quaffed. Unlike most red wines, it is often drunk slightly chilled. Provided you drink enough of it, and you are not President of the *Front National,* you could be admitted into *Les Compagnons du Beaujolais* whose crest is shown inset.

Similar *confréries* exist for Burgundy - *Les Chevaliers du Tastevin* and in the Loire, *Les Bons Entonneurs Rabelaisiens.* If you can get into the latter, you could in theory find yourself at a banquet next to Gérard Depardieu or Elizabeth Taylor.

Beaumarchais (1732-1799)
Adventurer, libertine and dramatist, author of *Le Barbier de Seville* and *Le Mariage de Figaro,* both of which were turned into operas by Mozart.

Beauvoir, Simone de (1908-1986)
When Simone de Beauvoir died, the paper *Libération* devoted its entire front page to a photo with just the words *'Une Femme'* and the next twelve to her achievements. De Beauvoir was the life-long partner of Jean-Paul Sartre whom she met at the Sorbonne where she came second to him in the *agrégation.* With him she

shared a life-long 'open relationship'. Although they never actually lived together they were seen as a couple, both as existentialist philosophers and espousers of most left-wing causes.

In addition to editing Sartre's voluminous writings she was a prolific writer in her own right. 'The Second Sex' (1949), arguably the first piece of feminist literature, was an account of woman's condition as the 'other' as compared to the masculine type against which women are measured and defined. It was placed on the Vatican's banned list for its advocacy of free love and threat to the family. In 1974 she formed the *Ligue du Droit des Femmes'*, a fore-runner of the *Mouvement pour la Libération des Femmes*. Her later book, The Mandarins, won her the Prix Goncourt and she also wrote a four-volume autobiography.

She was on the editorial committee of *Les Temps Modernes* a left-wing review which remained at the centre of French intellectual life for 25 years, and took up radical positions on both domestic and international issues.

Bébète Show

A daily, ten-minute, peak-time equivalent of 'Spitting Images', regularly watched by fifteen million viewers. Cassettes of the show sold over 300,000 copies. More influential than 'Spitting Images', two politicians, Le Pen and Edith Cresson, have complained about their characterisation. Le Pen was portrayed as 'Frankenpen' wearing a Prussian military helmet. He was changed to a stupid peasant girl from Brittany from where he originates.

Madame Cresson was originally portrayed as a panther under the name Amabotte. This was a *jeu de mots* on her name. 'Cresson' means 'watercress' which you buy in a bunch or *botte*. But *'botte* has a second meaning of 'boot' so that the expression *à ma botte* was equivalent to 'heel!' and implied that she was M. Mitterrand's poodle. When she complained she was changed to *Didi la Teigne* which means both a moth and ringworm. The President is portrayed as a frog, not from the English view that makes all French people frogs but from the play on the name Kermitterrand. He treated Amabotte with a familiarity which went some way beyond the normal courtesies between *Président* and *Premier Ministre*. But then he did say *'Elle est charmante, non?'* shortly after appointing her.

The programme is repeated each morning at 7.50 a.m. on the radio. If your French is up to it, you can tune in to *France Inter* and listen.

Bécaud, Gilbert (b. 1927)

'Monsieur 100,000 volts'. Singer/pianist/composer with massive, mainly middle-aged following. A person of considerable talent, he got as far as composing an opera which *malheureusement* sank largely without trace.

Beckett, Samuel (b. 1906-1989)

Although born in Dublin, where he was a friend of James Joyce, from 1932 Beckett lived in Paris. In 1953 his most famous work, *En Attendant Godot*, was first performed causing an instant sensation. He became a leader of the Theatre of the Absurd and won the Nobel Prize in 1969. Building on this, subsequent plays featured characters that were blind and paralysed, legless and confined to dustbins, and another person gradually disappearing up to her neck in a mound of sand. A later play, *'Souffle'*, had no actors and lasted for only thirty seconds during which a breath is drawn in and expired accompanied by 'a faint brief cry'.

Belmondo, Jean-Paul (b 1933)

Down-to-earth, dog-loving actor and stuntman, whose best-known film is *A Bout de Souffle*. A long-time *copain* of Ursula Andress. His father was a well-known sculptor; son Paul is a racing driver.

Belote

Card game played, often with considerable passion, in cafés. It uses a standard pack of cards minus all those below nine. The rules are a mixture of solo, rummy and bridge. Success is 75% a function of the cards you are dealt and 25% of the skill with which you play them. A more interesting game is Tarot which puts a greater premium on the play of the hand and whose cards can double up as aids to fortune-telling.

Bérégovoy, Pierre (b. 1925)

Appointed Prime Minister in April 1992 before which he was Minister of Finance. Unlike most of his predecessors he has little formal education, not even possessing the *bac*, but is a long-time ally of the President. One could draw a parallel between his succession to power and that of John Major, both also Treasury men following strong women. Except that he makes John Major look charismatic.

Berlioz, Hector (1803-1869)

Romantic composer, who wrote *somptueuse* (a favourite French word) dramatic music such as Damnation of Faust and *Symphonie Fantastique*.

Bernhardt, Sarah (1845-1923)

Golden-voiced actress of international renown, originally with the *Comédie Française*. She lost a leg in 1915 but carried on acting regardless. Shaw wrote *Salomé* in French for her. Rostand went one better by writing a play *'La Gloire'* in which she could remain seated throughout. Off-stage she was given to sleeping in a coffin.

Bibliothèque Nationale

France's greatest library created by Mazarin in the 17th century and originally stocked from the collections of various kings. Situated in Paris, it receives one copy of every book, periodical and piece of music published in France to help fill its 38 Km of shelves.

Bibliothèque de France

An author in his own right, President Mitterrand can lay a strong claim to being the most lettered of contemporary political leaders. It is totally appropriate, therefore, that his Presidency should be responsible for the building of the world's largest library. His political opponents take a more jaundiced view, linking this project with the Pyramid at the Louvre and the *Grande Arche* at *La Défense* in Paris (known locally as the 'wind tunnel'), to accuse him of delusions of grandeur, megalomania and of pretensions to emulate Louis XIV.

Construction is financed by the State but on ground donated by the city of Paris (whose mayor, Jacques Chirac, is not Mitterrand's greatest supporter). This has caused some hiccups, not least when the *Mairie* suspended building on the pretext of needing to rehouse some squatters who had inconveniently moved in nearby.

Births

With three invasions in under a hundred years, France has historically seen security and the birthrate as closely linked. In the Second World War, Germany was able to put almost twice as many men of military age as France into the field.

Today French family allowances remain among the highest in Europe and there are various other financial inducements to have children. Reductions in fares on public transport start at 30% if there are three children in the family going up to 65% if there are more than five. There is even a *Prix Cognacq-Jay*. This is given to families with more than eight children and both parents under 45, and to families of five or more children where both parents are under 35.

Possiby driven by such inducements, there was *le baby-boom (sic)* after the war, reinforced by immigration, so that the population of France grew from 41 million in 1941 to over 56 million today. More recently the danger has been that it will resume a long-term decline. To maintain population stability each woman of child-bearing age needs to have 2.1 children. Currently the national average is an insufficient 1.8.

In this cartoon from the Canard Enchainé *Mme Cresson, holding the INSEE report saying 'France is getting older', is saying 'The French are not having any more babies'. Mitterrand, in a reference to her statement that one in four Englishmen is homosexual, replies, 'No doubt, the influence of these English queers (pédés).'*

In 1991, at the height of the so-called charters affair (the plan to charter aircraft to repatriate clandestine immigrants), the government statistics institute, INSEE, did not help by pointing out that as a result of the low birthrate, the working population would need to be topped up with immigrants (in 1955 there were ten people of working age to support every one person in retirement; now there are only two). In fact existing immigrants are already doing their bit. The groups currently with the highest birthrates are Moroccan immigrants, with an average of 5.23, Tunisians with 5.20, Turks with 5.05 and Algerians with 4.29.

Bison Futé

The 'Crafty Bison' was invented to help you avoid traffic jams on your way through France. He does this by means of signposting recommended alternative routes *'Itinéraires Bis'* with green arrows. In summer a map showing the routes can be picked up free of charge at any autoroute *Bureau de Tourisme.* Since the suggested routes mainly follow the golden rule of driving in France, which is to stick to autoroutes and D-roads and keep off the *Routes Nationales,* his recommendations are mostly helpful.

However, his best advice concerns not where to travel but when. If you insist on returning from the South of France during the last weekend in August you are in trouble no matter which route you follow. Days are coded by colour as to anticipated traffic density and regular bulletins given out on the radio and television.

Blanco, Serge (b. 1958)

Holder of the world record for the most tries (38) scored by a full-back in international rugby and the French record for number of international appearances (89). He captained France during the latter part of the eighties. An inspirational attacking full-back whose turn of speed and adventurous style contributed to many famous victories, notably when he scored in the last minute of the semi-final of the first World Cup.

Although born in Caracas, he is a Basque and now runs a centre of thalassotherapy (therapy using the sea) at Hendaye in the *Pyrénées-Atlantiques.*

Blum, Léon (1872-1950)

Jewish intellectual, hated by the right, who became the first-ever socialist Prime Minister in 1936 at the head of the *Front Populaire.* During his brief period of office he found time to institute the 40-hour working week, holidays with pay and collective bargaining. Consequently in many quarters he became even more *populaire* after his death and his name is commemorated in many *rues* and *places.*

Bocuse, Paul (b. 1926 - *See Front Cover*)

Poacher turned *restaurateur extraordinaire.* Bocuse, the most famous chef of the century, perhaps owes his insistence on utilising what is fresh from the market on his early experiences poaching on the Saône. From there he learned his trade under the great post-war chefs - Fernand Point, Lucas-Carton - before returning to his home at Collonges-au-Mont d'Or, just outside of Lyon. Having first had to buy back the name of Bocuse which his grandfather had sold, he had, within six years gained the coveted three Michelin stars. In 1975 he was awarded the *Légion d'Honneur* and created a *Soupe Aux Truffes Valery Giscaird d'Estaing* for the inauguration.

His name is often wrongly associated with *nouvelle cuisine.* His own comments dispel that illusion: 'a tiny carrot jostles with a thin turnip, accompanied by a pea cut into four, the whole lot surrounding a skinny fillet of chicken from which both skin and bones have been taken off...' The real, and lasting, innovation for which Bocuse was responsible was managerial - the take-over of restaurants by the chefs where previously they had been run by businessmen with the chef hidden in the kitchen. No danger of Bocuse resting *invisible.* Provided he is not globe-trotting, spreading his message from the States to Japan, he will be there to greet and talk with you as you enjoy a superb meal. No dearer than a night at the opera, and just as much an experience, *ça vaut le voyage.*

The photo on the front of this book is printed with the kind permission of M. Bocuse. A Dutch advertising company, which had the bright idea of showing him dreaming of a Big-Mac hamburger, did so without such permission. Their explanation, in the face of a lawsuit, that 'Not many people have heard of M. Bocuse in Holland', did nothing to soothe the great man's wrath.

Boileau, Nicolas (1636-1711)

Founder of French literary criticism. His *L'Art Poétique* defined the Three Unities to which classical playwrights had to adhere. A play had to be situated in one place only, at one point in time and have only one plot:

> *Qu'en un lieu, qu'en un jour, un seul fait accompli*
> *Tienne jusqu à la fin le theatre rempli*

The effect of this is that the sub-plots, comic relief, battles and passage of time that characterise a Shakespearian play do not occur and the plays become predominantly studies of personality.

Bokassa Diamonds

A personal gift, unearthed by the *Canard Enchainé* and estimated by them to be worth one million francs, from the Central African, child-eating Emperor Bokassa to the then President, Giscard d'Estaing. The latter was seen at the time as economical with an explanation when questioned about them and they did little to help his chances in the 1981 Presidential elections.

In his autobiography published in 1991 he devotes 56 pages to the issue whilst contriving as far as possible to avoid the 'emotive' word 'diamonds'. He also puts their worth at only twenty thousand francs, accusing *Le Canard* of having confused the currency in which their value had been expressed.

Book Prizes *(Prix Littéraires)*

The French are immensely keen on book prizes as befits a nation that takes its language and culture seriously. At the latest count there were around 1500 prizes awarded every year with values ranging from nothing up to £30,000. Among the most prestigious are *le prix Goncourt, Prix Femina, Prix de Critiques, Interallié, Medicis* and *Prix Renaudot* to name but a few. In general they carry less money but considerably more prestige than their equivalents in England. The Goncourt, for example, brings the winner 50 francs as his or her prize but guarantees sales of almost half a million in this literature-loving country.

The prizes are thus highly sought after and as surrounded by controversy as to the winners as any such competition. There is even a suspicion that the major prizes are dominated by the holy trinity of *maisons d'édition,* Gallimard, Grasset and Seuil who will not infrequently have one of their own authors on the jury.

Bordeaux

Port on the estuary of the Garonne in South-West France, 100 Km from the sea. *Chef-lieu* of the region of Aquitaine. Beautifully situated, it has claret-producing vineyards to the east and miles of beaches and pine forests to the south. With almost three-quarters of a million inhabitants it is France's fourth largest city. Its mayor, Chaban-Delmas was Prime Minister under De Gaulle and this was not unhelpful in reviving a declining town with various projects such as a new arts centre.

One unsuccessful project was the cheque-book attempt (subsequently copied with more success by Bernard Tapie at *l'Olympique Marseille)* to make the Bordeaux side, the *Girondins,* France's top football team. In 1991 it collapsed with debts of £2.4 million and the team was relegated to the Second Division of the French Football League.

Boulanger, Général Georges (1837-1891)
Minister of War in 1886 who won popularity as a man of action and became the focus of an anti-republican movement which almost swept him to power. Unfortunately he was equally, if not more, enamoured of action with his mistress and at the crucial moment history passed him by. He finally committed suicide on his mistress's grave.
In this final gesture he was upstaged by his near-contemporary, President Félix Faure. Whereas Boulanger died on his mistress's grave, Faure died on his mistress. *'Au cours d'un rendez-vous galant'* is how the French described it. Shuffling off the mortal coil in this way was seen by Hamlet as:

a consummation
Devoutly to be wished.

Boulangerie
The bakers is a good place to practise the language. A knowledge of the different types of bread and *croissants* plus the ability to count in French will suffice.
Quatre croissants, s'il vous plait', should sort out breakfast. With that success under your belt, the family can next day have a chocolate *croissant* - referred to as chocolate bread *'pain au chocolat'*. For bread you have a wider choice. In increasing order of size you can buy *une ficelle, une baguette, une flûte, or un gros pain.**
When it comes to paying, cowards proffer a higher sum than the total, trusting to the honesty of the assistant. The result is a pocket weighed down with small change *(monnaie)*. The more adventurous attempt to construct the right amount, apologising, if appropriate, for getting rid of all their change on them - *Je voudrais m'en débarrasser'*. You will almost certainly be told that it is *'pas de problème'*. When you thank the assistant she may reply simply *'C'est moi'*. This is short for *'C'est moi qui vous remercie'* (it is I who thank you) - a sentiment less commonly heard in English shops.

Boules
There is a fiction surrounding the Olympic Games that to take part is more important than to win. But with *Boules* - with the exception of a *Concours de Pétanque* (another word for *boules*)* which you are unlikely to enter - it is true. *Boules,* which dates from the time of the Pharaohs, is less a game than a pastime, as much a social event as a contest of skill. As such there are seven million players in France. Since it is a social event it is one in which you should participate, preferably refreshing yourself from time to time with a *pastis.*
For an informal game on holiday, not just you but also the kids can join in. Not only will you fraternise with the natives, you will consolidate your command of the language. Only a few expressions are needed in order to become a pundit.

The prerequisite of participating is to know the rules and to have your own *boules*. The latter are easily acquired from a *supermarché* or local market. Ignore the matched sets complete with duster. Go for the cheapest you can find. After all, all that you are going to do with them is throw them at a small wooden ball. The rules are simple. The target is the *cochonnet* (little pig). At the start of each game the winners of the previous game throw it up the alley - not less than six metres and not more than ten. The teams then throw their *boules* as near as they can to the *cochonnet*. Throws do not alternate. Once one of your *boules* is nearest to the *cochonnet* the other side has to keep throwing until such time as they

* *As always, I refer to the Midi. In other parts of France, the names are reversed and you can buy something called* un bâtard.

* *The name* pétanque *comes from the old Provençal expression* 'pes tanques' *meaning 'feet together'. Originally you were allowed a run at it, as with English bowls, but since the end of the last century you throw from a stationary position.*

get closer. When all *boules* have been thrown you count up (bowls-style) by how many shots the winning side has won.

A *partie* is decided by the first team to reach thirteen. You can play almost anywhere that there is a suitable gravelly terrain. Most village squares in the *Midi* have an area specially set aside. If possible, however, you should choose the middle of a street. This will force any motorist into stopping until an end is finished. This shows the correct attitude towards drivers.

It is less important that you demonstrate any ability than that you adopt the correct style. Do not roll the *boule* as you would a bowl in England.* Before throwing the boule, cradle it gently in your hand and look meaningfully at the target. Then throw it out of the back of the hand so as to impart an imaginary back-spin. If you slightly roll it as though you were bowling a leg-cutter, *tant mieux.*

The trajectory is equally important. You should bend the knees - *fléchissez* as your ski instructor would say - so that the *boule* starts its flight from approximately 25cm above the ground. This allows an exaggerated parabola which again is meant to be efficacious in the *boule* stopping quickly after landing. Neither statistically nor aerodynamically is there compelling evidence that these two techniques contribute to the desired end. That is part of your education. Form is more important than function - a notion that is difficult for an Englishman to come to terms with.

The other important thing is to knock the *boules* together whilst waiting your turn. This gives a satisfying sound analogous to Chinese playing mahjong, Remember to keep your fingers out of the way whilst you are doing it. During *une partie* you should focus all attention on the game, even though you are not concerned with winning. In this way you keep the vocabulary you need limited to the game. All you need to know in order to demonstrate perfect familiarity with the game is the following:

Elle est bonne. Say this at any time when your opponent's *boule* finishes up closert to the *cochonnet* than yours. If yours is closest, but the opposition then throws one closer *'elle est meuilleure'* is appropriate. More generally you can say *'elle a gagné'*. If the *boule* lands well but then runs past, then your comment is *'elle est partie'* If it's your turn then just say *'C'est à moi'* if it's the opponents' *'C'est à vous'*.

When it is your turn to throw there are two options. You can either attempt to *'pointer'* your *boule* closest to the *cochonnet* or you can *'tirer'*, that is aim at an opponent's *boule* in an attempt to knock it out of the way. To let it be generally known that you are up with this distinction you could nominate one of your team as a *pointeur* and yourself as the *tireur.* The ultimate successful *tir* is when your *boule* knocks away an opponent's and stops dead in its place. This is known as a *carreau.* If, as is more likely, your *boule* disappears into the middle distance having failed to make contact, you could reflect that the world record for successful *tirs* is 501 out of 503.

You should occasionally evince an interest in the score. Nothing could be simpler: *'Quel est le score?'* you enquire. *'Sept à quatre'* indicates that you are slightly behind. If the scores are level it is *'huit partout'*. Once you have mastered these simple expressions you can quickly move on to more advanced ploys. If there is difficulty deciding which of two boules is *meilleure* then you could suggest a referee *'il faut un arbitre'*. When it's all over you could suggest a return: *'Encore une partie..?'* or *'la revanche'?*

* *Unless you are playing the Lyonnais version which has a longer pitch and bigger* boules *which you roll rather than throw.*

Boulez, Pierre (b. 1925)

Composer and conductor of both the BBC Symphony Orchestra and the New York Philharmonic. His own creative work centred on research into electro-acoustic technologies and in the exploration of the different relationships between text and music. Among his many international awards is an honorary fellowship at Cambridge.

Bourbon

Dynasty of kings starting with Henry IV in 1589, and lasting (with a brief interruption for the Revolution) until 1830. Of them it was said that they had forgotton nothing and learned nothing. The living heir to the line, and therefore pretender to the throne, is the *Comte de Paris.* Now that the French elect their monarchs every seven years his claims are less than pressing.

Bourgogne

The Burgundy *région* comprising the *départements* of Côte-d'Or (21), Nièvre (58), Saône-et-Loire (71) and Yonne (89) and numbering 1.6 million inhabitants. Its *chef-lieu* is Dijon but names like Nuits-St-George, Beaune and Mâcon slip more easily off the tongue or down the throat.

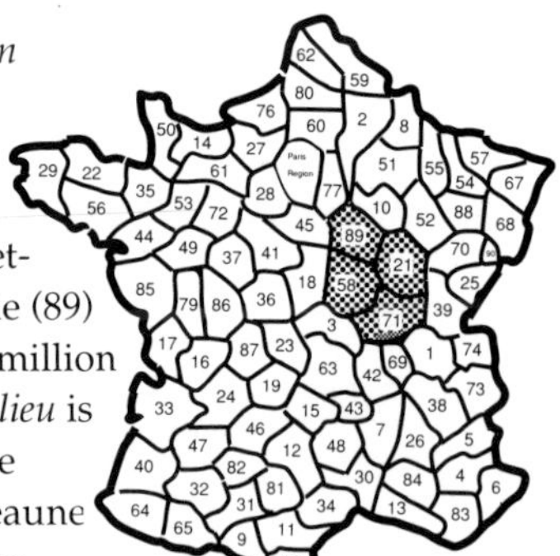

Most of the A6 autoroute from Paris to Lyon is through this region. It became a province (as opposed to an independent dukedom) in 1477.

Bourse

Literally meaning 'purse', *la Bourse* is the Stock Exchange. Although regional exchanges exist in Lyon, Marseille, Bordeaux and elsewhere, the Paris Bourse accounts for 95% of all business. Officially established in 1724 it has its own building in the Rue Vivienne. There is a viewing gallery from which you can see people waving arms wildly and shouting *'J'ai'* or *'Je prends'*

Braques, Georges (1882-1963)

Painter who started out with the *Fauves* * then, together with Picasso, invented Cubism. Best-known for his still-lifes.

Brel, Jacques (1929-1978)

Belgian-born singer and composer who enjoyed enormous popularity in France throughout the Sixties. His writing talents extended to an operetta which brought him fame in the USA.

In 1966 he took off to the Marquesas Islands in the Pacific (where Gauguin had been before him and next to whom he was subsequently buried). His comeback album on his return eleven years later sold a million copies in advance. After his death from cancer a charitable foundation dedicated to his memory was set up by his daughters. It now has offices in both Brussels and Paris. The Foundation exists to encourage cultural activities around the works of Brel and to use the funds thus raised to assist in research into cancer and help hospitalised children.

Fondation Jacques Brel, 25, rue Francois Ier, 75008 Paris

* *'Fauve', meaning 'wild beast' was a derogatory name applied to the paintings of Matisse, Derain, Vlaminck and Braques. As with 'impressionism' and 'cubism' a term meant initially as a disparagement, became the accepted (and respectable) name of a school.*

Brittany

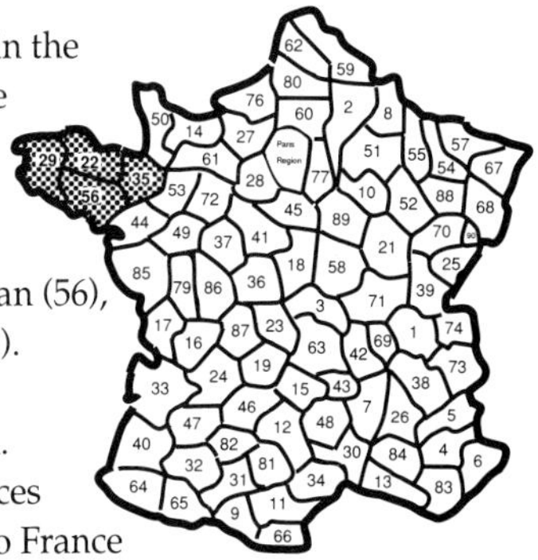

La Bretagne is a *région* in the North-West of France incorporating the *départements* of Finisterre (29), Côtes-du-Nord (22), Morbihan (56), and Ille-et-Villaine (35). *Chef-lieu:* Rennes; population 2.8 million. One of the last provinces to be incorporated into France (in 1532), it still retains a healthy air of independence, if not separatism. The Breton language is still spoken and efforts are made to keep it alive. One sign of the Bretons' independent spirit, allied to their love of the sea, was the formation of Brittany Ferries. This was set up, and is still majority-owned, by local farmers and has expanded to give a number of cross-channel connections with England. However, there is no equivalent to the Scottish Nationalists. When the first direct regional elections were held Breton nationalist parties received only a derisory vote.

A national record inexplicably held by this most beautiful region is for the highest incidence of suicide.

Bruel, Patrick (b. 1959)

Comparatively little-known actor who turned into a superstar singer and song-writer, with enormous popularity among the young. In 1991, the year of 'Bruelmania', his album *Alors Regarde* sold more than two million copies and he is by some distance the hottest property on the popular music scene. The words of the title song, 'Alors Regarde', are an invocation to 'look at' and speak out about oppression. An entertainer *engagé*,* he was the clear winner (34% against second place 23% for Alain Delon) of a *Paris Match* poll for the person with whom women would choose to have *une aventure de vacances.*

* *The nearest translation of* engagé *is 'politically committed'. Montand was* engagé *to left-wing causes, as was Sartre. Bruel's songs reflect a commitment to combatting oppression.*

C

Cafés

A quintessential aspect of French life where you can make a tiny cup of coffee last an hour - *à table* or, more cheaply, *sur le pouce* - without pressure to drink up. You can also eat and, in many, place your bets on the PMU. Though café society is not what it was, and *'les flippers'* are losing the battle against video-games, one in ten persons still goes to a café at least once a day.

Calendrier of Names

The much-used term, *dirigisme,* means roughly that the State knows best. It has been an enduring feature of French political life, whether the state is embodied in Louis XIV, the Jacobins, Napoleon, General de Gaulle or Mitterrand.

An everyday example of this is the *Calendrier* of Names. Until very recently French parents could not give their child any *prénom* that they wanted. Names had to be those of a saint taken from the *calendrier**. This accounts for the high proportion of double names - Marie - Noel, Jean-Paul etc - as parents struggled within the rules to give their offspring some form of individualism. Since every day of the year has its own saint, being named after one means that, in addition to your birthday, you have your own *'Jour de Fête'*, i.e. the day in the year on which your saint's day falls.

MAI		
MER	F. du TRAVAIL	1
JEU	S. Boris	2
VEN	S.Jacq.Phil.	3
SAM	S. Sylvain	4
DIM	Se Judith	5
LUN	Se Prudence	6
MAR	Se Gisèle	7
MER	Vict. 1945	8
JEU	ASCENSION	9
VEN	Se Solange	10
SAM	Se Estelle	11
DIM	Fête J. d'Arc	12

The requirement to refer to the *calendrier* was relaxed in the eighties with greater discretion given to the local *maire,* and was finally abolished on January 1st, 1992.

* *In France, therefore, you did not have to buy one of those books entitled 'What to call your baby'. You merely looked down the* calendrier. *This led to some children being called* 'Ascension' *and, so the story goes, others being christened* 'Fêtenat'.

This relaxation has already led to greater diversity as shown by the list of the most popular names in France. Whereas traditionally Michel, Jean, Pierre for boys and Marie, Isabelle and Monique for girls were the most popular, in the late eighties these were supplanted by names such as Julien, Nicolas and Jeremy for boys, and Aurelie, Mélanie, Elodie, and Julie for girls. One in thirty working-class parents now calls their son Kevin. The most common surnames are Martin, Bernard, Moreau and Durand.

Calvin, Jean (1509-1564)

Theologian who believed in the doctrines of justification by faith alone, denial of free will and the predestination of some to salvation and others to damnation. He established a theocratic dictatorship in Geneva and his intolerant brand of religion became the basis of that adopted by French protestants (known as Huguenots). This was unfortunate for them as it lead them into opposition to the authority of the catholic-dominated monarchy with generally unpleasant consequences.

Camargue

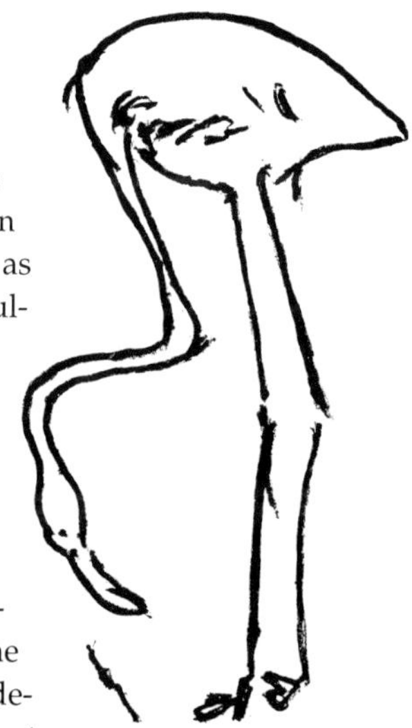

As it nears the Mediterranean the Rhône splits into the large and small Rhône and forms an extensive delta. In this delta is the large, often marshy, expanse known as the Camargue. Partly cultivated - it provides a fair amount of rice - it is best known as the home of white horses, black bulls and pink flamingos.

At the southern extremity of the Camargue is the town of Saintes-Maries-de-la-Mer. The name of this attractive resort evidences the legend that the two Marys came to this part of the world after the death of Christ. The area is classified as a *parc régional national* although it is doubtful that this will be sufficient to save it from having an electronic listening post built on it by the *Direction Générale de la Sécurité Extérieure.*

Camping
Camping is a good way to meet the natives as over five million French people go camping every year. This high number reflects the fact that there are many activities in France, such as camping and ski-ing, which are essentially the preserve of the middle-class in England but where no such distinction exists in the less class-conscious France.
There are different ways to camp. The first is to go to an international campsite. Facilities, coded by number of stars, will be good and there will be a complete mix of nationalities. Staff will speak English and you can import your little bit of England into France.
Alternatively you can go *camping à la ferme.* This will bring you closer to the real France. The campsite will be part of a farmer's property and facilities may well be home-built. This offers greater opportunities for getting to know people socially. Prices, and minimum standards, are controlled by the government.
Finally there is *camping sauvage.* Most communes now ban this but you could get permission from a local to pitch your tent. This approach is most appropriate for impecunious youngsters willing to trade off comfort against cash.

Camus, Albert (1913-1960)
Algerian international goalkeeper turned writer and moralist. As a writer his best-known works are *L'Etranger,* (the original manuscript of which recently changed hands for a million francs) and *La Peste.* He was awarded the Nobel Prize for Literature in 1957. As a journalist, together with Jean-Paul Sartre, he put the first paper onto the streets of Paris immediately after the Liberation - *Le Combat.* Similar to Orwell in his distrust of authoritarianism, he subsequently fell out of favour with Sartre owing to his (Camus) repudiation of Marxism. He was killed in a car crash at the age of 46.

Canals
The French have long been great canal builders. It was, after all, Ferdinand de Lesseps who built the Suez Canal, although Disraeli managed subsequently to buy it from the French. From there de Lesseps made a start on the Panama Canal but this fell foul of a financial scandal and it was left to the Americans to complete.
Back in the Hexagon canal building has been attended with greater success and one of the most relaxing ways of enjoying rural France is on a *péniche.* Their speed synchronises well with the pace of life as you get further south and vineyards appear to exert a magnetic effect on their courses. The *Canal du Briare* takes you through the Loire Valley; the *Canal du Bourgogne* winds lazily through central France and the 241 kilometers of the *Canal du Midi,* built in 1681, serve to join the Mediterranean to the Atlantic by way of the magnificent mediaeval town of Carcassone. The latter 'fairy-tale castle' attracts over 200,000 visitors a year.
Inland waterways are not only, or indeed predominantly, for tourists. Over ten billion tons of freight are transported annually on them.

Candide
Novel by Voltaire first published in 1759 satirising the prevailing philosophy of optimism as expounded by Leibniz and Rousseau. It was published under a pseudonymn but its author was immediately recognised. Balzac described it as *'le diamant de notre intelligence nationale'.*
Candide is assured by the philosopher, Pangloss that 'everything is for the best in the best of all possible worlds'. He roams the world meeting innumerable natural and man-made disasters - including the Spanish Inquisition (where Pangloss is hanged), shipwreck, slavery, cannibals and earthquakes - of a type to shake one's belief in the philosophy. Although Pangloss (miraculouly surviving his hanging) never loses his optimistic creed, in the end Candide rejects it in favour of a more modest conclusion that the world will go round better if everyone does good in his own particular sphere.

'Tout cela est très bien, mais il faut cultiver son jardin.'

Capetians
Third dynasty of French kings founded by Hugh Capet in 987and reigning until the death of Charles IV in 1328. This dynasty established the central monarchy and extended its rule over most of present-day France.

Carolignians
Second dynasty preceding the Capetians, ruling from 751 following the Merovingians. Starting with *Pépin le Bref*, the line included Charlemagne after whose death internal strife and external invasions caused the break-up of the kingdom. The dynasty survived until the death of Louis V in 987.

Cars
Over half of all French drivers own a car built by a French-owned company. The corresponding British figure is 12%. France has always been in the forefront of car manufacturing, through the originality of its engineers and the flair of its stylists. Renault (27% of the home market) and Citroen-Peugeot (33%) between them produce over three million cars a year and represent, with Fiat and Volkswagen, the major European constructors.
Renault was founded by Louis Renault in 1899. Guilty of collaborating with the Germans during the war, the company was taken over by the government. In principle it is run along private industry lines but government ownership came in helpful when it lost 33 billion francs in the early eighties.
Citroen is best-known for its 2CV - known in France as *'la deuch'*. Its original specification just after the war was for a car that could carry a farmer, his wife and a 50Kg sack of potatoes at 50kph. Production started in 1947 and was discontinued only in 1990.
Peugeot cars have performed consistently well in the gruelling annual Paris-Dakar rally (where Mark Thatcher got himself lost) and have acquired a deserved reputation for reliability. The 205 has been voted 'Car of the Decade'. In the seventies, the workforce at Peugeot took out a patent on the numbers 605 and upwards. When the company came to expand its range it found that these numbers had been patented and was forced to buy them back. But *ça, c'est du passé* (that's all in the past). Today Peugeot has withdrawn from the US market owing to declining sales, and revised quotas for the entry of Japanese cars into the Common Market pose a long-term threat to the French car industry. When Japanese video-recorders threatened the home industry they all had to pass through one tiny customs post in Poitiers. In today's climate such typically French subtleties are frowned upon.

Catacombs
Not as ancient as the Roman ones, these are full of the bones of six million graves cleared from Parisian cemeteries during the 18th and 19th centuries. They cover an enormous area underneath the *rive gauche* with some 300 km of tunnels. Only a tiny part is open to the public. If you want to see the rest you need to know the right manhole. The only one sure of being open is that outside the gendarmerie at Porte d'Orléans; others are regularly blocked up in an attempt to prevent the *cataphiles* from living down there and writing their subterranean magazines.

Eheu Fugaces!

Cathars
If your travels take you to the Languedoc-Roussillon area you are in Cathar country. The Cathars were an austere evangelical religious sect in the 11th - 12th century who believed in a dual Godhead of Good and Evil. They took Christ's teachings at his word and attempted to emulate his poverty, leading simple, virtuous lives doing no harm to anybody. Such an

example posed an obvious threat to the established church and successive Popes ordered crusades against them. The most famous culminated in the Albigensian Massacre in 1215. Shortly after this the Inquisition visited the area and in 1246 two hundred people were burned at Montségur. They have left behind many ruined castles, aptly named *Châteaux de Vertige* from their positions stuck on the top of hills.

Many rumours of fabulous treasures, including the Holy Grail, surround the Cathars and, later, the Knights Templars. An important find, made at Rennes-le-Château (Aude) in 1891, served to fuel this specultaion.

Centralism

France is a much more centralised country than the UK. Virtually every important decision - political, economic, cultural - is taken in Paris. One still-common measure of professional success - the extent to which one has *arrivé* - - is how close to Paris one works. There are clear historical reasons for this dominance of Paris in all aspects of French life..

A common way of looking at French history is the gradual subjugation of regions such as Burgundy, Aquitaine and Brittany and their integration into a unitary state. Centuries after Magna Carta had started the process of devolving power in England, Richelieu was busy centralising France in support of an absolutist monarchy. Later on his soul-mate Napoleon continued the process. The *Code Napoléon* was the ultimate attempt to apply pure reason to the administration of affairs of the State at all levels. Relatively small *départements* were easier to control than large provinces and each *département* was run by a *préfet* appointed by, and responsible to, the central government. *Divide et impera!* In reality the attempt to regulate everything by a central set of rules is self-defeating and spawns the *Système D* (for *débrouillard)* whereby people work their way round the system. Nevertheless, the system remained virtually unchanged until the Mitterrand reforms of the 80s which first gave the regions their own directly-elected *conseils généraux.*

This penchant for state planning and control is known in France as *étatisme* or *dirigisme.* It cuts across left/right political boundaries in that both de Gaulle and later the Socialists were largely sympathetic to it. In economic terms Paris, the seat of the Ministry of Finance and of the largely state-owned banks, is the major source of finance for both private and state industry and provides a large part of the funds for regional development.

The Chirac government from 1986-88, in the true spirit of Thatcherism, set about reducing this economic dependence on the government through a programme of privatisation, abolition of price controls and reduction of subsidies to lame ducks. How well France has been served by its centralist planning policies is part of the never-ending debate between planners and laissez-faire economists. It produced the TGV but also Concorde.

Centre

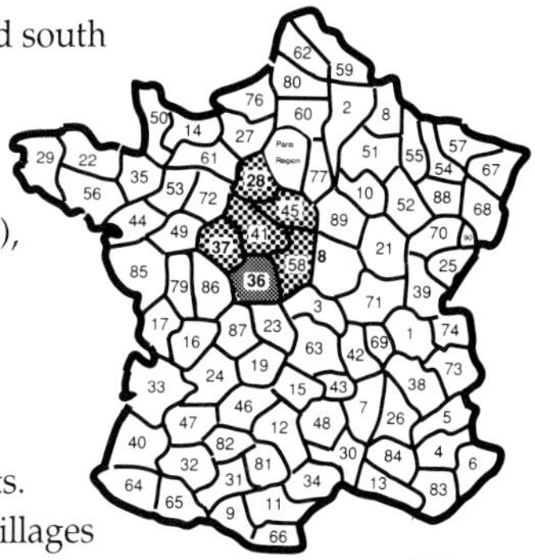

Région to the west and south of Paris comprising the *départements* of Cher (18), Eure-et-Loir (28), Indre (36), Indre-et-Loire (37), Loir-et-Cher (41) and Loiret (45).

Chef-lieu: Orléans; 2.4 million inhabitants.

Near Bourges three villages lay claim to being the precise geographic centre of France. The honour is generally given to Saulzais-le-Potier, a row of stone houses with a two-metre monument.

It is in the Centre that the Allier joins the Loire which till then is little more than a stream but soon becomes a majestic river. The region has the reputation of being the part of France where the purest French is spoken.

Centre Pompidou (a.k.a. Centre Beaubourg)

Opened in 1977, this oil-refinery look-alike attracts more visitors (25,000 a day) than any other monument in Paris. A cynic might say that this is less a tribute to the contemporary art displays on show than to its being the easiest place from which to get a good view over the city without having to walk up hundreds of steps. In addition to housing the *Centre National d'Art et de Culture,* it currently boasts a large digital clock on its exterior which is ticking off the seconds until the end of the millennium.

Cévennes

Area of forested hills and steep valleys to the south of the Massif Central and west of the Rhône Valley. The Cevennes epitomises what is referred to as *la France profonde,* that is the lowly-populated rural areas, often with poor soil, which have suffered greatly from *l'éxode rurale.* One of the surviving bastions of Protestantism, it still remembers the brutal wars against the *camisards* waged in the 18th century.
In 1878 Robert Louis Stevenson made his 'Travels with a Donkey' from north to south of the Cévennes.

Cézanne, Paul (1938-1906)

Born in Aix-en- Provence, the son of a wealthy banker, he was a friend of the Impressionists and of Zola. His paintings are mainly of still life, open air and bathers. The latter, in his early period, were violent, sensual works with swollen breasts and buttocks. Later in life he could not bring himself to paint women in the nude and his paintings are from memory.
The use of depth and colour in his paintings had great influence on succeeding generations of artists and he is often referred to as 'the father of modern painting'.
The *'route Cézanne'* past Mont St Victoire and Picasso's château at Vauvenargues is a favourite jaunt for inhabitants of Aix.

Champagne-Ardennes

Région to east and north of Paris comprising the *départements* of Ardennes (08), Aube (10), Marne (51) and Haute-Marne (52). *Chef-lieu:* Châlons-sur-Marne. 1.3 million inhabitants.

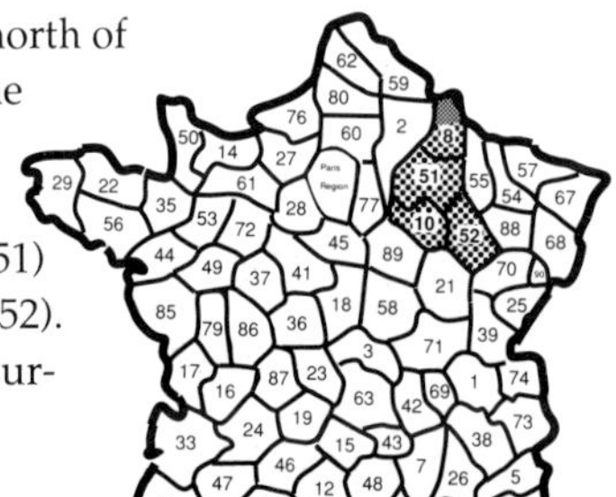

Less than three hours drive from Calais along the deserted A26 brings you into this historic area (to say nothing of its wine). All but three of the kings of France were crowned at Rheims including Charles VII who had to rely on Joan of Arc to get him there.

Chanel, Coco (1883-1971)

Her humble background gave rise to her economy of style as a couturier. Her first creation was a man's sweater over a pleated skirt tied together by a handkerchief. She is also credited with starting the fashion for suntan, thereby spawning an industry almost as great as the ragtrade. Like other couturiers she went into perfume, giving the world Chanel No 5 which has more than eighty ingredients and which, by her own testimony, was all that Marilyn Monroe wore in bed.

Channel Tunnel

A magnificent feat of engineering - the 9 million cubic metres of soil excavated would fill a pyramid 300 metres high.
The cost-estimating was not quite up to this high standard. Although compared to similar technologically-advanced projects - Concorde, Sydney Opera House, both of which exceeded their original estimates by a factor of thirteen - the overrun of roughly double is better than par for this type of project. Nevertheless, it means that shareholders will have to wait until the next century to receive dividends.
When the company was floated shareholders subscribing to £5,250 worth of shares were granted free crossings until 2040. In the UK this offer was taken up by over 10,000 people anxious to take Sunday lunch in Pas-de-Calais. When completed, hopefully as *prévu* in 1993, the tunnel will have the capacity of 4000 vehicles per hour in each direction - equivalent to a two-lane autoroute - with a journey time of thirty minutes at 160 kph. The tunnel carries an 'all risks' insurance against damage to the value of £500 million.

Chansons

Every teen-ager, without exception, useless at remembering anything you or their teachers tell them, exhibits total recall when the latest chart hits are concerned. Songs are a marvellous way to imrove your grasp of a language. A cassette of a French singer such as Gainsbourg, Michel Sardou, François Cabrel, Françoise Hardy or Piaf is a painless self-teach text. The important thing is to enjoy the tape independently of any linguistic benefit you may obtain from it. Once you have listened to it a number of times read through the words (most tapes or CDs now include them). It does not matter if you do not understand every single word or expression. Because they are already vaguely familiar you will soon pick them up.

There are even French rhymes as prevalent as 'moon' and 'June' - in sad love songs *'je t'aime'* is rhymed with *'problème'*; in happier ones, it's *'amour'* with *'toujours'*. To start you off, and allow you to join in, if not initiate, the singing, here is a popular drinking song. The verse involves picking on a person and challenging them to empty their glass, first having ceremonially touched their forehead, nose, chin, chest and 'sexibus' (untranslatable) with it. The chorus declares that, having emptied his or her glass, the person is 'one of us', who can be seen from his or her red nose *(trogne)* to be a drunkard

Ami François, ami François, bois de ton verre,
Et surtout, ne le renverse pas.
Et porte le aux frontibus, aux nezibus,
aux mentibus, aux ventribus, aux sexibus
Et glou, et glou, et glou, et glou..........
(repeated until glass is empty)

Il est des nôtres,
Il a bu son verre
Comme les autres.
C'est un ivrogne,
Ça se voit rien
Qu'à sa trogne.

Note that in both songs and poetry the final 'e' on words, silent in everyday speech, is usually pronounced.

Chanson de Roland

Getting lots of people killed, particularly if they are on your own side, has long been a guaranteed route to fame. Thus Roland is commemorated in a famous epic poem written in the twelfth century during the time of the crusades.

The incident that the poem commemorates dates from a battle against the Arabs four centuries earlier. Charlemagne had led an expedition into Spain against the Saracens but was forced to withdraw on account of trouble back home. On the way through the Pyrenean pass of Roncevaux, the army, betrayed by Ganelon, was ambushed. Roland, his friend Oliver, and all hands were killed, mainly because Roland stubbornly refused to blow his horn for reinforcements until too late.

Charlemagne (742-814)

The greatest of the Carolingian line of kings, he ruled from 768 to 814. During this time he subdued large regions of Italy, Saxony, Bavaria and Aquitaine and introduced them to Christianity, failing only to free Spain from Muslim rule. On Christmas Day, 800, he was crowned and anointed the first Holy Roman Emperor. Although unable to read himself he presided over a considerable cultural renaissance.

By the end of his reign his empire stretched almost from Denmark to Venice and embraced the whole of current day France with the exception of Brittany. After his death the Treaty of Verdun (843) shared it out among his three sons and not until Napoleon was a similar area under one man's (nominal) control.

La Chasse

Although their number is declining, there are still 1.8 million licensed hunters in France. 98.5% of these are men and 80% live in communes with less than 5,000 population. At 3.4% of the population this makes France the country with the most hunters per head of population.

Hunting is a part of everyday life in the Midi. Mostly it is for *sangliers* (wild boars) but can also be for deer or smaller animals and birds. The precise season varies depending on the area and on what is being hunted but essentially embraces autumn and winter. People hunt on average for thirty days a year.

Although hunting as we know it in the UK exists, a very different form is prevalent in France. Hunting in France is very democratic. *La chasse* is a local, as opposed to a class, activity. If you have a house in the area and pay your taxes you are entitled to hunt once you are over sixteen. You first need to obtain a *permis*. This involves a test to establish that you can tell a hawk from a handsaw, plus a fee in the region of 200 francs. Then you buy yourself a gun and blaze away.

For the hunt it is normal for a couple of villages to get together. They then deliberate where the *sangliers* are most likely to be found. That decided, they divide into shooters *(posteurs)* and beaters *(rabatteurs)*. The former position themselves strategically around the chosen hill or hills whilst the latter go in and beat out the *sangliers*. It is better to be outside firing in. There are on average twenty to thirty fatalities a year from hunting accidents. Even this is an improvement on 1976 when 63 people were killed.

If you are accustomed to a pack of well-drilled hounds, a motley collection of a limping retriever (having got in the way of a *sanglier* the previous week), moth-eaten terriers and friendly lap-dogs, may come as something of a surprise. You do not expect to be nuzzled by hounds.

At the end of the day the *sangliers* are taken to the centre of the village, disembowelled, cut up and shared out.

Sanglier rôti is likely to be on the menu at the local restaurant, and should not be missed.

Chateaubriand, Vicomte de (1768-1848)

Writer who, at the start of the Revolution, was sensible enough to go and seek his fortune in America. Having been wounded, he spent some time in England before returning to France when Napoleon came to power. In the long line of French writers turned politicians, he was Foreign Minister under Louis XVIII and an ambassador to England under Charles X. Ultimately he was disappointed by the Restoration and turned to preserving his place in posterity by writing his autobiography, *'Mémoires d'Outre-tombe'*. Unsympathetic to the conservative nature of his writings, Sartre's reaction was to take a special trip to where he is buried in order to urinate on the grave from beyond which his memoirs emanated.

Chevalier, Maurice (1888-1972)

Starting with Mistinguett in the music halls, he became an international entertainer and film star. His popularity in America was such that he was accorded a ticker-tape welcome on Broadway, the only foreign entertainer to whom this accolade has been extended. He is best known to British audiences for singing 'Thank 'eaven for little girls'.

Chirac, Jacques (b 1932)

Energetic, American-style politician, known as *'le bulldozer'* from the finesse and subtlety which characterise his political style. President of the RPR since 1976, he was Prime Minister under Giscard d'Estaing from 1974 to 1976 and again under Mitterand from 1986 to 1988. In 1988 he unsuccessfully stood against Mitterrand for the Presidency and is a contender for 1995. He is on the right of French politics and his periods as Prime Minister have been characterised by moves away from state control.

In 1977 he became the first Mayor of Paris and this remains his powerbase. In this position he has worked hard to make Paris more beautiful and regain its former pre-eminence as the city of culture.

Cinema

Although cinema attendance is in decline (from 424 million in 1947 to 119 million in 1990), the French still watch more films than any other country in Europe. On average they go to the cinema 2.2 times a year, compared with 1.4 in England.

This continuing patronage is appropriate to a country credited with the birth of the cinema industry when the Lumière brothers, Louis and Auguste, first showed a film to a paying public on December 12th, 1895.

Ever since, France has been a leading film-producer with such famous directors as Jean Renoir (son of the painter and father of Claude, the cinematographer), Jean-Luc Godard *(A Bout de Souffle, 1959)* and François Truffaut. The two last-mentioned graduated from film criticism in the intellectual *Cahiers du Cinéma,* to originators of the *'Nouvelle Vague'* whereby the director is seen as an author of the film. Truffaut is best known for *Les 400 Coups (1959)* and *Jules et Jim (1961).* Claude Berri has a distinguished list of films that he has directed or produced including *Tchao Pantin, Jean de Florette* and *Manon des Sources* and more recently, *Uranus.* Roger Vadim was another well-known film producer though his fame rests mainly on his propensity to marry his leading ladies - Bardot from *Et Dieu créa la Femme* and Jane Fonda from Barbarella. Three other film-star wives and a *union libre* with Catherine Deneuve marked him out as a man to be both envied and admired.

American films account for a half of all shown, French films for a third. In the hit parade of films since 1956 *La Grande Vadrouille,* a French film, comes top with 17 million viewers, followed by Once Upon a Time in the West (Italian), The Ten Commandments and Ben Hur. Bridge over the River Kwai is fifth. The only other British entry in the top fifty is Goldfinger.

It has been said that the French are still as devoted film-watchers as ever but that they now watch them on their televisions. Foreign films are either 'V O' (*Version Originale* - i.e. subtitled) or' V F' (*Version Française* - i.e. 'dubbed') - in which there is an unsettling disparity between the movement of people's lips and the sound that emanates.

Clemenceau, Georges (1841-1929)

Known as 'the Tiger' on account of his fighting qualities, Clemenceau was Prime Minister at the time of the First World War and encapsulated the French fighting spirit. After the war he fought hard to protect France's safety by reducing German power and was mainly responsible for the harsh provisions of the Treaty of Versailles. General de Gaulle said of him 'He was France' and started the tradition of saluting his statue on the Champs Elysées. The British representative was Lloyd George about whom Clememceau said 'If only I could piss as well as Lloyd George talks'.

His house is preserved as a museum exactly as in life, near the *Trocadéro* in Paris.

Clovis (465-511)
King of the Franks who defeated the Gallo-Roman king, Syragius, at Soissons in 486. Seven years later he married the Catholic princess Clotilda from Burgundy. She converted him and he was baptised into the Roman Church, thereby initiating the umbilical connection between monarchy and Church that was to characterise French history for centuries. The liaison was cemented by a fortuitous series of miracles involving Clovis. The first of these was a dove coming from heaven with sacred oil for his consecration. This holy fluid, always mysteriously maintained at the same volume, was thereafter used in the coronation of all French kings.
His new-found religiosity did not stop him murdering his relatives lest they became rivals for the throne. His less sanguinary descendents took to banishing rival princes to monasteries much in the way that politicians now bestow distant High Commissions on threatening rivals.
His fame in the history books stems from having increased the Frankish kingdom from an area at his accession running approximately from Calais to Cologne to one that, at his death, included almost the whole area west of a line from Strasbourg to Toulouse.

Club Mediterranée
A major cultural export, this up-market Butlins has spread from the original camps situated around the Mediterranean to locations throughout the world and embraces winter as well as summer holidays. All manner of entertainments are provided on-site for customers who are more easily parted from their money by the painless use of beads as currency. Anyone who has experienced the feeling that non-English money is easier to spend than the real stuff, will recognise this as a brilliant sales ploy. Its success can be measured in corporate profits which reached £58 million in 1989.
The phrase once applied, more from alliteration than accuracy, was that it allowed the middle classes to *'bronzer, bouffer, baiser'*. A translation that preserves the alliteration would be 'suntan, stuffing and screwing'.

Cocteau, Jean (1889-1963)
A creative artist of great versalitity and talent. An aesthete and dandy with an irresisitible urge to shock people, he was foremost a poet. Like De Quincey he became addicted to opium, from which he recovered. In the early years of the century he was very much part of the 'in' set centred on Picasso. He almost won the *Croix de Guerre* for bravery in the First World War, and later won a bet with a national newspaper by going round the world in eighty days. He turned to writing plays in the 1920s and became associated with the Surrealist school though never part of it. In 1930 he wrote *La Voix Humaine* for Piaf which consisted entirely of her alone on the stage talking for the last time on the telephone to a man she loves.

Cohabitation
Not two people living together without being married - *ça c'est normal* - but the period 1986-88 when Mitterand, a Socialist president, had a conservative government with Chirac as his *Premier Ministre*. This is perfectly possible under the Fifth Republic as elections for Presi-

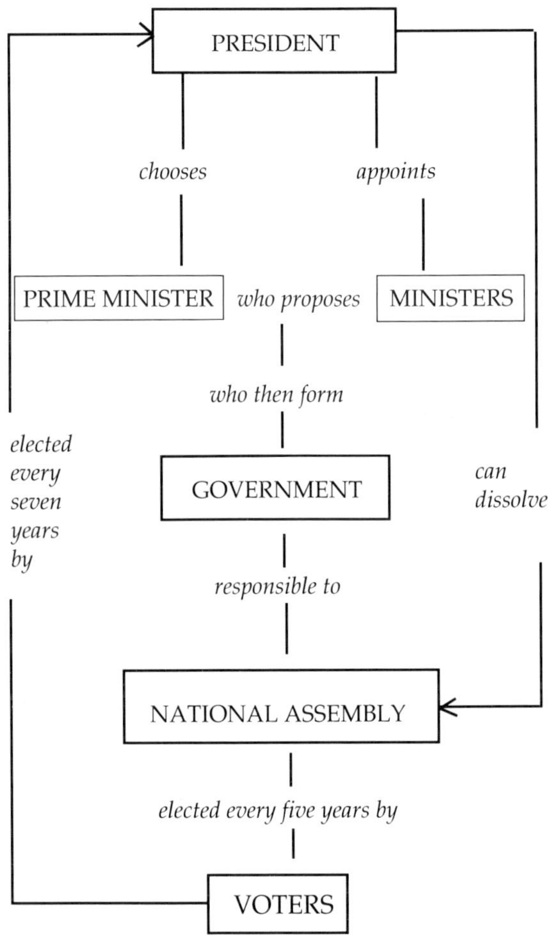

dent and the National Assembly are at different intervals (although there is much discussion about reducing the Presidential term to five years to overcome this problem).

The Constitution of the Fifth Republic was created by De Gaulle who gave its drafters the instruction to 'keep it short and keep it vague'. That they took him at his word is shown by the fact that it contains only 8,000 words and 92 articles. It greatly increased the powers of the President which suited the General as he then became the first incumbent.

Ministers, including the Prime Minister, may be appointed from outside the Assembly. If they are *députés* they have to give up their place in the Assembly which is then taken by an *adjoint* - a successor pre-nominated so as to avoid by-elections both in this eventuality and in the case of the death or resignation of the sitting member. The problem for any Prime Minister under the Fifth Republic is that the President has the power to dissolve the Assembly when he thinks fit. It is thus the President who controls the calling of elections. Whereas a British Prime Minister will always select the most propitious moment (and possibly even engineer that), the French Prime Minister has no such valuable weapon. This does not matter if President and Prime Minister are of the same party. But when of different parties there is the irresisitible temptation for the President to dissolve the Assembly at the low, rather than high point of the government's popularity.

In the current Assembly elected in 1988 the respective party strengths, from left* to right, are : Communists 27, Socialists 276, UDF (Giscard's lot) 130, RPR (Chirac's supporters) 128, assorted right-wing parties 13, National Front 1.

Colbert, Jean-Baptiste (1619-1683)

Finance Minister to Louis XIV and one of the select band of politicians with their own 'ism', Colbertism. This is predominantly the offering of state aid to private industry and is as such is associated with the now-unfashionable *dirigiste* approach, whereby the state plays an interventionist role in industry. In other areas Colbert attempted to lower taxes through reducing government expenditure. Unfortunately court extravagance and Louis XIV's propensity to fight wars made this difficult.

The tradition of state aid to industry survives but now risks falling foul of EEC policy on competition. The government has already been ordered to return £700 million in subsidies to Renault and has had problems with its desire to inject money into the electronics giant Thomson and the ailing computer company, Machines Bull.

** Literally, since the modern left/right classification results from the seating arrangement - in a semi-circle rather than across a divide - which started with the Revolution.*

Colette (1873-1954)

Cat-loving writer and actress, bisexual before her time. A larger than life personality, a sort of female Oscar Wilde, who once said *'Le difficile, ce n'est pas de donner, c'est de ne pas tout donner'*. (The problem is not to give, it is not to give all one has). She wrote a series of books called *Claudine* based on her schooldays and published under her husband's name to immediate acclaim. She was also author - in her own name - of *Gigi*, the book of the film starring Lesley Caron. She spent almost ten years on the music hall stage, some of them as a mime artist at the *Moulin Rouge*, at other times appearing in drag. She was both the first woman president of the *Académie Goncourt*, and the first woman to be granted a state funeral, to which Parisians turned out in their thousands.

Collaboration

The period starting shortly after the fall of Paris in June 1942 and lasting until the Liberation, during which a puppet French government under Marshal Pétain was established in Vichy. Following the armistice, the southern part of France became a free zone. From a mixture of motives - anti-Bolshevism, desire to repatriate French POWs, but mostly to make the best of a crushing defeat - the government collaborated with the Germans. Ministers of the 3rd Republic were imprisoned, De Gaulle was sentenced to death in absentia, Jews were deported to German death camps, and Resistance fighters killed.

Liberté, Fraternité, Egalité was replaced by the slogan *Travail, Famille, Patrie* (Work, Family, Country). By the end of 1942 the government had lost what little influence it ever had. From then till the Liberation France was subjected to Nazi terror, hunger and allied bombing.

No-one can hope to understand the divisions in the French political life without an appreciation of the extent to which a section of the right - represented by big business and the Church - supported the Nazis. During the period of Nazi occupation some three million *lettres de délation* were written by French people betraying their fellow-citizens. Jean-Louis Malle's award-winning film, *Au revoir les enfants,* brilliantly captures this era.
After the war the left-wing had its revenge and hunted down suspected collaborators. The search for one, the former chief of militia in Lyon, lasted until 1989 during which period of time he had been protected by a succession of religious houses. The book, and film, *Uranus* gives a vivid insight into France immediately after the Liberation.

Collège de France
Prestigious teaching institution in Paris set up by François Ier in 1530 to counteract the dogmatism of the Sorbonne. Composed of 52 of France's most eminent professors, being elected a *Professeur* of the College is like becoming a Fellow of All Souls, and about as onerous. Their only duty is to give an annual series of lectures on new ideas and developments in their field - *la science en voie de se faire.* Lectures are free and open to all. This can attract a bizarre audience of *clochards* and eccentrics who tend to undermine the original purpose of disseminating scholarship.

Coluche (1944-1986)
Born Michel Colucci in a tough suburb of Paris, he became, under the name Coluche, one of the nation's most-loved comedians and highest paid actors. He started his career at the *Café de la Gare,* a *café-théâtre* in Paris which became a breeding ground for actors and satirists. He personally won a *César* for best actor in Tchao Pantin.

In 1981 he declared himself an 'anti-political' candidate for the Presidency and ran a joke campaign until the electorate started to take it as a serious attempt, thereby causing a hasty withdrawal. At its height 16% of the population declared they had a 'lot of desire' to vote for him.
He was killed in a motor-cycle accident. His enduring fame springs from having set up the *Restaurants du Coeur,* a series of soup-kitchens at which in winter poor people can get food and advice for nothing. His widow continued running these after his death and they are well-known throughout the country.

Comédie Française
Founded by Louis XIV in 1680 this famous company of actors, situated next to the *Palais Royal* in Paris, has a repertoire, not exclusively of comedies, based on the classical dramatists but also including work of modern and foreign playwrights. Since 1981 the subsidy to French theatre has doubled to £116 million a year, the number of *Centres Dramatiques Nationaux* has gone up from 23 to 42 and the number of grant-aided companies from 146 to 398. As with opera, the provinces are sharing in the popularity. The Avignon Drama Festival each summer has four hundred productions making it the foremost theatre festival in Europe.

Comité d'Entreprise
Workers committee which any company employing more than fifty people must by law set up through internal elections. It has rights to financial information concerning the company and to consultation over matters of pay and personnel. Introduced by De Gaulle as a first step towards greater worker participation, in reality they have rarely got beyond organising social activities such as subsidised holidays.

Common Agricultural Policy
Iniquitous French-inspired policy whereby the British taxpayer allows M. Martin and his sons to make a living out of handkerchief-sized strips of lands cut into hillsides. Any attempt to deprive French farmers of their inalienable right to grow more produce than people can possibly buy immediately provokes the Gallic revolutionary instincts. Whereas Parisians put up barricades and throw cobble-stones, farmers form a convoy of tractors on the autoroute, dump tomatoes or burn sheep. Partly because of this, but also because of its climate, fertile soil and large cultivable area, agriculture accounts for 4% of the Gross Domestic Product, much larger than the UK. France is second

only to the USA as an exporter of agricultural produce. Mme Cresson was formerly Minister for Agriculture so is unlikely to let France's interests go unprotected in international trade discussions.

Communist Party

French politics was for decades bedevilled by the existence of a Communist Party capable of polling up to twenty per cent of the popular vote. In part this stemmed from ancient French divisions and anti-clericalism, bolstered by the party's leading role in the Resistance (particularly after Hitler had attacked Russia). The electorate's fear of letting them into any form of power deprived the left for decades of the opportunity to govern with a clear majority - until the Socialists won in 1981. Then, despite the Socialists having an overall majority in the *Assemblée,* they were offered some minor Cabinet posts. They accepted this poisoned chalice but withdrew from the government two years later when the Socialists did a U-turn on economic policy. Nevertheless, it has been their continuing support for the government in the lobbies that has kept the Socialists in power.

Initially their decline was due to their failure to come to terms with the changes after Stalin. They have remained the most Stalinist party in Europe outside (until recently) Albania. Their leader, Georges Marchais, is the quintessence of the apparatchik and blocked all moves towards modernisation along the lines of so-called Euro-communism. With the final collapse of the Soviet empire and discrediting of communism as an ideology, they are consigned to the history books, polling less than 7% of the vote in 1988 and likely to do much worse in the nineties. As if to show the brittleness of their commitment to the ideology, a high proportion of their supporters switched directly to the National Front during the last elections.

Concubine

To the English the word 'concubine' conjures up visions of King Solomon's harem; in France it is a recognised and widespread legal status. Couples (they must be heterosexual), in *union libre,* (getting on for two million at the last count) and not wishing, or unable, to marry can go to the *mairie* and sign a statement of *concubinage* conferring legal rights and entitlement to social security on each other. One thing they cannot confer in this way is *les droits de succession* - the right to inherit each other's property.

Corneille, Pierre (1606-1684)

Seventeenth century playwright, contemporary of Racine, who wrote classical tragedies. His major works are *Le Cid, Horace, Cinna* and *Polyeucte.* Whereas Shakespeare wrote in iambic pentameters - i.e. ten syllables to a line - French poets had to contend with Alexandrines, which have twelve syllables, usually divided into two sets of six. You can see the difference by comparing:

Now is the winter of our discontent
Made glorious summer by this son of York

with:

Mais le trône soutient la majesté des rois
Au-dessus des mépris, comme au-dessus des lois

This metre is uncommon in English poetry and its ponderousness to English ears was satirised by Alexander Pope in his Essay on Criticism, where he follows a conventional iambic pentameter with a line of twelve feet:

A needless Alexandrine ends the song,
That, like a wounded snake, drags its slow length along.

Corsica ***(La Corse)***

The answer to the question, 'Which *département* is also a region?' is Corsica, *département* 20, also known as *l'Ile de Beauté.*

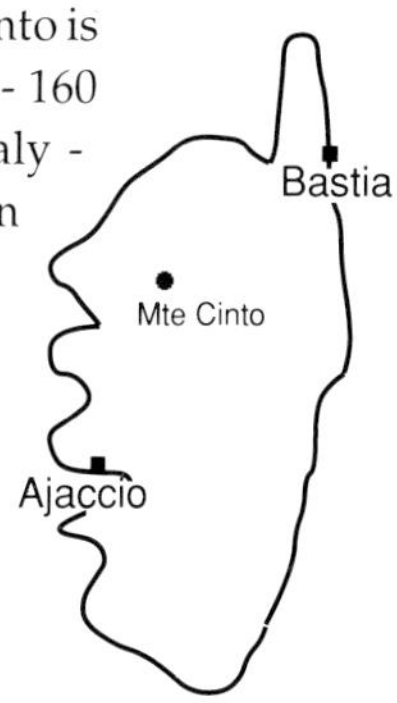

A mountainous island - Monte Cinto is 2710m - its geographic situation - 160 Km from France and 80 from Italy - means that it has swung between independence, Italian domination and being part of France. It was finally sold to France in 1768. The fact that Napoleon was born there helped to cement the union. Nevertheless, there is still a strong nationalist movement, the FLNC, giving to blowing up buildings. Perhaps because of this, Corsicans, of whom there are only 250,000, came bottom of an opinion poll measuring the popularity of the inhabitants of the different regions of France. Their compatriots see them as *fainéants* (lazy) and unwelcoming.

Cousteau, Jacques-Yves (b.1910)
Inventor, with Gagnan, of the aqua-lung which he used to become the world's most famous sub-marine explorer in his boat, Calypso. Academician, turned environmentalist film-maker and propagandist, he now tends to pip Abbé Pierre to the post as France's most popular personality. He was influential in the signing of the Madrid Agreement which banned the exploitation of minerals in the Antarctic for fifty years and has now turned his attention towards the problem of population. He had less success as a businessman, His *Société du Parc Océanique* went bankrupt owing eight million francs. This confirms Peter's Second Principle that people who are so outstanding as never to achieve their level of incompetence in their chosen profession switch to a different one at which they can fail.

Cresson, Edith (b. 1934)
'Et Dieu nomma la femme' was the headline in Liberation's edition of May 1991 when Mitterrand plucked Edith Cresson from obscurity - former Minister of Agriculture and Socialist mayor of Châtellerault since 1983 - to become his fifth Prime Minister. Presumably he felt the need for a strong woman in his life following the overthrow of Mrs Thatcher. That explanation of Madame Cresson's unexpected elevation is at least less scurrilous than most that abounded at the time. Unlike the President Mme Cresson speaks flawless English which she learned from her governess.
On taking up office Mme Cresson immediately called the Japanese 'ants', the English 'queers*' and government ministers 'creeps'. An analysis of her speeches found them to contain the word 'I' 7% of the time (even Mitterrand has never got above 5%), without counting the royal 'we'. Within one month she suffered a disastrous fall in the ratings, threatening to drag the President with her. For the next few months she contented herself with comments on the weather.
However, her initial decline was probably less to do with her free tongue than her decision to raise *cotisations* (social security payments). In so doing she was merely following the first rule of government - which is to do all the unpopular things early in one's term of office. But the second rule is to blame these on your predecessors. Unfortunately for her (in common with John Major) she was following a Prime Minister of her own party.
The popularity of this so-called 'Cardin socialist' continued its nosedive throughout her period in office. With the disastrous showing of the Socialists in the regional elections of March 1992, her days were numbered and she was replaced shortly afterwards. From saviour to scapegoat in ten months.

Crosswords *(Mots Croisés)*
If you enjoy doing English crosswords there is no reason why you should not equally enjoy French ones. In addition to which you will impress the locals and add to your vocabulary (though not as usefully as you may expect). But, as with songs, it is a means of learning as a by-product of something that is intrinsically enjoyable. You are *déconseillé* to try the cryptic sort; stick to the straightforward ones - particularly the *Mots Fléchés* to be found in papers and magazines.
French crossword compilers work differently from their English counterparts. Their object appears to be to minimise the number of black squares. Typically both 1 and 2 across *(horizontalement)* will stretch the complete width of the crossword. It is no simple matter to find two seven-letter (or longer) words which allow you to make legitimate vertical connections. This leads to the first characteristic of French crosswords - the preponderance of two-letter words. You need a Scrabble-type knowledge of such words (see page 143), all the chemical symbols and notes of the scale.
The second characteristic is given by the fact that adjectives have to agree. Thus if an adjective clue has a feminine ending, so must its solution. The same applies to past participles. So you can fill in a few 'e's and 's's even if you do not know the answer. The same principle holds good for verbs. If the clue ends with *'eraient'*, so will the answer. Add to this the fact that the vast majority of infinitives end with 'r' and you are already well under way.

* *To be fair, this is not strictly accurate. The 'queers' comment came from an interview she had given some years before for a book about women. It had not been included in the book but suddenly had the dust blown off it when she came into the public eye. Which goes to show why politicians are best off saying nothing at all times.*

The combined effect of infinitives, adjectives and past participles is that compilers end up needing lots of words which contain 'e', 'r' and 's'. Particularly short words. Thus *'Reflexive'*, *'Sélénium'* or *'Direction'* are all clues to 'SE'; *Département* of five letters is likely to be Isère, if four, Eure. Many a compiler has been grateful for the town called *'Is' ('Sur Tille'* is the clue, as that is the river on which it lies) not to mention the river *'AA'*. Another helpful river is the *'Eule'* which, as you are probably aware, is a branch of the Oubangui. A two-letter Siberian river will be the 'Ob'; an eight-letter one, much valued for its letters is the 'Iennisse'. Forsaking geography you need to know the sound that deers make - *reer* (clued as *'Bramer'*).

From this you may conclude that the vocabulary you pick up is not exactly *la langue de la rue*. It is never easy to introduce into one's conversations *Arête* (fishbone), *Us* (customs), *Esse* (a butcher's hook - literally) or the obselete word for anger *Ire*.
A good place to start with crosswords is with the magazine *Sport Cérébral*, from which this example is taken. This helpfully has a list at the back of all words used in the fifty or so crosswords that each issue contains. As shown by the worked solution on page 141, this assistance is both useful and necessary. The original crossword is given below. *Essayez!*

Culture
France takes culture seriously. Seriously enough to have a Ministry of Culture. This Ministry, created by De Gaulle as part of putting France back onto the cultural world stage, was initially occupied by the distinguished writer, André Malraux. In 1988 it assumed even greater importance and was expanded to the Ministry of Culture, Communications, Great Projects (such as the Louvre Pyramid and other monuments to Mitterrand's reign) and the Bicentennial. France devotes almost one per cent of the state budget to the arts.
The long-serving Minister for Culture, Jack Lang, was one of the most popular members of the government. A fluent Italian speaker, he once addressed a conference in Vienna in Italian as a protest against the proceedings being conducted in English. A member of the radical chic, he had the nickname in the right-wing press of Jack the Rapper. He is now Minister for Education.

Horizontalement
1 Film avec Liza Minelli.
2 Airelle canadienne.
3 Marquera.
4 Initiales du premier couple. Paradis.
5 Pensées.
6. Arbuste à fleurs blanches.
7. Signal de départ.
8. Relatif à l'os cubital.
9. Poète et romancier espagnol.

Verticalement
1. Répertoire.
2 Foyer. Récipients.
3. Pièce vestimentaire féminine. Romain. Neptunium.
4. Parviendrai à
5. Amiral allemand. Branché.
6. Brame. Monnaie scandinave.
7. Refroidi. Particule étrangère.

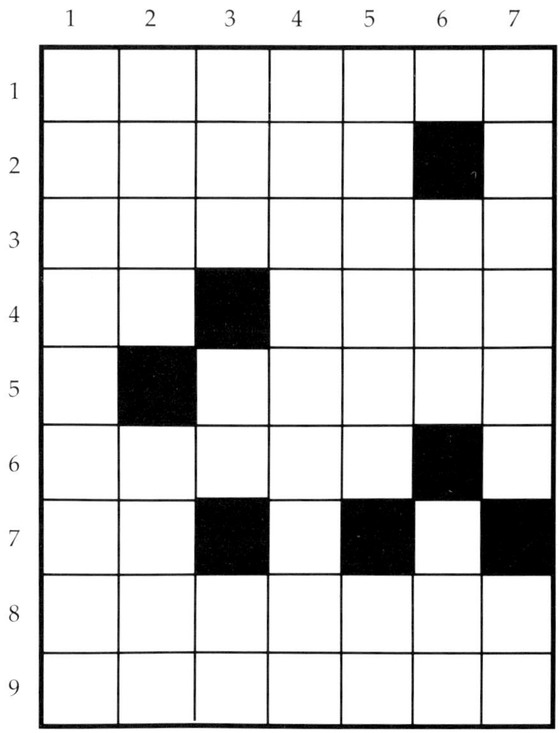

Curie, Marie (1867-1934)
Born in Warsaw, she lived in Paris where she worked with her husband Pierre. Together they conducted research into radio-activity for which in 1902 she was awarded the Nobel prize for physics. In 1911 she became the only woman ever to win two Nobel prizes when she was awarded the prize for chemistry for the discovery of radium. She died of leukemia caused by handling radio-active products. Her daughter continued her mother's work after her death and was herself awarded the Nobel prize in chemistry.
In 1993 she will become the first woman, *à part* goddesses and the like, to have her portrait on a French banknote.

Currency
The most obvious manifestation of not being at home in a country is a failure to handle money. When travelling to any foreign country it is always worth the investment of time in becoming familiar with its paper currency and coins. Not least, this may save your being short-changed. Colloquially francs are referred to as *'balles'* (the equivalent of 'quids' in English); ready money is *'liquide'* or *'espèces'*, and small change is *'monnaie'*. If you are discussing large amounts of money, as when house-buying, people will switch into *anciens francs* - that is, the franc before it was devalued in 1958. One pound sterling is worth a thousand *anciens*. This makes things much easier when discussing large amounts such as house prices as, for instance, *quarante millions* translates into forty thousand pounds.

Cyrano de Bergerac
Play by Rostand, written in 1899, about a *chevalier* with a large nose and an unrequited love for his niece, Roxane. Christian is also in love with her and has a regulation size nose. Moreover his love is returned. His problem is that he is unable to express his love. Cyrano therefore gains vicarious pleasure by writing his love letters for him and helping him generally with his wooing. Christian is killed in action but Cyrano helps Roxane to keep his memory alive. Only as Cyrano is dying does she finally become aware of his love and the role he has played.

In the film, released in 1991, Cyrano is played by Gérard Depardieu.

D

Dagobert (600-639)
A famous member of the Merovingian dynasty, Dagobert is credited with being the first king of all France (from 628). He also founded the *Abbaye de Saint-Denis*, where he is buried, possibly in atonement for the limitless debauchery for which he is reputed.

Danton, Georges Jacques (1759-1794)
A powerful orator, he rose rapidly to prominence during the Revolution and became responsible for national defence at a time when the Revolution was under threat from abroad. After the defeat of the Girondins he was for a while the de facto leader of the Revolution. He became the foremost member of the Committe of Public Safety but decided to take a break in the country with his new wife. As C P Snow has pointed out, absence from the centre of power is the major political mistake - in Danton's case a capital one. Robespierre took his place on the Committee and by the time Danton returned his head was metaphorically (soon to be literally) in the frame. At his trial his impassioned speech in his own defence was said to be audible on the opposite bank of the Seine and threatened to sway the audience to him. It was therefore cut short, as, soon after, was he.

Dassault, Marcel (1892-1986)
Aircraft designer and founder of the aircraft company of his name. A Jew, during the Collaboration he was offered honorary Aryan status if he would make planes for the Nazis. He refused and was incarcerated in Buchenwald.
After the war his company produced planes of the quality of the *Mystère* and *Mirage* jet. Well over a thousand of the latter were sold to regimes such as Libya (with whom France nearly found itself at war over the Chad), Israel and South Africa. During its early nationalising days, the Mitterrand government took a majority interest in the company, which it still maintains. It is now working on an advanced fly-by-wire fighter aircraft, the *Rafale*, estimated to cost 100 billion francs, after the withdrawal of France from the European Fighter Aircraft project. Dassault was reputed to be the richest man in France by the time of his death at 94.

Daudet, Alphonse (1840-1897)
Minor novelist famous for his sketches of Provençal life. His best-known work is *Lettres de mon Moulin*, a set of short stories which are both agreeable and easy to read for the keen French student. Although these were written in Paris rather than Provence, the mill is preserved as a musuem near Arles.

Debussy, Claude (1862-1918)
D H Lawrence look-alike who wrote sundry *préludes* and *études* such as that for a fawn's afternoon; also an opera, *Pelléas et Mélisande*. A highly original composer, his music embraced and fused many different styles from plainsong to Wagner. He had a profound influence on 20th-century music.

Déclaration des droits de l'homme et du citoyen
The Manifesto of the Revolution approved by the *Assemblée* in 1789. Among its provisions are:

> *Man is born free and equal in rights...social distinctions can only be based on the common good.*
>
> *The natural rights are liberty, property, security and resistance to oppression.*
>
> *Liberty consists in the freedom to do anything that does not harm anyone else.*
>
> *The law is the expression of the general will.*
>
> *Free speech and opinion are the most precious rights of man.*

Five years later most of its authors had been deprived of their right to life without which the others are a trifle academic.
It would appear that, despite the Revolution's egalitarian zeal some were more equal than others and that *'homme'* is gender-specific (an interpretation reinforced by *'citoyen'*). Feminists of the day clearly thought so. Arguing that since women were allowed the right to

ascend to the guillotine they should also have the right to ascend to the *Assemblée,* they published the *Declaration des droits de la femme et de la citoyenne.* The main author of this was Olympe de Gouges. Alas, all she got for her pains was for herself to mount the scaffold.

As Mrs Thatcher, accurately but a trifle tactlessly, pointed out during the bicentenary celebrations, the Rights of Man did not originate with the French Revolution. Many of the ideas of Montesquieu and Voltaire derived from their admiration of the English system of government. England, she added, had also had a revolution but, being English, we did not make such a fuss about it. The revolution she was referring to was the Glorious Revolution of 1688 when William and Mary were imported in order to keep England safe from Catholics. The closer comparison, however, is with our Civil War. We also chopped a king's head off but since we did it 150 years earlier we are more civilised.

Defence

France is Europe's biggest spender on defence after the UK. Under De Gaulle it withdrew from the unified command of NATO and has maintained its own *force de frappe* of nuclear weapons. Its six nuclear-armed submarines are now over twenty years old and due for replacement by the year 2000. Most spending on hardware goes to the largely state-owned manufacturers such as Aérospatiale and Thomson-CSF. The Exocet missile is one of the former company's main export earners.

Degas, Edgar (1834-1917)

Associated with the Impressionists but not one of them. An aloof intellectual, he always worked in a studio, preferring artificial light to outdoor and seldom working directly from nature. He is best known for his pastels of ballet-dancers and studies of horses, characterised by a genius for capturing movement. The 'e' in his name does not have an acute accent and its common pronounciation of 'Daygas' is therefore inaccurate.

Delon, Alain (b 1935)

Leading film star and enduring female heartthrob despite approaching *le troisième age.* First married to Nathalie, then a long-time *copain* of Romy Schneider until her death in 1980. A favourite of the gossip magazines, Paris Match devoted fourteen pages to his 'coming out' with the latest women in his life - Rosalie and their daughter, Annouchka. The same event accounted for the highest sales of the year for the 'TV Times' equivalent, *Télé Sept Jours.*

Delors, Jaques (b. 1925)

President of the European Commission who inspired the memorable slogan 'Up yours, Delors' when found guilty by the Sun newspaper of multiple crimes of attempting to federalise Europe and bring in socialism by the backdoor. He is quoted as saying that '80% of economic policy, and perhaps tax and social policy legislation' will be decided in Brussels. This is not so much socialism as good old French centralism. In reality, this devout Catholic, jazz-loving workaholic is a formidably able politician. A former banker, then adviser to the Gaullist Prime Minister, Chaban-Delmas, he later served as Minister of Finance in the first Mitterrand administration. Here he was largely responsible for implementing the U-turn that marked the end of the attempt to usher in the Socialist millennium. His austerity program, considerably more rigorous than that of Barre which had preceded the Socialist victory, did marvels for the economy but helped the Socialists to lose the 1986 elections.

He is a fancied contender for the Socialist ticket in the 1995 Presidential elections and possibly for a return to Paris

THE Sun

FREE Turtles photos - coming tomorrow only in your Sun

UP YOURS DELORS

At midday tomorrow Sun readers are urged to tell the French fool where to stuff his ECU

£292,000 LOTTO · Page 9 · £31,000 BINGO

as Prime Minister before then. His daughter is keeping a Cabinet seat warm as Minister of Employment in the current government.

Démon de Midi

The *'midi'* in question means midday and the expression is the French equivalent of 'the mid-life crisis' i.e. the demon that makes middle-aged men elope with their (female) secretary.

However, it could equally well be *le midi* in its other meaning of the South of France as the same crisis often manifests itself in an uncontrollable desire to quit the rat race and take up sculpting in Provence.

One of Professor Parkinson's Laws states that when a company attains a sufficient size it no longer needs to have contact with the outside world. It can survive by sending internal memos. The number of sculptors, potters and other assorted artists in Provence is rapidly attaining this critical mass where they can exhibit at each other's expositions and massage each other's egos without the tedious necessity to deal with the general public (to whom, in any case, their works are caviar).

Deneuve, Catherine (b. 1943)

Film star of classic beauty, enduring reputation and unassailable hold on French hearts. Formerly married to the photographer, David Bailey, she won the *Lion d'Or* at the 1967 Venice film festival. A one-time model for Marianne, the symbol of the *République,* she was voted *'la plus belle femme du siècle'* by 48% of Frenchmen. This opinion appears not to have been shared by Gérard Depardieu who enigmatically described her as 'the only man I would like to have been'. Her change to a short hairstyle merited a feature article in Paris Match which also records her work in favour of AIDS charities.

Depardieu, Gérard (b. 1948)

Leading French actor, star (with his actress wife, Elizabeth) of *Jean de Florette,* of its sequel, *Manon des Sources,* and of *Cyrano de Bergerac, Uranus* and Green Card. He received five nominations for an Oscar for Best Actor in 1991 but failed. This may have been because the nominated film, *Cyrano de Bergerac,* was in French, which the judges could not understand, or, as the French prefer to think, because he was cheated out of it by the resuscitation of an old allegation of having been present at a rape at the age of nine. Perhaps his latest role as Christopher Columbus will appeal more to American judges.

He is a man who lives life to the lees, or more accurately to the *marc,* since he makes his own wine in his *château de Tigne* in Anjou.

Départements

Caesar described Gaul as divided into three parts. Until the Revolution it was divided into between fifteen and twenty provinces depending on which century you take. In 1790 the *Assemblée Générale* rearranged it into what are now 95 *départements.* The size of a *département* was governed by the ability of someone in a stage coach to reach the principal city in a day. They are mostly named after their main geographical features, usually rivers or mountains.

As Paris outgrew 75 (Seine), it had to be sub-divided. The numbers above 91 are the suburbs. From 01 to 89 the *départements* are numbered alphabetically, starting with Ain and finishing with Yonne. Since all French number plates *(plaques)* end with the *département* number, you can immediately tell where anyone has come from. If the person next to you on the campsite, or in the adjoining *gîte,* has a 05 plate, you have an immediate opening conversational gambit available. *'Vous habitez où dans les Alpes?'*

Where people live is a subset of the language in which you can quickly become fluent. The dedicated francophile will take the trouble to memorise the numbers. The easiest way is initially to learn 10, 20, 30 and so on. Conveniently, these are (almost) all monosyllables:

> Aube, Corse, Gard, Landes,
> Manche, Oise, Haute-Saône, Somme.

Then there are sets such as the three Alps departments, the three Pyrenees and the various derivatives of the Loire. Many occasions then present themselves for demonstrating your familiarity with French geography. 'Typical Lyonnais', you mutter as a '69' cuts you up on the Autoroute; or 'All Parisians are pigs', if the offender is a '75'. The numbers are:

01 Ain
02 Aisne
03 Allier
04 Alpes de Haute Provence
05 Alpes Hautes
06 Alpes Maritimes
07 Ardèche
08 Ardennes
09 Ariège
10 Aube
11 Aude
12 Aveyron
13 Bouches-du-Rhône
14 Calvados
15 Cantal
16 Charente
17 Charente Maritime
18 Cher
19 Corrèze
20 Corse
21 Côte-d'Or
22 Côtes-du-Nord
23 Creuse
24 Dordogne
25 Doubs
26 Drôme
27 Eure
28 Eure-et-Loire
29 Finistère
30 Gard
31 Garonne (Haute)
32 Gers
33 Gironde
34 Hérault
35 Ille-et-Vilaine
36 Indre
37 Indre-et-Loire
38 Isère
39 Jura
40 Landes
41 Loir-et-Cher
42 Loire
43 Haute-Loire
44 Loire-Atlantique
45 Loiret
46 Lot
47 Lot-et-Garonne
48 Lozère
49 Maine-et-Loire
50 Manche
51 Marne
52 Haute-Marne
53 Mayenne
54 Meurthe-et-Moselle
55 Meuse
56 Morbihan
57 Moselle
58 Nièvre
59 Nord
60 Oise
61 Orne
62 Pas-de-Calais
63 Puy-de-Dôme
64 Pyrénées Atlantiques
65 Hautes-Pyrénées
66 Pyrénées-Orientales
67 Bas-Rhin
68 Haut-Rhin
69 Rhône
70 Haute-Saône
71 Saône-et-Loire
72 Sarthe
73 Savoie
74 Haute-Savoie
75 Seine Paris
76 Seine-Maritime
77 Seine-et-Marne
78 Yvelines
79 Deux-Sèvres
80 Somme
81 Tarn
82 Tarn-et-Garonne
83 Var
84 Vaucluse
85 Vendée
86 Vienne
87 Haute-Vienne
88 Vosges
89 Yonne
90 Territoire de Belfort

Descartes, René (1596-1650)

Famous mathematician and philosopher who devoted much of his existence to the question of whether he existed. Does matter exist? Is life a dream? These were the sort of questions over which he drank many a pastis in his local café. Finally he coined the famous expression 'Cogito ergo sum', 'I think, therefore I am' as the irreducible basis of self-existence. This was on the grounds that if he did not exist he would not be able to wonder whether he did exist or not. Starting from that he built up a complete philosophy. Needless to say, later philosophers managed even to cast doubt on this seemingly self-evident proposition.

Descente

A journey down a river, such as the Tarn or through the *Gorges de l'Ardèche,* by canoe or kayak. The latter *descente* involves the negotiation of several rapids at which latter-day *tricoteuses* eagerly assemble to watch you smash yourself against the rocks.

Discussing a *descente* provides the opportunity, beloved of the French, to make another *jeu de mots. Avoir une bonne descente* is the colloquial expression for being able to hold one's drink.

Devos, Raymond (b. 1922)

Fat, Belgian comedian with dry line in verbal humour much appreciated by the French but wholly incomprehensible to the English.

Diderot, Denis (1713-1784)
Together with Pascal, the original polymath - scientist, man of letters, philosopher. Mainly remembered for editing the *'Encyclopédie'*, to which Voltaire, Montesquieu and Rousseau were among the original contributors.

Diên Biên Phu
Garrison in Vietnam besieged for six months by Vietminh forces. Its fall in May 1954 marked the end of French involvement in what had until then been French Indo-China.

Dior, Christian (1905-1957)
Couturier who initially gained fame with the 'New Look', the first design to rebel against the conformity of post-war fashion. He did not rest on his laurels and followed this up in later years with other influential and commercially successful lines such as the 'H' and 'A' lines. In common with other couturiers he diversified into perfume producing Miss Dior (1947) and *Eau Sauvage*.

Distel, Sacha (b. 1933)
Musician, songwriter and actor. Starting as a talented jazz guitarist, he progressed by way of Brigitte Bardot, to becoming the universal New Year's Eve anchorman - a sort of Terry Wogan with sex.

Doctors
The first thing to realise about French doctors is that for you, if not for the French, they are the point of last resort. Before you go to the trouble of locating the local practice, finding out *les heures d'ouverture* and turning up at the correct time, you should first try the *Pharmacie*. French pharmacists, to a much greater extent than their English counterparts, see themselves as para-medics. In England one goes to the chemists to buy something one has already decided upon, or to fill a prescription. In France you can go with the original problem. If you have a stomach upset, *c'est pas la peine* to go to the doctor. He will charge you F100 for advice that the *pharmacien* will give you for nothing. The only phrase you need is *'je désire quelque chose pour...'* followed by whatever is wrong. Your English/French dictionary will supply the illness.
The range of potential cures that are stocked by *la pharmacie* is staggering. If you have an ear infection they will give you some drops. But, if you are lucky, they may also sell you *une poire*. This simple rubber bulb with a pointed end is a DIY ear syringe. This is incomparably more fun than having your ear syringed by a doctor. Back at the campsite you can squirt water into your ear at a satisfyingly high speed any time that it takes your fancy.

Cela dit, there will be times at which you need to visit the doctor. You will immediately feel at home. There may not be the same protective receptionist (doctors are self-employed and do not all make enough money); but the magazines are recognisably three years old - *Paris Match* replacing *Country Life*. Training or experience has equipped most doctors with a smattering of medical English. If not, all you need is *'mal à'*. You then point to the offending area and adopt a painful expression. If it is *mal à l'estomac* you could embellish your description with an exaggerated pewking motion but in most cases he will get the idea.
The next thing to know is that symptoms fall into two groups - muscular and those that involve your running a temperature. The first of these will be treated by putting you in plaster; the second, by giving you pills - mainly anti-biotics. Irrespective of the illness, the remedy will *obligatoirement* involve some form of analgesic in the form of suppositories that you have to insert *dans le derrière*. French doctors have an anal fixation. They are never happy unless either they are sticking a needle in your rear end or prescribing something for your spouse to administer in the same area. At the end of the consultation the doctor will take your E111 form and write up a long list of medicaments that you will go to the *Pharmacie* to collect. He will also fill in his fee which you pay on the spot. Afterwards you will take the *vignettes* off the bottles that you get at the *Pharmacie* and stick them on the form, returning all to the Department of Health in England upon your return. Some months later, if you are lucky, you will receive a *remboursement* of 70% of the cost.

Most French people have some supplementary form of insurance *(Mutuelle)*, often subsidised by the company they work for, which will pay the other thirty per cent. Should you have to go to hospital the procedure is reversed. Now the E111 suffices to get you treatment and you subsequently are billed for the net cost - normally about 30% of the total.

Other services may on occasions be available. According to an opinion poll 43% of doctors have been subjected to sexual advances by their patients. Of these, 54% were taken up.

DOM-TOM

The name given to those parts of France which are *outremer* (overseas, as opposed to *métropole*).

DOM are *Départements d'Outre-Mer - Guadeloupe, Guyane, Martinique, Réunion, Saint-Pierre-et-Miquelon* - which are *départements* in exactly the same way as *Seine Maritime* and *Isère* i.e. with *députés* elected to the *Assemblée.*

TOM are *Territoires d'Outre-Mer*, such as New Caledonia, French Polynesia and other small islands mostly in the Pacific. TOMs are administered by the French government but have no representatives in the Assembly.

French civil servants - *fonctionnaires* - posted to DOM-TOM are known locally as *les oreilles.* This is because being unused to the climate their ears tend to go red in the sunshine but also because they are assumed - with no conceivable justification - to be the eyes and ears of the government back in France *Métropole* reporting back on any subversives not sufficiently appreciative of the benefits of French rule.

Double-entendres

"In English, the sentences, 'I pull the branch aside' and 'I have an extra toe on my foot have little similarity.... In Shawnee Indian these two statements are closely similar. In fact, they differ only at the tail end."

This magnificently useless piece of information is difficult to insinuate into a conversation, but it is a show-stopper if you succeed. It is taken from the book 'Language, Thought and Reality' by B L Whorfe. In it the author advances the theory that a people's language influences how they perceive the world. The connecting point in Shawnee between the two apparently totally different statements is the sense of 'forkedness' that comes from pulling a branch or having an extra toe. Other slightly less esoteric linguistic phenomena are more widely known. Eskimos have different words for snow depending on its state - falling, ground, packed, slushy, wind-driven. By contrast, the Aztecs, not seeing so much of it, have only one word to cover cold, ice and snow. In Japanese there is one word to express the colour of the sea, sky and grass. Conversely, the Arabs have many different words for 'camel'.

It is interesting to speculate on whether the French tendency - by English standards - to use exaggerated language is purely linguistic or whether is is a reflection of a propensity to feel more strongly. In support of the latter explanation one could cite an opinion poll in which citizens of various European countries were asked to express their attachment to concepts such as family, freedom, equality, democracy, money. Irrespective of the order in which different nationalities placed these, the French across the board were more likely to claim a 'strong attachment' than other nationalities.

The situation in which a purely linguistic difference is seen between French and English is where the French have two words for which there is only one in English, and vice versa. French has no word with which to render the English concept of conscience (which may give some insight into their foreign policy over the years). The French word - *conscience* - does not differentiate between consciousness and conscience. Where we have only one word for 'wave', the French have two - *vague* and *onde.* Similarly all fires come alike to the English, whereas French differentiates between *un feu* and *un incendie.* The former is applied to any type of fire; the latter, specifically to those that you need to put out, such as a forest fire. Generations of schoolchildren have been tripped up in exams by the difference between *savoir* and *connaître* in rendering the one English word 'know'.

Another interesting example is the word *doubler.* In French this can mean to 'dub', as in superimposing French voices on an English-speaking film, to line a coat and to overtake. The connection, that of two things where normally there is one, is not reflected in the English langauge. Where we see such a concept - as in 'doubling' at bridge, the French see none; the French for 'to double' at bridge is *'contrer'*. The English word 'free' does the work of two French words - *libre* (as in freedom) and *gratuit* (as in not incurring a cost).

These different perspectives are a common source of confusion when speaking the language. Is a micro-wave a *micro-vague* or a *micro-onde?* (It is the latter). When do we translate day by *jour,* and when by *journée?*

Dreyfus

France has the largest Jewish community in Europe (700,000). Despite, or resulting from, this, anti-semitism has a long and discreditable history in France. The best-known manifestation of this was *'l'affaire Dreyfus'* at the turn of the century.

In 1894 Captain Dreyfus, a military officer of Jewish descent, was accused of passing military secrets to Germany. Convicted on evidence subsequently shown to be falsified, he was imprisoned on Devil's Island. The uncertainty of the conviction provoked continuing calls for a retrial. These had no effect until four years later when Emile Zola took up the cause in a famous article entitled *'J'accuse!'*. In the time-honoured tradition of bureaucrats, the French army did everything in its power first to frustrate the demands for a retrial and, when it happened, to engage in a cover-up. The appeal to *'l'honneur'*, whether of the army or the state, is a powerful one in France and only after a fight lasting twelve years was Dreyfus exonerated and restored to his rank.

Driving

Are the French really bad drivers? Generalising about a nation's driving habits is as dangerous as attempting to cross a road in Paris. In 1972 total traffic-related deaths were 16,500. Successive safety campaigns involving seat-belt laws, reduction of speed limits in town and crackdowns on drink-driving reduced this to under 10,000 by 1990. But this is still almost twice as many fatal accidents per cars on the road as in the UK. In France 410 people are killed on the roads for every million cars; in the UK the comparable figure is 183.

Various measures are being taken to reduce the toll. On January 1, 1992 an equivalent of an MOT test was introduced in an attempt to reduce the 20% of accidents attributable to mechanical malfunction. The test will apply to all cars over five years old although it will start with ten year old cars and only catch up on the backlog by 1995. The certificate will be *valable* for a period of three years.

Drivers in France risk a fine of F250 if they are caught without driving licence, car registration and insurance documents. If caught doing more than 30 kph in excess of the speed limit you incur an automatic fine of F900 (reduced to F600 for payment on the spot). You are more likely to be caught in a radar speed trap than by a pursuing police car. You do not even know you have been done until you receive a summons complete with

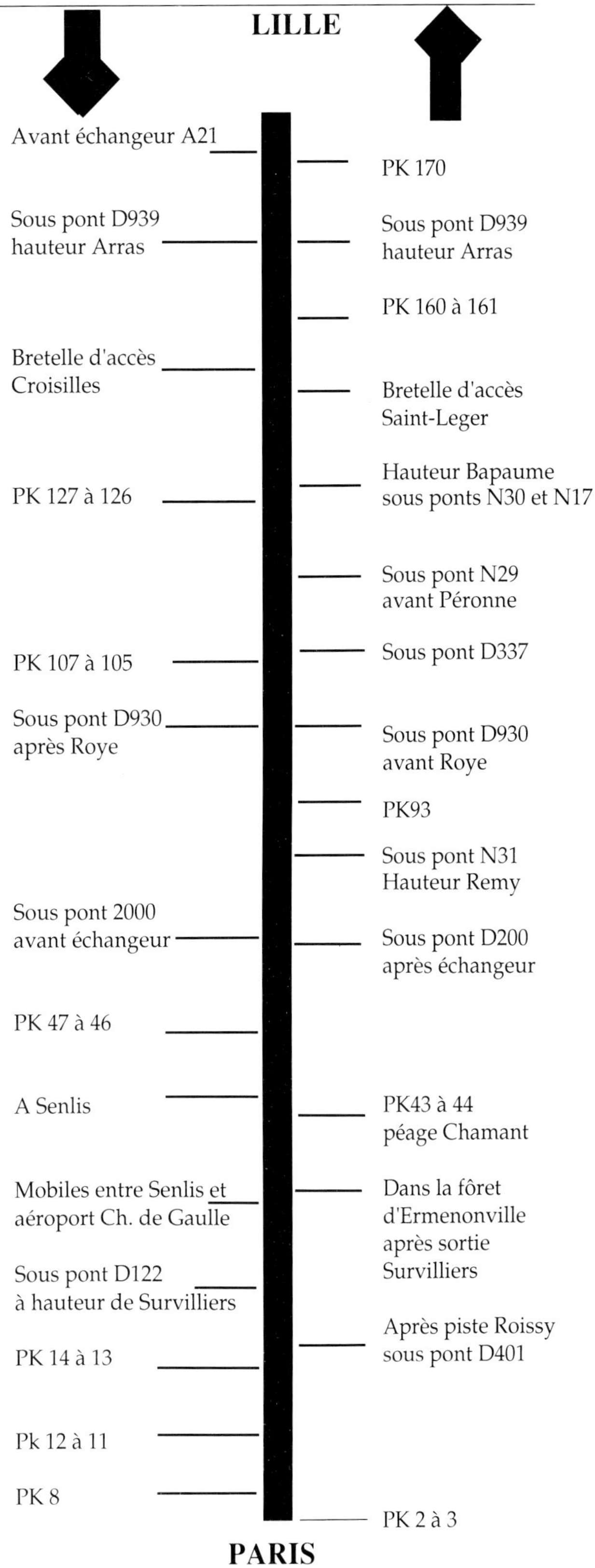

photograph of your car and a speed read-out through the post. Do not, therefore, be fooled by the apparent lack of police cars on French roads into thinking you can break the speed limit with impunity. The seriousness with which this campaign is now pursued can be gauged by the map of speed traps between Lille and Paris (preceding page).

Later in 1992 a points system for traffic offences is being introduced. Points, ranging from one for a minor infringement to three for a serious, will be recorded on a central file accessible to the police through terminals. Motorists will start with a total of six points. Once this total is reduced to zero their license will have to be handed in to the *préfecture* and they will have to sit a new driving test. Points will automatically be deleted three years after the offence or motorists can knock off two points by doing a sixteen hours *'stage de perfectionnement'* i.e. retraining course, at a cost of 1500 francs.

Parking fines are *largement* ignored, unless your car has been taken off to the pound - *mise en Fourrière* - when it will cost you F900 to get it out.

Alcohol is an influence in 38% of fatal accidents. For the under-45 age group being killed in a traffic accident is the most common cause of death. Women drivers have 10% more accidents than men, but the latter's cost 30% more. The drink limit is the same as in England but testing is random. In practice the police do everyone in a blanket test or they do no-one. Penalties for driving over the limit tend to be slightly lower than in England.

Road tax - *la vignette* - varies according to *département* and, to a more significant extent, according to engine capacity. It also halves for cars over five years old. Thus taxing an ancient *deuch* in Lozère may cost only £12 whereas a new, top of the range Renault in Paris would be nearer £1000.

For the first twelve months after passing the driving tests *jeune conducteurs* have to display a *disque réglementaire* and cannot exceed the speed shown on it of 90 kph.

Drucker, Michel (b. 1942)

Journalist turned television presenter of both current affairs and variety programmes on TF1. A passionate football fan, he commentated on the World Cup series in the seventies and has written books about the subject. During the Gulf War he smuggled a French baby out of Baghdad in a suitcase. His brother is head of a rival chain M6.

Dumas, Alexandre (1802-1870)

Author of The Count of Monte Cristo and the Three Musketeers. Firmly in the French tradition of voluminous output, he told Napoleon III that he had written 1200 books. Most of these were probably ghost-written with Dumas taking a planning and editorial role rather than writing all the words himself. Like Balzac he had trouble with creditors.

His son - *Alexandre Dumas fils* - followed in his father's footsteps and wrote *La Dame aux Camelias* which Verdi used for La Traviata.

Duras, Marguérite (b. 1914)

Writer of *nouveaux romans* among which are *Hiroshima, mon Amour* and *l'Amant.* Her style of writing revolves round what she refers to as a leitmotif of 'musica'. From this it can be deduced that the books are in the line of writings that are somewhat difficult to understand and therefore trendy.

E

Economy

Wth a GNP in excess of £500 billion, France has the fourth largest economy in the world, although only fifteenth in terms of competitiveness. West Germany is by far its largest trading partner although trade with UK and Spain has increased since successive enlargements of the EEC. In recent years, compared with the UK, inflation has been lower and unemployment slightly higher.

Edict of Nantes, 1598

An edict, promulgated by Henry IV, giving a measure of religious freedom to Protestants and marking the end of the *Guerres de Religion*. Under its provisions Protestants were granted liberty of conscience, guarantees of civil rights to enter universities and the professions, the freedom of public worship and were allowed to have a hundred *villes fortifiées* - most notably La Rochelle, Montpellier and Montauban. More an armistice than, as usually portrayed, an act of tolerance, it was never accepted by the Catholic factions and was finally revoked by Louis XIV in 1685. The latter act caused a migration of Protestants taking their skills - not least of *viniculture* - with them.

Eiffel Tower

As with all new building financed by the State, this was the centre of a great controversy when it was built to commemorate the centenary of the Revolution. All one can say is that of the 700 designs submitted for the competition it could possibly have been the least bad. Others were for a lighthouse to illumine the city and for a tower shaped like a guillotine. It was probably saved from demolition only by virtue of becoming an important radio and telegraphic centre in the First World War*. Familiarity breeds consent and it was classified as a national monument in 1964.

An average of three people a year commit suicide by throwing themselves off it including one whose fall was filmed by a BBC cameraman who happened to be passing at the time.

Eleanor of Aquitaine (1122-1204)

Fecund, uncontrollable wife of Louis VII by whom she had two daughters. She refused to accompany Louis on a Crusade and instead consoled herself with her young uncle. Louis did not take kindly to this and in 1151 had the marriage annulled. Eleanor went, taking Aquitaine with her. A year later she married Henry Plantagenet soon to become Henry II of England. For him she bore four sons. She is buried, with other Plantagenets, including Richard *Coeur de Lion*, at Fontévraud in the *département* of Maine-et-Loire.

Elections

Under the constitution of the Fifth Republic there are five types of national elections - Presidential, Parliamentary, Regional, Municipal and Cantonal. For the most part they work under the 'Second Ballot' system whereby there are two lots of voting a week apart. The French say that you vote with your heart on the first ballot, and your head on the second. To win, a candidate must gain an overall majority of the votes cast. With four or five candidates contesting the first round, this is virtually impossible. The two candidates with the most votes in the first round go through to the second round.

The intention of this form of voting was to stop the fragmentation of parties that occurred under the Fourth Republic. In practice minority parties such as the National Front and (formerly) the Communists wield considerable influence on the major parties as their preferences become vital for the second round. The major parties may have to 'trim' their policies, for example on immigration, in order to pick up the votes of the supporters of these parties.

Presidential elections take place every seven years. Elections for the *Assemblée Nationale* take place every five. In principle, and in practice, this can land the

* *There is a recorded case of a man living close to the Tower whose teeth picked up the signals. Every time his metal fillings came into contact with each other he emitted pop music or a phone-in. He had the fillings replaced and the problem disappeared.*

President with a government of a different political persuasion to his own. They then have to co-habit. It is likely that the presidential term of office will be reduced to five years in order to make it coincide with that of the *Assemblée*.

Elections to the Upper Chamber, the *Sénat*, are indirect. Voting is restricted to *députés* (M.Ps) and elected representatives of the *départements*. Senators are elected for nine years, with one third being up for re-election every three years. The Senate has marginally more power than the House of Lords.

An interesting phenomenon is that the government of the day can - and does - change the electoral system. Only the most naive would believe they do this other than to their own perceived benefit. A law to change the system can be passed through the *Assemblée* in exactly the same way as any other law, with no delay in implementation. Thus in 1991 President Mitterrand could declare that he might change the system for regional elections the following year as little as three weeks before voting was due to take place. In 1985 (and possibly again in 1993) the socialist government changed the legislative elections to a system based on Proportional Representation. This was not unconnected with damage limitation to the left by dividing the two main right-wing parties. One malign effect of this was to give the National Front 35 seats. The 'success' of the new system restricted the RPR/UDF to a majority of only three. Once they were in power, however, the new government immediately changed the system back again.

In addition, parliamentary constituencies are not drawn up by an independent Boundaries Commission but by the Minister of the Interior. In extremis the Constitutional Council could intervene to prevent gerrymandering but providing it is not blatant the government can expect to get away with it.

If, as at present, the government does not have an overall majority in the *Assemblée* it becomes a bit more difficult to change the system. Now it has to have recourse to the eminently useful Clause 49.3 of the Constitution. This allows the government to declare any Bill a question of confidence. It is then automatically passed unless there is an absolute majority against it. This means that the Opposition must get 289 votes out of the total of 577, abstentions counting as votes against the motion. Since this entails the right and the Communists voting in the same lobby the chances of this happening are minimal.

The Presidential electoral system, *par contre*, is written into the constitution and can only be changed by referendum.

Elysée, Palais de l'

Originally lived in by Madame de Pompadour, from 1873 it has been the official residence of the *Président de la République*.

Environmentalism

Although there is a Minister responsible for the environment, he tends to fight a losing battle. A country as wedded to nuclear power as France is unlikely to be a fertile ground for environmentalists. They appear likely to lose the battle over the listening station in the Camargue. The next battleground is the extension of the TGV-Sud through Provence. If the environmentalists do win this it is as likely to be because of the interests and opposition of local farmers than through any groundswell in favour of green politics.

One attitude that does assist the environment is the French concern for their *patrimoine*, whether personal or collective. The concept of maintaining what previous generations have handed down to you is much stronger in France than in the UK where the word 'patrimony' is seldom used. Combined with the clout of the tourist industry, this, more than any political ideology, explains why such concern is frequently shown for preserving the natural beauty of the country.

There are two environmentalist political parties, whose support fluctuates more according to people's disillusionment with conventional parties than as a function of firm commitment to the cause. Founded in 1984 they won 3.8% of the vote in the 1988 Presidential election. In the regional elections in March 1992 they achieved 13% of the vote, their best-ever score in a nationwide election. However, as tends to happen in such quarters, they are split between an idealistic party, hostile to any compromise with establishment parties, and the pragmatic *Génération Ecologie* headed by Brice Lalonde who was Environment Minister in the Cresson government. The 1992 vote was split roughly equally between them. However, their seats make them a prime courtship target as allies at the regional level.

Escoffier, George Auguste (1846-1935)
Chef and food-writer. His *Guide Culinaire*, published in 1920, was a seminal work in disseminating the art of good cooking. He was head chef at the Savoy (where he was asked to leave on account of a *petit problème* with accounting). Among his most famous eponymous dishes are *Pêche Melba* (created for Dame Nelly) and *Tournedos Rossini*.

Etrennes
Seasonal presents that it is wise to give to tradesmen or to your *concierge* at the New Year. The latter title, in the manner of rat catchers and rodent control officers, has now been superseded by *'guardien(ne)'*.
In case you are prone to lapses of memory the postman each year delivers you a *Calendrier de Poste* or *Almanach du Facteur* containing useful information such as local maps and transport guides together with services provided by *la Poste*. If your amnesia runs not to the need for a tip but to the appropriate amount the postman can probably advise you of what you gave last year.

Euro Disneyland
Opened in April 1992 at Marne-la-Vallée, 32 Km east of Paris. The site occupies 5,000 acres and the Metro delivers you from Paris directly to the foot of Main Street, USA. It is thirty minutes by car from either Charles de Gaulle or Orly airport. The TGV will stop there as from 1994.
Costing £100 million to build, when finished it will have six hotels with 5200 bedrooms, an 18-hole golf course in addition to Frontierland, Adventureland, Fantasyland and Discoveryland. Shown here is Sleeping Beauty's castle - *le Château de la Belle au Bois Dormant*.
Eleven million tourists are *prévus* for the first year and it is estimated that it will increase the Gross Domestic Product by 0.25%.
It is, however, labouring under one enormous disadvantage. As Rabelais pointed out:

Un repas sans vin est une journée sans soleil

Yet at Euro Disney alcohol is totally banned. For the average Frenchman to sit down to lunch without the prospect of *un petit verre de vin* may quickly turn him from Happy to Grumpy.

Exile
France is the favoured bolt-hole of many a retired dictator. Most of them live in considerable luxury from the proceeds of their previous occupation. Apart from Edward VIII and Grahame Greene, there are few instances of English people who have sought exile, temporary or permanent, in France. Traffic the other way has been much more intense.
Starting with Voltaire who found it expedient to spend three years in England, the list includes Rousseau, Chateaubriand, Louis-Philippe (after his abdication), Napoleon III (twice), Zola and General de Gaulle.

F

Fashion

With names such as Dior, Chanel, Balmain and St Laurent, France is the undisputed home of *haute couture.* Even the bikini was invented there, as was the blue denim of which jeans are made (the word comes from *de Nîmes* the town in the Gard where the material originated). Magazines such as *Elle* and *Marie-Claire,* in addition to Vogue and Cosmopolitan, devote innumerable column inches to what women, and to a lesser extent men, should wear. It goes without saying that French women are the best-dressed in the world.
Yet as fashion shows get even more outrageous and divorced from what Mme Martin is actually likely to wear, so expenditure on clothes plummets. Although 58% describe themselves as ' attentive to fashion', expenditure on *haute couture* represents only 7% of outgoings compared to 33% on women's ready-to-wear, 23% on men's clothes and 37% on accessories.
As a result Balmain, after losing £3 million, pulled out of the *haute couture* market in 1990 to concentrate on 'ready to wear' and the Managing Director of Dior received his marching orders.
One area where the French do spend money is on their feet. The French are Europe's greatest buyers of shoes with an average of 5.2 pairs a year pushing the English (4.9) into second place.
Despite these problems with the home market France still commands half of the world's £30 billion market in fashion and luxury goods including two-thirds of the Japanese market.

Faux Amis

Faux amis (false friends) is the name given to French words which are spelt exactly like, or closely similar to (actual/*actuel),* an English one but have a different meaning. Thus *agréer* means to accept rather than to agree, and *user* means to become worn out rather than to use *(utiliser).*
An excellent book, which uses *faux amis* as the starting point for a comparison not only of the language but also culture and society with English, is 'Faux Amis & Key Words' by Thody and Evans, published by Athlone Press.

Faux Pas

Attention! More dangerous than *faux amis* are words in French which can land you in trouble. Take 'kiss' for example. The French do a lot of it. If you consult your French/English dictionary you will see the word *'baiser'.* And it is perfectly OK to give someone a *baiser,* always provided that you know them well enough. But as a regular -er verb *baiser* is dangerous. Articulate a desire to *baiser* someone and you are in for a surprise - exactly what sort depends on whether the answer is affirmative or negative.
Nor should a woman literally translate 'I'm full up' to *'je suis pleine'* as an excuse for refusing an extra helping. The French phrase means 'I'm pregnant'.
Not so much a *faux pas* as a misunderstanding was when a friend in the Ardèche commented *'Toujours fidèle?'* when he saw me on holiday. I blushed at this intrusion into my private life. In fact he was not questioning my sexual peccadilloes but commenting on my faithfulness to the Ardèche. *Fidèle* is applied more widely in France - e.g. *rester fidèle à Renault* - than its literal equivalent 'faithful' is in England.

Feminism

France is an arid soil for those aspects of Women's Lib that seek to diminish the differences in personality, outlook and roles between men and women. This is not to say that French women, who make up 41% of the work force, do not believe in equal pay for the same work, equality of opportunity for personal advancement and, increasingly, sharing of household tasks. Just that they want to preserve *la spécificité* of the two sexes. And why not, when life expectancy for a woman is 81 against that of 72 for a man?
The *Mouvement pour la Libération des Femmes* was founded in 1968. Given that until two years before then women needed their husband's permission to work and until two years later to put their child into school, it can be deemed necessary. Among the Movement's most noteworthy successes was to stop all cyclones being named after women. Part of the impetus was lost through winning battles such as the creation of a Ministry of Women's Rights in 1981. Considering that women only got the vote in 1945 this represents considerable political progress.
France recently became the second country in Europe to legislate against sexual harassment, which now incurs a fine of £10,000 or a year in prison, or both. The current female Prime Minister seems unlikely to initiate a prosecution herself. In her famous interview published in the Observer she lamented the fact that English men did not *draguer* women as they do in France.

The illustration alongside, showing legs that are the equal of, well, Angela Rippon's, is not of a contestant for the Miss World competition but of Elizabeth Guigou, the *Ministre des Affaires Européennes*. She concedes that, in the men's world of politics *'une jolie fille est avantagée'*.

Fête Votive

During the *haute saison* virtually every commune, especially in the Midi, has its *Fête Votive*, usually extending over two or three days. Originally a religious celebration of the patron saint of the commune, it now has more to do with tourism. It typically comprises a *Grand Concours de Pétanque*, a set of seedy sideshows characteristic of the worst kind of fairground and a *'Bal Gratuit'*. The latter will involve lots of music, from Beatles to Bécaud, all played at a high number of decibels. This ensures the impossibility of anyone within five kilometres sleeping through the ball and therefore maximises attendance.
Doing the waltz, in addition to 'rock', has none of the negative connotations of 'Come Dancing' in England and the French are more accomplished dancers than the English. 1988 was designated the 'Year of the Dance' by the Minister of Culture. The *Fête* is supported by all ages and grandmothers and children happily do a turn together on the temporary dance floor.

Fire Brigade ***(Sapeurs-Pompiers)***

Hopefully you won't have occasion to call upon the services of the fire brigade (who also double as ambulancemen in the case of an emergency). In the *grandes villes* firemen are much as we know them in England. In other words we don't know them and we hold them in the awe that is reserved for the professions. Elsewhere the fire brigade is frequently a largely voluntary *(bénévole)* affair. In fact throughout the country of a total force of 230,000 only 20,00 are full-time professionals. You should not therefore be surprised if Serge, whom you last saw emptying the dustbins or pruning his vines, is first through the door.

The second difference is that, for small incidents, calling out the fire brigade is a social activity. We once used our local brigade to deal with a nest of hornets that had ensconced themselves high up in the wall of our courtyard. When they arrived we were *à table* in the courtyard. As it turned out, all of the firemen bar one were known to us. Thus there was much shaking of hands to be gone through. It seemed only polite to offer them an *apéritif* since the bottle of *pastis* was on the table. Twenty minutes later they enquired as to the whereabouts of the hornets' nest. They then mounted a ladder and sprayed poison into it. After that a *digestif* seemed the least we could offer them by way of thanks.
Whereas an *arrêt préfectoral* of 1936 survives which specifically bans the solicitation of *étrennes* by dustmen, you are allowed to give them to your local fireman.

Flaubert, Gustave (1821-1880)

Nineteenth century novelist, noted for the perfection of his style. He lived largely as a recluse in his native Normandy which was for the best since he declaimed aloud all his writing to make sure the sentences were sufficiently mellifluous. When his most famous work, Madame Bovary, appeared he was prosecuted for foisting pornography on the public. He never married but found some consolation and inspiration with his mistress, Louise Colet, who was herself a poet.

Fontainebleau

Royal chateau and forest of mediaeval origin but reconstructed for Francis Ier with his emblem, the salamander, much in evidence. Because of the excellent hunting most kings spent time there. Louis XIV revoked the Edict of Nantes there and it was the setting for Napoleon's abdication in 1814.

Football

Highly popular sport, organised professionally along the same lines as the Football League, with four Divisions, and a *Coupe de France*. France, as host nation, won the Nations Cup in 1984 and were quarter-finalists in the 1986 World Cup defeating the holders Italy and Brazil on the way. They failed to qualify for the 1990 World Cup in Rome.

Following that failure they appointed as manager Michael Platini (inset), formerly their best player and much-feared as taker of free-kicks. Since taking over he has wrought a transformation in the national side to the point where they won eight successive internationals in 1991 and go to the finals of the 1992 European Championship as the only team ever to have qualified with maximum points. However, their run of nineteen matches without defeat was brought to an end in 1992 at Wembley where they maintained their record of never having scored a goal.

Leading club sides import expensive overseas players such as Glen Hoddle, whose talents were more recognised in France than England and who helped Monaco to win the League in 1988. Chris Waddle and Trevor Stevens play for the leading club *l'Olympique Marseille.* Best-known native French footballer is Jean-Pierre Papin, who also plays for *l'OM* and is the country's leading goalscorer. A National Football Centre of 143 acres is currently under construction at Rambouillet south of Paris.

In general the French prefer individual sports to team games but football is an exception which numbers 7.5 million *pratiquants.* Nevertheless, Platini claims that one of his problems is that French football has 'spectators not fans' who regard entertainment value as almost as important as winning.

Foreign Legion

Motto: *Legio patria nostra* - the legion is our homeland

Part of the French army renowned for its bravery and *élan.* It was created in 1831 originally to fight outside French territory. All officers - but no other ranks - are French. Non-French nationals may enlist for a period of five years (and gain French citizenship after ten years' service). Around 7,000 people apply each year of whom about 25% are accepted. 10% of the total force of 8,500 are British. Enlisters do not have to give their true identity and are guaranteed anonymity and have protection from any actions against them arising from past misdeeds. Criminals, others than *criminels du sang,* or those sought by Interpol, are admitted.

The price they pay is to become virtually a non-person; they cannot marry, buy a house or even a car. Originally based in Algeria, thereby giving them their image of desert warriors beloved of films, their HQ is now at Aubagne, east of Marseilles.

Franche-Comté

Région in the east of France comprising the *départements* of Doubs (25), Jura (39), Haute-Saône (70) and the Territory of Belfort (90). *Chef-lieu:* Besançon. The Jura is a chain of mountains whose folded formation gave rise to the adjective Jurassic and which are the most densely-wooded in France with a highest point of 1723m. The region has more rain than any other which possibly explains why under 900,000 people choose to live there.

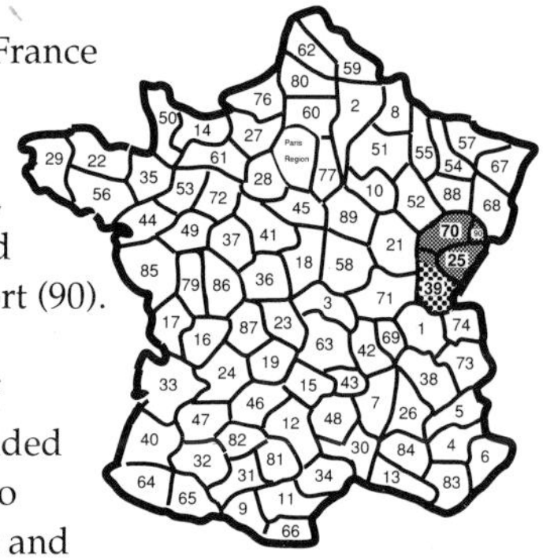

Historically, it was long under the control of the *ducs de* Bourgogne. It put up stiff resistance to Richelieu, scared off Mazarin and did not finally become part of France until 1678.

If you had not heard of Franche-Comté before seeing this map you are not alone. It ranks bottom of the list of regions whose whereabouts British people can accurately identify.

Francois Ier (1494-1547)

One of France's most famous kings. Captured and imprisoned by the Italians during an unsuccessful invasion, he brought back the Renaissance with him on his release and became a patron of the arts. Leonardo da Vinci accepted his invitation to live at court and died at Amboise in 1519. A contemporary of Henry VIII, the two kings met in 1520 at the *Camp du Drap d'Or* (the first historic sign that travellers from Calais see). This competition in finery - the French had 300 tents many covered with gold leaf - was meant as a substitute for the two countries going to war. In this it was a failure as shortly afterwards Henry VIII allied himself with François' opponents.

Franco-Prussian War

Disastrous war declared by France on July 19, 1870. A crushing defeat at Sédan lead to the fall of the Second Empire, exile of Napoleon III and occupation of Paris by the Prussians. In the peace treaty, signed by Bismarck at Versailles, France lost Alsace.

The traumatic effect of the war on France's self-esteem is everywhere seen in the literature of the latter end of the nineteenth century in writers such as Maupassant. It was not fully exorcised until the German defeat in 1918.

Francophonie

> *La francophonie n'est pas une language mais une civilisation capable d'assurer l'avenir du monde.*
> (French is not a language but a civilisation capable of assuring the future of the world.)
>
> *Malraux*

The French are rightly proud of their language which was as much the language of diplomacy as English was of commerce. In the nineteenth century every European royal house spoke French. Since then a worthwhile but rearguard action has been fought, and is continuing to be fought, to preserve the usage of French throughout the world.

In 1988 a Secretary of State was given responsibility for *francophonie* with a £5 million budget. In 1987, and again in 1991, President Mitterrand, one of the few top French politicians who does not speak English, convened a summit of (generously-defined) *francophone* countries to rally to the defence of the French language. *Le Journal Officiel* fights a losing battle to hold back the intrusion of *franglais* words such as *'le fast food'* in place of which it offered *le prêt-à-manger*. In the official language hit parade (itself a *franglais* word, replaced by *palmarès),* French rates only sixth place. When the test is habitual usage, it drops to eleventh.

An ancient law exists forbidding the use of *franglais* terms but allowing only private prosecutions. Nevertheless many have been brought. Presumably the Channel Tunnel will be exempt from these. It appears that some form of *franglais* will be the means of communication between cross-Channel train-drivers.

Francophone francophiles might like to test their knowledge of the language on the following two questions:

- Which is the longest word in the French language?

- Which word has the most accents?

Answers are at the foot of page 148.

G

Gabin, Jean (1904-1976)
Paris-born film actor between thirties and fifties who achieved fame playing the leading roles in films by Marcel Carne, Julien Duvivier and Jean Renoir.

Gainsbourg, Serge (1928-1991)
Un grand des grands. Actor, producer, singer, but above all song-writer. The song with which most English people are familiar, as a result of its being banned by the BBC, is *'Je t'aime, moi non plus'*. This is a three-minute orgasm set to music . It was originally recorded on a single by Gainsbourg with his then wife, Jane Birkin, and later with Brigitte Bardot on an album. Both of them sang and sighed meaningfully, Mlle Bardot with such gusto that the recording was withheld from issuing for twenty years at her request.
Never seen without a glass of whisky in his hand and a cigarette in his mouth, one of his best-known songs is *'Dieu est un fumeur de Havanes'*. His compositions are full of humour, often black. *Le Poinçonneur* is about a person who punches holes in tickets - *des trous d' seconde classe, des trous d'première classe* - at a Paris metro station. *'Trou'* also has the meaning of 'grave' and the headline in *Libération* on his death was *'Le Dernier Trou'*. *Paris Match* gave him a thirty-page obituary.
Among the various stunts on which his notoriety was based are:

- singing a reggae version of the *Marseillaise*
- setting fire to a five-hundred franc note on a TV chat show
- propositioning Whitney Houston on another *(là, il a mal choisi!)*
- getting the young and innocent France Gall, fresh from winning the Eurovision Song Contest with his song *Poupée de Cire, Poupée de Son,* to record a song entitled *Les Sucettes.* The literal translation of *'sucette'* is 'lollipop' but it has a strong sexual connotation which, although lost on Mlle Gall, was not on anyone else.

When he died he was buried with full honours, a bottle of whisky and packet of cigarettes. If the devil has all the good tunes then his life as *dragueur* will have ensured that he has gone to the right place.

Gambetta, Leon (1838-1882)
Orator and devoted opponent of Second Empire whose downfall he engineered after the defeat at Sedan in 1870. It was he who proclaimed the 3rd Republic of which he became President for a very short time. He escaped in a balloon from Paris in 1871 when under Prussian occupation and tried unsuccessfully to organise resistance from Bordeaux.
His funeral was attended by enormous crowds and in 1920 his heart was removed to the *Panthéon.*

Gambling
Louis XIV was the first to realise that gambling could provide a useful form of income and set up a state-controlled momopoly to capitalise on it. No government, however imbued with the spirit of free enterprise, has thought of including it in any privatisation plans. Today LOTO is played by twenty million punters (80% of them, men) with over twelve million tickets bought each week at 13,500 *points de vente,* LOTO is based on numbers similar to Premium bonds. The record amount staked was 350 million francs on November 11th, 1989. There are many different ways in which you can contribute to the state's coffers.
Loto Sportif - the nearest equivalent to the pools - was launched in 1985, the proceeds going to the development of French sport. A year later an anonymous player staked a thousand francs and won a record-breaking 14,464,731 tax-free return.

Even more popular is PMU *(Paris Mutuel Urbain)* which has eight million players who bet £3 billion annually. PMU is based on horse-racing. There is a bewildering variety of different types of bets that can be made but the most popular - *le tiercé* - requires picking in the correct order the first three horses past the post. However grave the international crisis, the results of the *tiercé* are included in all news bulletins on most French radio stations.

On one occasion the wrong result was announced - at odds of 4000 to 1. The rules of the competition forbid the correction of such a mistake and a few lucky people cashed in. After the ensuing uproar from holders of the correct numbers the government stepped in to pay them as well.

Yet another alternative is the *Tapis Vert* which requires you to guess four cards from a pack of 32 playing cards. The draw is made nightly on TF1 at peak time.

Gastronomie

Il faut manger pour vivre
Et ne pas vivre pour manger
Molière

This advice - to eat to live and not live to eat - is thankfully ignored by most French people. It has been estimated that the average person consumes some 50,000 meals in his or her life, spending around twelve years in this occupation. The French reverence for food is thus well-placed.

More pressurised life-styles mean that the old traditions of painstakingly prepared home cooking are giving way to eating out and *le fast food.* On average the French spend only twenty minutes a day in the kitchen compared with an hour less than ten years ago. But respect for *la gastronomie* is not lost. Your ready-to-serve meal purchased in Leclerc may well carry the imprimatur of Bocuse. The food industry has concentrated increasing attention to the pre-packed market as the trend towards smaller households - 11.5 million of one or two people - makes convenience food more attractive. Spending on food has plummetted from 36% of the family budget in 1959 to under 20%. In line with current trends, and with the French preoccupation with their health, there is a swing towards low-fat and low-sugar products.

Nevertheless, the special occasion, whether celebrated at a restaurant or privately, is still an occasion for fine food and good wine. In an opinion poll 79% of French people still regarded France as the country of the *'grande bouffe'* - the 'good blow-out'. The parts of France in which, according to the French, you eat best are, in order, Perigord, the Lyon area, Alsace and Burgundy. *L'Académie de Gastronomes* apes the *Académie Française* in having forty self-electing members, although it is still all male. Many other societies, such as the *Chevaliers du Tastevin* in Burgundy, exist to promote enjoyment of good food and wine.

Gauguin, Paul (1849-1902)

Post-impressionist artist who gave up a successful career as a stockbroker at the age of thirty-four in order to take up painting. Eight years later he abandoned his wife and five children and settled in Tahiti whence derive many of his best-known paintings, among which is that shown below - *Femme de Tahiti,* painted in 1892.

He returned to Paris for an exhibition which was a failure, as had been his attempt to work with Van Gogh in Provence. He wisely went back to Tahiti and then to the Marquesas Islands where he died in 1903. His method of covering flat surfaces with bold colours anticipated the Fauves and Abstract Art.

Gaulle, Charles de (1890-1970)

Head and shoulders above any other French personality of the twentieth century, first as soldier and war-leader, then as statesman (but never as politician).
After a distinguished military record in the First World War, he emerged as a lone military theorist who understood the importance of tanks. Since the military establishment is always one war behind in its thinking, his views were disregarded.
As an under-secretary of State for Defence he refused to accept the armistice after the defeat by Germany and launched the *Comité français de libération nationale* from London. From there, with virtually no cards in his hand, he passionately defended France's interests worldwide, making himself unpopular with his allies in the process. Churchill described him as looking like 'a female llama surprised in her bath.' Roosevelt offered to equip him a complete division, provided that he would lead it.

But who can believe that without de Gaulle's influence France would have become a permanent member of the UN Security Council after the war?
Entering liberated Paris he became President of the newly-formed government. Unable to stand the *jeu des partis,* he walked out in 1946 and left them to it. He retired to his home at Colombey-les-deux-Eglises to write his memoirs and await a second call to save his country. This came in 1958 as a result of the Algeria problem. Brought back to keep Algeria French, he gave them their independence shortly afterwards. He was also responsible for the Constitution of the Fifth Republic which has served France so well
Having said *oui* to Algeria, he then said *'non'* to Britain's first attempt to enter the Common Market. The *événements* of May 1968 shook the throne and he walked out for a second time in 1969 following the failure of a referendum on reforming the Constitution. He is buried in a simple grave in the churchyard of his home town.
After his death Roissy airport, north of Paris, was named after him and the *Place de l'Etoile* was renamed *Place Charles de Gaulle.* A new bridge under construction over the Seine will also bear his name.
His tangible legacy is the Fifth Republic. His less tangible legacy is that of his pride in France, his total integrity and lack of self-interest. With the current political malaise and disillusionment with politicians gripping France there is more than one person saying 'De Gaulle, thou should'st be living at this hour'.

Gauls

Earliest inhabitants of what is now France, commemorated by the helmet on a packet of Gaulloises. In common with other early tribes they regarded mistletoe as having magical qualities ('Balder Dead' by Matthew Arnold describes a similar belief in Norse mythology).
Their subjugation by the Romans is described in Caesar's Gallic Wars. A reconstruction of their way of life, and of the Roman defences at the battle of Alésia, can be seen, without leaving the Autoroute, at the *Archéodrome* at the Aire de Beaune/Tailly on the A6.

Gault-Millau

Guide, named after two influential food critics, for those who wish to know where they should be seen eating. It christened the term *nouvelle cuisine* which it has since worked ceaselessly to promote. Whereas Michelin awards stars, Gault-Millau awards *toques* (chef's hats).

Gender

Much acrimony has been generated in English-speaking countries on the vexed question of gender-specific words. Perhaps we English are more prone to it simply because our language is not gender-based as are most. We, fortunately, have only one article instead of the two French ones or three German.
It is interesting to compare how another language such as French copes with the problem of gender-specific words. Sometimes they have two gender-specific words where we have one non-gender-specific. Anyone hearing radio announcers saying goodbye to *'auditeurs et auditrices'* must be grateful for the economy of mere 'listeners'. Similarly we only need say 'Goodbye to all', not *'à tous et à toutes'*. In a different situation they have

no guilt in specifying that the male form of 'they' has precedence over the female form when the 'they' refers to people of both genders. By using the impersonal pronoun *'on'*, they do not so much run into the difficulties we have over 'he or she' or its ugly concatenation 's/he'. And the consequent 'his or her' is not at all a problem since the possessive pronoun takes its gender from the noun it qualifies rather than the person doing the possessing.

The French, mercifully, are much more relaxed about sexism in language, as they are about sex generally, and do not search for offence where none is intended. In any case, in French there appears to be a perfectly random use of the feminine or masculine when a non-gender-specific word is required. Madame Cresson is *le Premier Ministre;* any member of the National Assembly is *un député,* irrespective of their biological sex. All victims are feminine. But before any significance is read into this, so are all stars (in the sense of 'stage and screen' whether the French word *'vedettes'* is used, or the *franglais, 'stars'),* And with the quintessentially generic term 'person', the female embraces the male - *'une personne'*.

For the first time we men can experience what it is like to be subsumed into a feminine term. If a man is injured or killed in a traffic accident the report must start with *'la victime était M. Durand..'* If in the next sentence the reporter switches to the personal pronoun, he (or she!) would be forced to use *'elle'* in order to agree with *'la victime'*. To get round this, a different noun has to be introduced, such as *'le blessé'* (the injured man) in order to allow the switch to *'il'*.

Gide André (1869-1951)

Avant-garde essayist, critic, novelist and dramatist. His works are mostly about the struggle between individualism and organised religion often in the domain of sexuality. He won the Nobel Literature Prize in 1947. His most accessible book for the casual reader is probably *La Symphonie Pastorale.*

Giscard d'Estaing, Valéry (b. 1926)

The ultimate political egg-head, having been educated at all the right schools. An inescapable air of haughtiness is compounded by the common knowledge that the aristocratic part of his name *'d'Estaing'* was purchased by his uncle - the erstwhile plain Réné Giscard - in 1923. Nevertheless he was President from 1974 until 1981 when he was defeated by Mitterrand. In which defeat the Bokassa Diamonds played their part. He stood for President again in 1988 but was eliminated in the first round of voting.

In the third instalment of his autobiography, published in 1991, he reveals that he became so sensitive to criticism that for seven years he avoided reading any political article or watching any political programme on TV. Also, that being obsessed that he was getting uglier, he never looked in a mirror except to shave, which he did in a half-light.

Despite these oddities, the avowal of which might be thought to prejudice his chances, he has experienced something of a revival of late and is keen to try his hand again at the Presidency in 1995. In an attempt to become more a man of the people he has taken to appearing on chat shows and letting it be known that he enjoys watching the appalling American soap, Santa Barbara.

Gîtes

Self-catering holiday cottages offering exceptional value for money. So popular is this form of holiday that many different types of *gîtes*, and variations on the theme, are now available:

Gîtes Ruraux - rentable for a weekend or several weeks a *gîte* rural is self-contained, self-catering accommodation usually near a farm of village. You deal with the owners.

Gîtes de Pêche - as above, but with convenient fishing nearby.

Gîtes d'Enfants - a place to get rid of the kids by sending them to stay with a French family.

Gîtes d'Etapes - situated close to walks this is a place where you can stop-over for a night or two.

Chambres & Tables d'Hôtes - up-market bed and breakfast, often with evening meal. You are welcomed as friends by the proprietors. Depending on the area, it is helpful if you can *vous débrouiller* in French.

Addresses can be found in the five different *Guides Nationaux*, available from *Maison des Gîtes de France, 35, rue Godot-de-Mauroy, 75009 Paris.*

Goldman, Jean-Jacques (b. 1951)
Singer/composer of immense popularity among the young. His song *Il changeait la vie* sold 1.7 million copies in 1990.

Golf
The sport that is fastest-growing in popularity. In the last ten years the number of players has gone from 40,000 to 200,000 (compared with 2.2 million in the UK) and there are now over three hundred courses of which half have been constructed in the last three years. The still-low number of players, relative to the UK, means that there are 2.09 courses per 1000 players in France compared to 1.08 in England.
Among the players is President Mitterrand who is a member of the fashionable St Cloud club to which the Duke of Windsor used to belong.

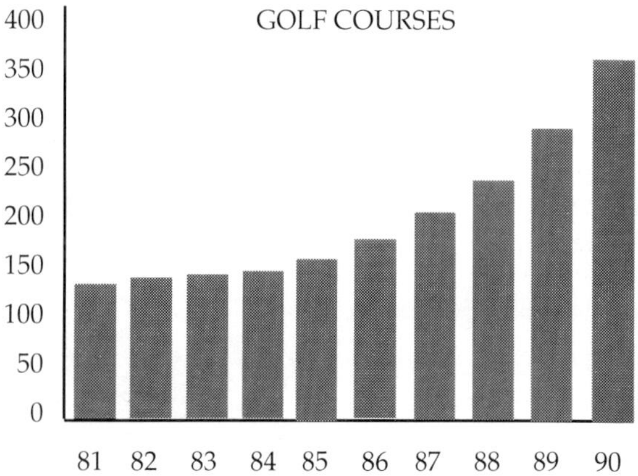

Goodbyes.
Taking your leave of the French is not a simple matter of *'au revoir'*. First, you have to make your excuses to leave. *'Eh bien, il faut partir'* (we have to go) will do nicely here. Standing up should compensate for any deficiencies in your pronunciation. You now go through the same hand-shaking or kissing routine that you started with. The French love long farewells. Even now it is too early to say *'au revoir'*. The word that you are now in need of has only one letter *'à'*. In this context it means 'until'. If you will see them again tomorrow, *'à demain'* is correct. 'See you later', with its useful lack of definition is *'à tout à l'heure'*. If the parting is for a longer, indeterminate time then *'à la prochaîne fois'* (until next time) is *très courant* (even more so, if you leave off the *'fois'*).[1]
You should always try to find an expression starting with *'bon* (or *'bonne')*. Simplest is *'bonne journée'* - the exact equivalent of 'Have a nice day'. *Bonne soirée,* of course, if it is later in the day - even *bonne fin de soirée,* if the evening is already under way. If you wish someone *bonnes vacances* as they set off, you can wish them *bonne route* or *bon retour* when they leave to go home. *Bon appetit* is, of course, *obligatoire*[2] before a meal. Encouragement in some difficult endeavour can be offered with *bon courage.* If all else fails just wish them well in doing whatever it was that they were doing before you interrupted them with *bonne continuation*[3]. Then you can finally go, leaving *'au revoir'* as your parting shot.
As if that is not complicated enough, try getting off the phone. There is a minefield of expressions that one has to navigate through - including *'Je t'embrasse'*, *'mes amitiés à votre femme'* and so on. Unless you are very quick the person at the other end always beats you to the punch leaving you with lame *'et à votre femme'* replies.
Finishing a letter is just as full of traps. In business the expression *'Veuillez agréer, Monsieur, l'expression de mes sentiments...'* can be followed with any number of adjectives depending upon subtle gradations of formality. *'...les plus distingués'* is the most formal (too formal ac-

* *This entry again betrays how badly connected I am. Françoise advises...*

1. *Only acceptable with* 'fois'; 'à bientôt' *is at all times to be preferred.*
2. Au contraire, *not for use in polite society.*
3. 'Quelle horreur!'

cording to Françoise), *'les meuilleurs'* would indicate that you have probably met, *'devoués'* that there is some element of familiarity. Perhaps the safest is *'Je vous prie de croire, cher monsieur, à l'expression de mes sentiments respectueux'*

For personal letters *'A bientôt'* or *'au plaisir de te lire (ou revoir)'* strikes the right balance between excessive formality and the more familiar *'amicalement'*.

Between members of the same family *'Grosses Bises'* are sent. If you are writing to your lover you can sprinkle the bottom of the page with the even more familiar *'Bisous'*.

Grandes Ecoles

For a country dedicated, at least nominally, to *Egalité*, France has the most elitist educational system in the world. Sitting on top of the university system, and disastrously reducing its value, are the hundred or so *Grandes Ecoles.* Unlike the universities, entry to these is by fiercely competitive examinations and aspiring post-bac students renounce sex, drink and social life, as they attend special crammers in order to get a place. Such dedication is well-rewarded, if successful, as a degree from the top *Grandes Ecoles* is an even surer passport to a life in the top drawer than a first at Oxford. Students are paid a salary during their studies and the average cost to the State of a student at a *Grande Ecole* is 250 thousand francs compared to seven thousand at university. The best-known of the *Grandes Ecoles* are:

Ecole Polytechnique, originally founded by Napoleon as a military school but currently less military and more engineering. No-one refers to it by its full name but as *'l'X'* from its badge of crossed canons.

Ecole des Hautes Etudes Commerciales (HEC), the top representative of the growing emphasis on management training for which the nearest English qualification would be an MBA. Graduates walk into top jobs in industry and finance.

Ecole Normale Supérieure (ENS), counting Jean-Paul Sartre amongst its alumni, it specialises in the humanities and in turning out teachers. Slightly less in fashion in the new vocational world of technology and business.

Ecole National d'Administration (ENA): Most recent and most prestigious. It is a forcing ground for top civil servants and politicians. The final exam classifies students in order of merit and the top ten take their pick of the best jobs in government administration. A roll-call of ENA graduates, known as *énarques*, is sufficient to show its influence - Giscard d'Estaing, Fabius, Rocard, Chirac (i.e. three Prime Ministers, two socialist, one conservative, in a row). Pompidou (ENS), Barre and Mitterrand, the other major politicians of the eighties, were all too old to have gone to ENA which was established by De Gaulle *exprès* to develop the governing class.

In a demonstration of political courage *sans pareil*, Mme Cresson is moving ENA out of Paris to Strasbourg. As may be expected this is being opposed strenuously by people who, whilst agreeing firmly with the move in principle, can find all sorts of reasons in practice why it cannot be done.

Grands Corps de l'Etat

Crème de la crème of the civil Service. Less Greats- more technology-orientated than the mandarins of 'Yes, Minister' but equally influential. The technocratic élite of French life, they have been educated by the *Grandes Ecoles* to know that they know better. Examples of the *Corps* are the *Inspection des Finances* and the *Cour des Comptes* (which regulates government expenditure), the *Conseil d'Etat* (sorting out legal issues affecting the citizen vis-à-vis the state), and the *Corps Diplomatique.*

Once you are in, you are in for life and continue drawing a salary even if you pass on to higher things such as political office.

Grappelli, Stéphane (b. 1908)

Violinist who has done more than anyone to make the violin an accepted instrument for jazz. In the thirties he was a member of the Hot Club of France with Django Reinhardt. Latterly his genius was recognised also by classical musicians and he has frequently played with Yehudi Menuhin.

Gregory, L'affaire

The case surrounding *le petit Gregory* is a long-running murder story of the type for which the French, or at least their magazine writers, have an insatiable curiosity. It started in October 1984 when the four-year-old Gregory was found drowned in a river near his home in the Vosges in eastern France. His hands and feet were both bound. Anonymous telephone calls, a letter signed *'le corbeau'* (the crow), posted before the body was discovered, taunted his father.

His uncle, Bernard Laroche was accused of the murder on the evidence of his fifteen-year-old daughter-in-law. She retracted her evidence and he was released. The father, Jean-Marie Villemin, believing nevertheless that he was guilty, shot him and was imprisoned for this crime.

Meanwhile suspicion for the original murder turned to Gregory's mother, Christine. Handwriting tests were made in an effort to determine whether she was the *corbeau* and she was accused *(inculpée)* of the murder of her own child. She was released pending further enquiries.

The first *Juge d'Instruction* left the case and was replaced by one who promptly suffered a heart attack. The enquiry lost momentum. In 1991 a new witness came forward, only to suffer sudden losses of memory about critical parts of her evidence. Meanwhile Jean-Marie was released and he and his wife had two more children. A new *juge d'instruction* has now been appointed and promises to get to the bottom of things. That will for starters mean reading the 18,000 pages of the dossier so far. Meanwhile Christine is still *inculpée...*

Guillotin, Joseph-Ignace (1738-1814)

Not, as is commonly believed, the inventor of the guillotine, but the person who proposed beheading as the method of execution during the Revolution. This was for humane, practical and sentimental reasons. Humanely, Dr Guillotin described it as 'a cool breath on the back of the neck'. Practically, its 70lb blade got through a lot fast (once dispatching 21 victims in 38 minutes).*

Romantically, the guillotine extended to all the traditional aristocratic privilege of decapitation. Prior to this there was a system of class distinction:

- Nobles were beheaded (with a sword or axe according to their station)
- Highwaymen were stretched on a wheel after having their arms and legs cut off
- State criminals were drawn and quartered
- Tricksters were boiled in oil
- Heretics were burned

The *Assemblée* adopted the proposal and it was built by a German engineer to the specification of a Dr Louis, then secretary of the French College of Surgeons. The job of executioner is traditionally kept in the family. The incumbent during the Revolution was M. Sanson, one of six generations of the same line who filled this position. Somewhat improbably he personally died in his bed. The guillotine was first used on 25 April, 1792 and last used in 1977. The last public execution took place in 1939.

The Mitterand government abolished capital punishment for murder as one of its first acts in coming to power in 1981.

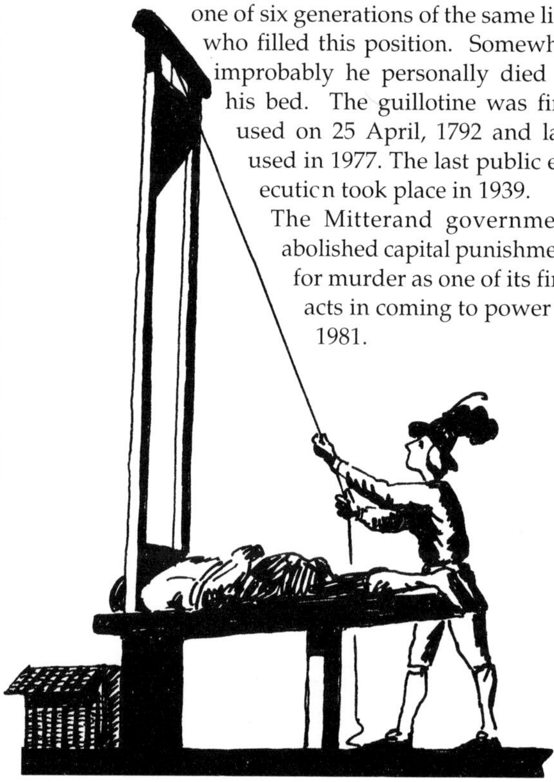

* *Although even this was too slow for the authorities in the Vendée. They drove victims into barges and scuttled them in the Loire.*

H

Hallyday, Johnnie (b. 1943)
Leading pop-singer, song-writer, actor and lover of Harley-Davidson motor-bikes. He is as well-known in France as he is unknown in Britain, the darling of *Paris Match* and like magazines who follow his private life with all-consuming interest. The latter is too volatile to be chronicled in a book such as this. At the start of writing he had just celebrated the first anniversary of his marriage to Adeline, the daughter of his best friend. Photos of them in appropriate loving poses were proffered as evidence to confute growing rumours of their imminent separation. By publication they were in the divorce courts. His son, David, is following in his father's footsteps, at least as far as singing is concerned. So far he is still married to his first wife.

Hand-shaking.
In France one should always *serrer la main,* both when greeting and leaving. That is unless one has progressed beyond this to kissing. If you are in the middle of doing the washing up, emptying the Portaloo or getting in the coal, then proffer your wrist. This is very French. One of my neighbours is a *cantonnier.* He works for the local council grading the roads, cutting hedgerows, and emptying the *poubelles.* The common denominator of all these activities is that Serge can never offer you his hand. I have rubbed wrists with Serge more times than I have shaken hands with most people. When confronted with a wrist or other part of the anatomy you can either grasp it firmly with your (clean) hand or respond in kind.

Harkis
Native Algerians who fought on the side of the French in the Algerian war and consequently found it expedient to settle in France. Concentrated, like the *pieds noirs,* in the South, the second generation is demanding (and rioting in support of) special rights from the government.

Haussmann, Baron (1809-1891)
Architect of the great building programmes in Paris in the 1860s that gave Paris ten new bridges and the broad boulevards which open up the city. The motivation for these was not entirely aesthetic. Wide streets made erecting barricades more difficult and firing at potential revolutionaries more easy. Beneath the surface he helped to build the famous Paris sewers a quarter of whose total length of 1600 Km can be visited from the *Pont de l'Alma.*

Health
In a farce by Jules Romains *'Knock ou le Triomphe de la médecine',* Dr Knock arrives at a small practice in the mountains to find that there are no patients. Launching a highly successful drive for patients with the slogan 'Every healthy person is an ill person who is not aware of it', he quickly fills his surgery.
The French have taken Knock to heart. It is no accident that the French equivalent of 'Cheers' is *'Santé'.* The nation is obsessed with its health. No-one ever gets mere indigestion as a result of all that good food. No, it is a *crise de foie* - which can only be cured by swallowing a lot of medicaments. The French take almost three times as many medicaments a year as the English. By the year 2000, if current trends continue, they will spend more on health than on food and drink. If the

pills don't get you, the scalpel will. The French perform three to four times as many appendicectomies as the rest of Europe.

Because of the worry that their health causes them, they consume more tranquillisers, sleeping pills and anti-depressants than any other country, the quantity having multiplied five times in the last twenty years. Given that the health service is semi-privatised, these figures could give pause for thought to those who hold that treatment free at the point of delivery of the service is the only possible way to ensure proper take-up.

France devotes double the percentage of its GDP to health (9.7) compared to the UK (4.8). Far from having the British problem of waiting lists, there are estimated to be 20% more hospital beds than there are patients to fill them. In France the results of privatised hospitals and independent doctors is an over-provision of both.

Héloise and Abélard

Famous pair of twelfth century lovers. Abélard was a brilliant theologian and teacher but a glittering career was cut short when he impregnated one of his pupils, Héloise. They were secretly married after the birth of their child but Héloise's uncle had Abelard's balls (literally, he had him castrated).

Following this reverse, Héloise got herself to a nunnery (again, literally) and became its Abbess. Lacking now the means, and presumably the inclination, to pursue their physical relationship, Abélard then wrote her the letters which have given them a permanent place in history among pairs of lovers.

Henry IV (1533-1610)

If you are able to slip the phrase *'Paris vaut bien une messe'* into a conversation you will gain great history-credibility. In one of the first and most comprehensive examples of what is now referred to as a political U-turn Henry de Navarre (as he started) began life as a Protestant, became a Catholic when captured by Henry III, reverted to Protestantism when he escaped and back again to Catholicism in order to cement his hold on the throne. Hence the sentiment that if the price of gaining entry into Paris was to say a mass, he was willing to pay it.

Henry IV is one of France's most famous and popular kings. His reign saw an end to the *Guerres de Religion*, bringing both internal and external peace, and his Minister, Sully, was a great administrative reformer.

His other well-known expression is that he wanted every peasant to have a *poule au pot* every Sunday - a sort of early 'Never had it so good'. The political analogy is not too far out as Henry IV was as much a forerunner of Presidents as a king.

Henry IV is in third place,after Louis XV and Louis XIV, for the number of mistresses. This did no harm to his popularity and he was known as the *Vert Galant*. There is a delightful square of this name just behind his statue at one end of the Ile de la Cité in Paris. Among his many *copines* was the famous Gabrielle d'Estrées, who had also been around. She is commemorated in a famous double portrait that can be seen in the Louvre having her nipple tweaked by her sister, apparently an indication that she is pregnant.

Henry IV was the first recorded victim of Paris traffic jams. Caught in his coach in a *bouchon*, he was assassinated in 1610 by a mad teacher called Ravaillac.

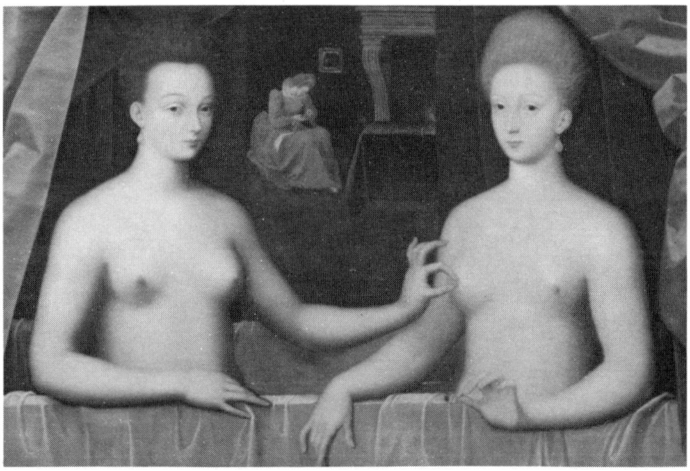

Hersant, Robert (b. 1920)

Right-wing newspaper magnate who started with his own local papers and went on to buy *Le Figaro, France-Soir* and many important regional papers such as *Le Progrès de Lyon.* A member of the European Parliament he is a multi-millionaire whose personal fortune will be only slightly dented by the financial problems of *la Cinq,* the financially-troubled television channel in which his companies have an investment.

L'Héxagone
The French's own way of referring to France. A cursory glance at any of the maps of France in this book will show that 'the hexagon' is a reasonably accurate description of its shape. At 549,000 Km2 it is, following the reunification of Germany, the third largest European country. With 55 million inhabitants it has one of the lowest population densities in Europe. Mont Blanc is 4807m but despite the Alps, Massif Central, Vosges and other ranges, two thirds of the country is less than 250m above sea-level.
France's situation means that it can be viewed as two different halves, either on a north/south axis - the north being Germanic, the south, Latin, or on an east/west axis - the east looking towards the heart of the continent, the west towards the Atlantic.

Hill, Benny (b. 1924)
English television comedian whose brand of slapstick humour and sexual innuendoes has made him a firm favourite with French audiences.

History
What has made France the way it is? What events determined her current borders, what factors led to her system of government, what influences explain her national characteristics?
For a variety of reasons France's history has followed a very different course from that of England. Lacking an easily-defensible Eastern border made it prey to successions of invasions by land to go with the many sea-borne ones resulting from her long coastline. Over the centuries she has been invaded by Romans, Franks, Huns, Arabs, Vikings, English, Prussians and Germans.
Secondly, France is twice the size of England. Before the seventeenth century it was impossible for the king's writ to run throughout the land and the difference in area between that which a king nominally ruled over and that which he controlled was large.
These two factors provide two themes: The gradual unification of France - by marriage, treaty or conquest - from a set of changing provinces into its current geographical borders. And the accompanying process of centralisation by which power was ceded by the provinces to the central authority (or, more accurately, taken by the centre). Two other strands help to understand her history. The differing path that religion took in France compared to England, and the propensity for change to be revolutionary rather than evolutionary. For a short overview of French history it is convenient to define three broad phases:

- Establishment of France: Roman conquest to 1437
- From Reformation to Revolution (1437-1789)
- The Revolution to the Fifth Republic (1789-1958)

After that history becomes current affairs.

The Establishment of France
Caesar conquered Gaul - *veni, vidi, vici* - immediately prior to turning his attention to Britain. Lyon became the administrative capital of Roman Gaul and towns such as Nîmes, Arles and Marseille were centres of Roman architectural and cultural influence. The Roman aqueduct at *Pont du Gard* has two million visitors a year and has been declared a *patrimoine de l'humanité* by UNESCO.

When the Roman Empire declined and fell, Gaul was invaded by Attila the Hun. He was defeated and the first post-Roman king was Clovis (486). The Merovingian dynasty founded by Clovis lasted until the accession of the first Carolingian king, Charles Martel. The latter, by defeating an invading Arab army at Tours in 732, set the geographical limit of the Arab conquests of the eighth century and kept France free from Arab influence. Charles Martel's grandson was the Holy Roman Emperor, Charlemagne.
Shortly after this time the Viking invasions began, continuing until they were bought off with Normandy in 911. Whence came William the Conqueror in 1066. A century later the English had their revenge. Marriage and warfare meant that by 1188 the English crown, under Henry II, had acquired Normandy, Aquitaine,

Anjou, Brittany, Gascony and the western half of the Pyrenees - effectively the whole of Western France. Henry's successor, Richard I, preferred Crusades to managing England which he left to King John who promptly lost virtually all that Henry had put together. However, the real Franco-English dispute was yet to come. A source of problems to French royalty throughout the ages was the refusal to allow the succession through the female line. When taken in conjunction with the propensity of kings to die well before their three score years and ten, this frequently gave rise to succession problems. One such struck in 1328 when Charles IV died leaving only a daughter. The English crown claimed the French throne on behalf of the Black Prince and in 1339 the Hundred Years War began, lasting, in fact, 114 years. This was the war that gave the English, Crecy and Agincourt. It gave the French Joan of Arc. At its end in 1453 English power in France was permanently broken. Normandy and Brittany were brought under the control of the French king by the end of the century and the territorial limits of France were largely established with only the eastern border changing since then.

From Reformation to Revolution (1437-1789)
Having successfully fought the English, the French now fought among themselves. The Reformation in France took a Calvinist turn which guaranteed problems in a state that remained overwhelmingly Catholic. The latter half of the 16th Century saw the *Guerres de Religion* as the Catholic League, headed by the de Guise family endeavoured to stifle Protestant influence. The wars finished with Henry IV's U-turn although, as we have seen, even this was not enough to save him from the same fate as that of his predecessor, Henry III, namely assassination.

Henry IV's untimely end meant that his widow took over as regent for their young son, Louis XIII. Cardinal Richelieu then set about a mission to centralise power under the monarchy and more civil fighting ensued. The reign of Louis XIV - *le roi soleil* - saw the monarchy at its absolutist height. But the failure to reform, the insolence of the aristocracy, the new ideas of Rousseau and Montesquieu, the unfair tax system, the emergence of a powerful new class - the wealthy, educated bourgeoisie - was building up discontent which had no effective democratic outlet. In 1789 it exploded.

Revolution to Fifth Republic (1789-1958)
It is always easier to pull down than create, particularly when it comes to political institutions. The Revolution certainly destroyed the *ancien régime* but what was to be put in its place? Between 1789 and 1958 there is a succession of different attempts. The best way to get to grips with these is to look at the forms of government that were tried and the reasons for their replacement.

Monarchy	1789-1792	Execution of Louis XVI
Republic (1)	1792-1799	Coup d'état (Napoleon)
Consulate/ Empire (1)	1799-1815	Military defeat (Waterloo)
Monarchy (1)	1815-1830	Revolution
Monarchy (2)	1830-1848	Revolution
Republic (2)	1848-1852	Coup d'état (Napoleon III)
Empire (2)	1852-1873	Military Defeat
Republic (3)	1873-1940	Military Defeat
Collaboration	1940-1944	Liberation
Republic (4)	1944-1957	Restoration (De Gaulle)

The nineteenth century was an era in which France tried various forms of government - monarchy, republic, empire and round again - with a mixture of success.

After Napoleon there was a Restoration of the monarchy. Louis XVIII ruled tolerably well from 1814 to 1824 (with a break of a hundred days or so for Napoleon's curtain call). He was succeeded by his brother Charles X who tried unsuccessfully to turn back the pages of history and was deposed by the 1830 revolution.

The latter ushered in an attempt at constitutional monarchy under Louis-Philippe (whose title was 'King of the French' as opposed to 'King of France'). This ended with a revolution - that of 1848. For some time Napoleon's nephew, with a name - Louis Napoleon Bonaparte - which covered most eventualities, had been fancying his chances. In December he was elected President of the Republic but on completion of his four-year term of office he followed in his uncle's footsteps and declared himself Emperor Napoleon III. Thus the period from 1854 to 1871 is known as the 'Second Empire'. It is described in the entry for Napoleon III.

Following Napoleon's exile and the collapse of the Empire as a result of the Franco-Prussian War, the Third Republic was established on the 4th of September, 1870, a date commemorated in many street names. Its constitution virtually guaranteed weak government and the ensuing seventy years saw a succession of crypto-royalist, republican, radical and socialist Presidents trying first to recover from the defeat by the Prussians, then survive a variety of scandals such as those of the Panama Canal and Dreyfus, combat and ultimately defeat German militancy in the First World War and then negotiate the tricky inter-war years. The latter period, in the face of the growing menace of Hitler, saw 44 governments and twenty different Prime Ministers. Although legally the Third Republic survived until 1946 it was de facto replaced by the Vichy government in 1940.

Detail from 'Liberty guiding the People' Delacroix Commemorating the Revolution of 1830

Constitutionally the Fourth Republic was little better, again suffering a string of weak governments caused mainly by the system of Proportional Representation under which they were elected. It ended in 1958 when De Gaulle, profiting from the lessons of the past century, wrote a new constitution embodying much stronger Presidential power.

An interesting post-script is that there appears with hindsight to be very little correlation between the type of political set-up, even less the particular head of it at any one time, and the level of economic growth, national well-feeling or any other indicator. It was, for example, during the musical chairs of the Fourth Republic that France's economy grew and self-respect returned. Perhaps Alexander Pope had it right:

For forms of government let fools contest
Whate'er is best administered, is best.
Essay on Man.

HLM

Habitation à Loyer Modéré (moderately-priced rental housing). HLMs are the nearest thing to council housing and account for 14% of all residences. Immigrants account for 43% of their occupants.

Holidays

French has two words for holidays - *vacances* for long holidays such as the *vacances scolaires* and *congé* for days off work granted by your employer, such as *congé de maternité.* Whereas England has eight days of public holidays, the French have eleven. May is particularly blessed with Labour Day, VE day, Ascension, and *Pentecôte* (Whitsun). Frequently people will *faire le pont* (bridge the gap between a *jour férié* and the weekend) by taking off the days in between.

The *grandes vacances* are in July and August during which time industrial production drops by 30%. So entrenched is the ritual of these holidays that specific nouns exist - *juillistes* and *aôutiens* - for people on holiday in these months. In an attempt to relieve congestion on roads and at popular resorts, French schools are banded into zones and the dates of half-terms and long holidays are staggered by zone.

Horse-racing *(Le Turf)*

There are 15,000 race meetings a year in France, at 250 different race courses. One of them, Longchamps, is widely regarded as the most beautiful race course in the world. There are no on-course bookmakers as all betting is controlled through the State-run PMU.

The French equivalent of the Derby is the *Prix de l'Arc de Triomphe* run on the first Sunday in October over 2,400 metres with £500,000 going to the winner.

Hôtel de Ville
Do not try to check into this hotel. You will for starters have great difficulty finding *'Réception'*. This is not surprising since an *Hôtel de Ville* is the equivalent of our town hall.

Hôtel Matîgnon
It is just as difficult to get *une chambre* here as at an *Hôtel de Ville. L'Hôtel Matignon* is the official residence of *le Premier Ministre* - the equivalent of 'Number 10'.

Hugo, Victor-Marie (1802-1885)
Greatest French poet of the 19th century with an international reputation in his own time. In all he wrote 100,000 lines of verse, none more beautiful than *A Villequier,* lamenting the death through drowning of his idolised nineteen-year-old daughter:

Maintenant, o mon dieu! que j'ai ce calme sombre
De pouvoir désormais
Voir de mes yeux la pierre où je sais que dans l'ombre
Elle dort pour jamais;

Maintenant, qu'attendri par ces divins spectacles,
Plaines, fôrets, vallons, fleuve argenté,
Voyant ma petitesse et voyant vos miracles,
Je reprends ma raison devant l'immensité

Toute traduction est trahison. The verses relate how, on returning some years later to the spot where the tragedy occurred, he can now look upon her stone, softened by the surrounding beauty and recover his sanity.
His second daughter, Adèle, whose life ended in madness, was the subject of a François Truffaut film starring Isabelle Adjani.
In addition he was a novelist and dramatist of the Romantic movement who spent fifteen years writing *'Les Misérables'*. He also wrote 'The Hunchback of Notre Dame' which has yet to be set to music.
A fiery republican and champion of the oppressed, he became a *député* in 1848, but found it expedient to leave France when Napoléon III became Emperor. He spent twenty years in the Channel Islands where he got involved in spiritualism. He returned to France following Napoleon's own fall and exile. More than one million people lined the streets of Paris for his funeral procession to the *Panthéon.*
His house near the Bastille is preserved as a museum and provides ample evidence that he was also an artist of some genius.

I

Ile-de-France

The 'Greater Paris' *région,* cradle of France, comprising the *départements* of Paris (75), Seine-et-Marne (77), Yvelines (78) Essonne (91), Hauts-de-Seine (92), Seine-St-Denis (93), Val-de-Marne (94) and Val-d'Oise (95). *Chef-lieu:* Paris.

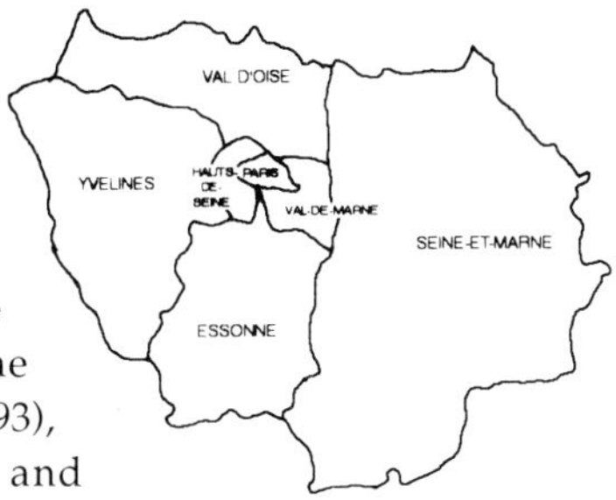

Although with 10.6 million *habitants* it is by far the most populous region, it also boasts the forests of Fontainebleau, Rambouillet and Compiègne, the *châteaux* of Versailles and Fontainebleau and the Brie cheese from Seine-et-Marne.

Immigration

As in Britain, the word 'immigrant' only incidentally refers to people coming to live in the country. As evidence of that statement, the number of English choosing to retire to Provence has not become a political issue. That is because most English people (and all who buy houses in Provence) have a white skin. Of the estimated four and a half million foreigners in France almost two million are from within the EEC. The largest number of immigrant workers in France is the Portuguese with just under a million and they have few problems of assimilation. The 650,000 blacks, mostly French citizens from the Antilles and Africa, are easily accepted.

No, when 'the immigrant problem' is mentioned it is a reference to the large number of Arabs, mainly from North Africa, that live, legally or illegally, in France. Originally brought in to do jobs that others spurned, the problem has worsened as unemployment has increased. The legacy of the Algerian War still lingers, nor have Arab terrorism and political assassinations helped the immigrants' cause.

Unlike England, France has a strong *Front National* always ready to fan the flames. The influence of Le Pen has been seen in the language of other politicians of the less extreme right. Chirac has talked of an 'overdose' of immigration and criticised the smells that Arab families make when cooking; Giscard has spoken of an 'invasion' and made references to French nationality being determined by *le droit du sang* as opposed to the *droit du sol. 'On naît français si on naît d'un père ou mère français'.* The implication is that those wishing to acquire French nationality would need to demonstrate French ancestry and not automatically be entitled to it through length of residence.

The problem manifests itself in different forms. First, non-Arab families tend to move out of areas in which Arabs settle, thereby producing ghettos and giving rise to the so-called *'problème des banlieus'* .

Secondly, Arabs are Muslims. Islam is a theocratic religion which places religious observance above duty to the State. This does not go down well in any democracy and particularly not France where, after centuries of religious conflict, the Catholic Church was disestablished in 1905 and which is now a secular society. To the extent that their religion and customs, such as the veil, make them unwilling to integrate into French society, immigrants attract hostility. Specifically, problems arise over the question of religious education in schools.

Third, there is the 'right to vote' question. At what stage should immigrants be granted the right to vote, and should this be contingent on in some way losing their cultural identity? Should they, for instance, support the French football team against the Cameroons? A recent opinion poll showed 75% against the right to vote in municipal elections.

On top of this is the problem of the *clandestins.* Estimates, starting at 300,000 and going up, vary as to the number of illegal immigrants in the country. A country with such a length of frontier - 6,000 Km - will always have difficulties in preventing illegal immigration. The Mediterranean is more a conduit than a barrier. It has been estimated that to prevent illegal immigration would require 100,000 frontier guards (against the current complement of 4,000). But what to do with them if they slip into the country and are then discovered, as approximately 4,000 are each year? The answer is to send them back where they came from. Unfortunately many *clandestins* ignore *le fairplay* and destroy their personal documents so that you have no idea where to send them back to. *En plus,* commercial airlines are notoriously unhappy about having scheduled flights disrupted by unwilling repatriates being manhandled on board. Hence the emergence of *les charters* - i.e chartered planes to repatriate illegal immigrants - as a political issue.

Impressionism

School of painting generally acknowledged as starting with Manet's *'Déjeuner sur l'herbe'*, which was considered too way out to be accepted for showing in the 'Salon' alongside the works of those household names, Cabanet, Winterhalter and Flandrin. Instead, in 1863, it was put into a special show called the *'Salon des Réfusés'* along with those of other outrageous affronters of official taste such as Pissarro, Renoir, Monet and Cézanne. Seven thousand visitors came on the first day but mainly only to join in the general hilarity. The term 'impressionism' was not coined till ten years later when a show included a painting by Monet called 'Impression: Sunrise' (inset). A critic, wishing to ridicule the group of exhibitors, called them 'The Impressionists'.
Other critics were also unimpressed. 'Five or six artists have joined together and exhibited their works. They take a piece of canvas, colour and brush, daub a few patches of paint on it at random, and sign the whole thing with their name. It is a delusion of the same kind as if the inmates of Bedlam picked up stones from the wayside and imagined they had found diamonds.' In 1875 you could have picked up a Monet for 200F or a Renoir for half that amount.

Inheritance

Liberté, Fraternité, Equalité are so ingrained as the rallying call of the Revolution and the motto of the Republic that it passes unnoticed that there is in many situations an inbuilt conflict between liberty and equality. Where this is so, in most cases it is equality that gets precedence and often the State that intervenes to accomplish this. Thus in France you do not have the *liberté* to leave your estate to whom you wish. Napoleon laid down that the *patrimoine* must follow the *droit du sang* (right of the blood); in other words it should stay in the family - even to the extent of disinheriting the surviving spouse. He or she can benefit from the *usufruit* - that is the right to enjoy the assets - live in the house, receive the interest from investments - but does not automatically inherit the assets - indeed cannot. This goes to the children *who cannot be disinherited.* If there are no children then it goes in order of precedence, to the grandchildren, parents of the deceased, grandparents and cousins.
The estate is divided into two parts - the *réserve héréditaire* and the *quotité disponible.* The *réserve* cannot be touched and its amount and division among successors is according to a strict formula which depends mainly on the number of children. Thus if there is one child, he or she has to get half of the estate and the other half is *disponible* to whom the testator decides. With two children the *réserve* amounts to two-thirds of the estate; with three or more, three-quarters. Moreover, all children must receive equal shares in the estate - which accounts for the many small parcels of land and the problems of multi-ownership of that house you are trying to buy.
The remainder of the estate can go to whom the testator wishes. Even here, however, the *dirigiste* state puts in its oar. The amount of tax paid is determined by the recipient. If money is left to relatives it is taxed, broadly speaking, at 50%. If you leave it to the cats' home or ex-mistresses it is taxed more punitively*. Another alternative is not to leave it to anyone by the simple expedient of spending it. You can even release the money tied up in your house by selling it *en viager.* You then continue to live in it until your death at a rent agreed between vendor and purchaser.

Ionesco, Eugène (1912-1989)

Playwright, friend of Samuel Beckett, who lived in Paris and wrote surrealist plays such as the Rhinoceros, which are highly regarded on account of their being difficult to understand. His plays *La Cantatrice Chauve* and *La Leçon* have been running non-stop since 1957 at a theatre in Paris. This is not quite as impressive a statistic as for 'The Mousetrap' since the theatre holds only ninety seats but it nevertheless represents a total audience of close on a million .

* *The French, loth always to legislate against sin, occasionally tax it. A similar use of the fiscal system is seen in the higher tax rate imposed on pornographic messages on Minitel.*

J

Jarre, Jean-Michel (b. 1948)

Composer and impresario who stages enormous *'Son et Lumière'* spectacles. On July 14th, 1979 the Place de la Concorde display had a million spectators. The show staged in Lyon during the Pope's visit used a backdrop five Km long. The attempt to run a similar event in Docklands ran up against problems with the local councils. He is married to the actress, Charlotte Rampling. Composing runs in the family; his father, Maurice Jarre, wrote the music for Lawrence of Arabia and Doctor Zhivago.

Jaurès, Jean-Leon (1859-1914)

Philosophy teacher turned socialist politician and orator, founder of *'L'Humanité'* which started life as a socialist newspaper before turning communist. A dedicated pacifist, he was assassinated in a Paris café (by a non-pacifist) just before the outbreak of the First World War.

Jeanne d'Arc (1412-1431)

France's most famous maid. Born at Domrémy on the Meuse, Joan heard voices telling her to save France from the English. She therefore set off from her home town at the age of sixteen to stiffen the resolve of the weak Charles VII. She talked him into letting her relieve the siege of Orléans, which she succeeded in doing in 1429 (commemorated there on May 8th every year). Captured by the Burgundians, she was sold to the English for £10,000. She was put on trial as a heretic, condemned to death by a French judge and burnt at the stake in Rouen. She was canonised in 1920. One of her less salubrious companions was Gilles de Rais who was also burned at the stake for innumerable crimes of torturing babies, ritual murder, apostasy, sacrilege and violating ecclesiastical rights. He is the historical model for Bluebeard.

Juge d'Instruction

There is a fundamental difference between the French and English legal systems as embodied in the *juge d'instruction (examining magistrate).* Whereas in England the police force is the body responsible for gathering evidence and bringing prosecutions, in France the latter function is performed by an independent magistrate. A suspect is *inculpé* (arraigned) and may be held in jail - *garde à vue* - for 48 hours or released pending further investigation. It is also for the *juge d'instruction* to order a reconstruction of the crime. The system is held to be fairer to the defendant who will, for example, have facilities equal to those of the police to gather and analyse forensic evidence.

K

Kings

French kings tended to be given nicknames reflecting their physical appearance or character. Thus they have Charles the Fat, Pepin the Short, Louis the Stammerer, Charles the Bald, Louis the Pious (who tortured his nephew to death), Charles the Simple, Charles the Affable, Charles the Wise, (succeeded by Charles the Foolish), John the Good, Charles the Well-served, Louis the Spider, Louis the Blind, Louis the Fat, Charles the Beloved to name but a few. In addition a whole series was grouped together as *les rois fainéants* (do-nothing). The least fortunate was Jean I. He was known as *'le Posthume'* on account of posthumously succeeding his father, Louis X who died with Jean still four months away from birth. He lived and reigned for five days before himself turning up his toes.

Kingship is actuarially a bad risk. Owing no doubt to the stresses of court intrigue, wars, demanding mistresses, nagging queens and recalcitrant nobles, no French king has made it to eighty. The nearest was Charles X who died in exile only a few days short.

Kir

A refreshing drink often served as an *apéritif* consisting of white wine and cassis (blackcurrant). It is named after a mayor of Dijon and resistance hero, twice condemned to death by the Nazis and twice reprieved.

Even more refreshing is a *kir royal* in which the white wine is replaced by champagne.

Kissing

The French are inveterate kissers. If you get *intime* with them then ultimately you will have to start kissing instead of shaking hands. When you do, the first thing to realise is that you are not required to plant a smacker on your hostess's lips. If your lips make contact at all it is with her cheek and the merest brush. This is even more the case if a bloke is kissing another bloke. Now it is more a cheek-to-cheek rub.

Once you sense that the moment has come you still need to know how many times and on which side to start. Getting either of these wrong can leave you stranded in mid-air or with a nasty collision of noses.

The right number of kisses varies from region to region. In the Ardèche it is three; elsewhere in the Midi it is often four; in Paris and Lyon two is usually right. The number is also inversely related to the social class - the higher, the fewer. In common with many social customs, kissing is prone to inflation so do not be surprised if you draw away only to find your partner looking for a fourth or even fifth. Try to cultivate an 'educated hover'.

As to the starting side, in the Ardèche it is the left cheek, in Lyon and Paris, the right. If in doubt, aim to finish up on the recipient's left cheek. Quick reflexes are *l'ordre du jour*.

But the real problem, as with addressing people as *tu* rather than *vous*, is when do you start? It is not as simple as to say that you kiss anyone you *tutoie* and shake the hands of anyone you *vousvoie*. Nor should you be caught kissing the good-looking men or women and shaking hands with the rest.

My best advice (in the context of this book) is to get into it. English people are reluctant kissers. If you are to make the grade as an honorary Frenchman or Frenchwoman, err on the French side. In any case, as a foreigner, any over-exuberance will be treated kindly.

L

Lafayette, Marquis de (1757-1834)

Born with a silver spoon in his mouth and a name to go with it - Marie Joseph Paul Yves Roch Gilbert de Motier, Marquis de Lafayette. An aristocrat who fell in love with the idea of liberty. In 1777 he emigrated to America and fought on their side in the War of Independence, becoming a close friend of George Washington. Returning to France he was elected to the first *Assemblée* in 1789. Appointed head of the National Guard, his main preoccupation was to reconcile the king with the Revolution. Failing in this, he sensibly emigrated in 1792 only to be imprisoned for five years by the Austrians. He later returned again and resumed his political career, serving as a liberal *député* during the period of the Restoration.

His reputation was always higher in America than in his own country. When he died he was buried in American soil that he had brought back with him. The American flag flies over his grave at 35 rue Picpus where are also buried the victims of the guillotine. When General Pershing landed with the US forces in 1917 he is reputed to have said: 'Lafayette, we are here'.

La Fontaine, Jean de (1621-1695)

> *Je me sers d'animaux pour instruire les hommes*
> (I use animals to educate men)

La Fontaine's delightful fables are mostly cameos of life drawn using animals, often exploring poverty and hard times and finishing with a moral such as *'un tiens vaut mieux que deux tu l'auras'* (a bird in the hand...). Among the best-known of his fables are *Le Corbeau et le Renard* and *La Cigale et la Fourmis.* Although initially he had troubles at the court of Louis XIV where he was suspected of being a subversive influence, he ultimately became well protected by rich patrons.

Lamartine, Alphonse de (1790-1869)

As a result of his first work, *Méditations Poétiques,* he was hailed as the master of the romantic poets. He later turned to politics (French writers are much more likely to be politically active than English) and for a short time in 1848 was Foreign Minister and de facto head of government.

Languedoc-Roussillon

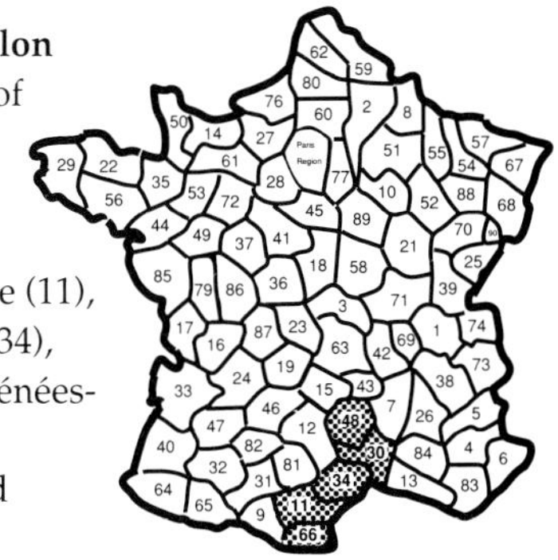

Région in the south of France bordering the Mediterranean comprising the *départements* of Aude (11), Gard (30), Hérault (34), Lozère (48) and Pyrénées-Orientales (66).
Its *chef-lieu* is the old university town of Montpellier and the population is just over a million. Containing all the Mediterranean resorts from Aigues-Mortes to Perpignan, its main industry is tourism, although a lot of wine is grown. This used to be inferior *pinard* (plonk) but the quality has been forced to increase in order to compete. The name 'Languedoc' comes from the old southern word for yes,'oc' and the local language *occitan* is still kept alive.

Larousse

In 1866 Larousse first published the *Grand Dictionnaire Universel du XIX Siécle,* a fifteen-volume encyclopedia. The French equivalent of Encyclopedia Britannica, it now covers all ages and countries and has been supplemented by the *Grand Dictionnaire de la Langue Française.* The latter now runs to seven volumes; the *Grand Dictionnaire Universel* to twenty. Both are more readily accessible in *'petites'* versions of which over 25 million have been sold.

Lascaut

Well-preserved examples of prehistoric cave murals and engravings dating from 17,000 BC. Unfortunately whilst they remained unharmed for centuries the impact of tourists made them begin to degrade. In consequence the caves are closed to the public who have to content themselves with an air-conditioned replica.

Latin Quarter

Famous Bohemian area of cafés, restaurants and bookshops, on the *rive gauche,* so-called because the scholars of the Sorbonne in the heart of the *quartier*, spoke Latin. It contains Paris's smallest street - *la rue du Chat-qui-Pêche* - the *Panthéon* and the gracious Boulevard St-Michel (referred to as Boul' Mich if you are *branché).* Former watering-place of writers such as James Joyce, Ezra Pound, Henry Miller and Hemingway.

Laval, Pierre (1883-1945)
Right-wing, appeasement politician of 3rd Republic who became Vice-Premier of the collaborationist government following its establishment at Vichy in 1940. Fanatically anti-British, anti-Bolshevik and openly in favour of a German victory, he assumed effective control of the government in 1942. As such he stands guilty of many of the worst excesses of the regime. Following the Liberation he was tried, sentenced to death and executed by firing squad.

Leclerc, Edouard (b. 1926)
Breton, founder, at age of 23, of the *'Centres Leclerc'* retail shops, of which there are now over five hundred . As with similar family companies in the UK, his aggressive retailing and insistence on selling at the lowest prices possible, have much benefited French life. Not unlike his counterparts in England he exhibits a social conscience and regularly pursues cut-price policies aimed at benefiting the poorest members of society. This has latterly led him and his brother into areas such as petrol, medicines and funeral parlours where cosy cartels were seen by them to be operating against the public interest.

Le Corbusier (1887-1965)
Although Swiss-born, Le Corbusier spent most of his life in France. He is the most influential architect of the 20th century famous for his concept that a house is ' a machine for living in'. His writings spread his theories which were an attempt to maintain the human element in architecture in a machine-driven, functionalist age. In his early work, particularly around Paris, he was influenced by *'L'Esprit Nouveau'* which drew inspiration from engineering principles. In his later work he adopted a style reflecting his love of peasant and monastic communities. He was the architect for the *Cité Radieuse* in Marseilles.

Le Pen, Jean-Marie (b. 1928)
President of the National Front since 1972 who described the Nazi gas chambers as a 'detail' of the war.

Born in Brittany he served as a paratrooper in Indo-China and again in Algeria, hence his appeal to veterans. He manifests an inbuilt dislike of all foreigners, particularly Arabs, with the possible exception of Saddam Hussein whom he was content to leave in control of Kuwait.
He was the youngest *deputé* in the NationalAssembly at the age of 27 and remains a Euro-MP. A powerful political figure he polled 14.5% in the first round of the 1988 Presidential election. His estranged wife appearing semi-nude in the French version of Playboy did not seem to harm his career. He lost an eye in a street brawl during one campaign.
His opposition to immigration and the support which he finds for such opinions forcibly expressed has forced his political opponents to trim their own views whilst advancing his own vote.
In March 1992 he failed in his attempt to get elected for the seat of Bouches-du-Rhône in Provence in the regional elections.

Limousin

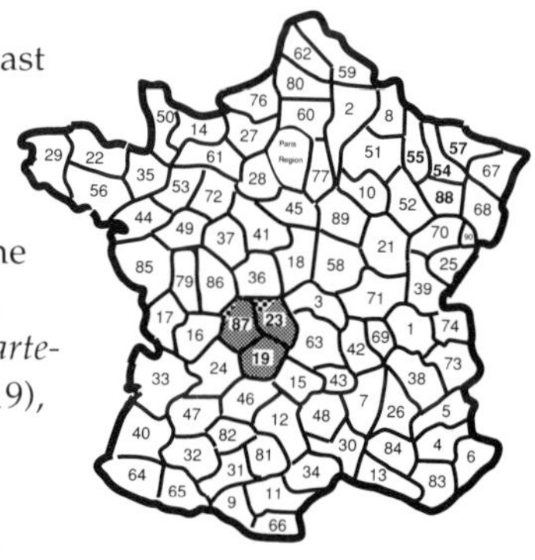

The smallest and least populous (720,000 inhabitants) of *régions*, situated to the north-west of the Massif Central and comprising the *départements* of Corrèze (19), Creuse (23) and Haute-Vienne (87). *Chef-lieu:* Limoges.
During the First World War unsuccessful generals were sent to Limoges giving rise to the verb *'limoger'* meaning to demote for incompetence. The verb 'to Stellenbosch' had the same meaning, for the same reaon, during the Boer War. During the Second World War the Nazis murdered all inhabitants of the village of Oradour-sur-Glane whose charred ruins remain as a memorial to the crime.

A meat-producing region, for a long time a fiefdom of England, it was annexed to the crown of France by Henri IV in 1607.
With Nord-Pas-de-Calais, it was in 1986 one of the only two *régions* to elect a Socialist government. In 1992 the latter lost control of both regions so strongly was the anti-Socialist tide running.

Logis
Small hotels of excellent value for money recognisable by the green *'Logis de France'* sign. For some inexplicable reason they all sport wallpaper covered with large, usually brown, floral patterns which belie the French reputation for *bon goût*.
The Logis Guide is on sale at most large bookshops in England but can be obtained from:
La Fédération Nationale des Logis de France, 83 avenue d'Italie, 75013 Paris. Tel: 010 33 1 45 84 70 00

LOGIS DE FRANCE

Lorraine
Région de l'est comprising the *départements* of Meurthe-et-Moselle (54), Meuse (55), Moselle (57) and Vosges (88).
Chef-lieu: Metz; population 2.3 million.

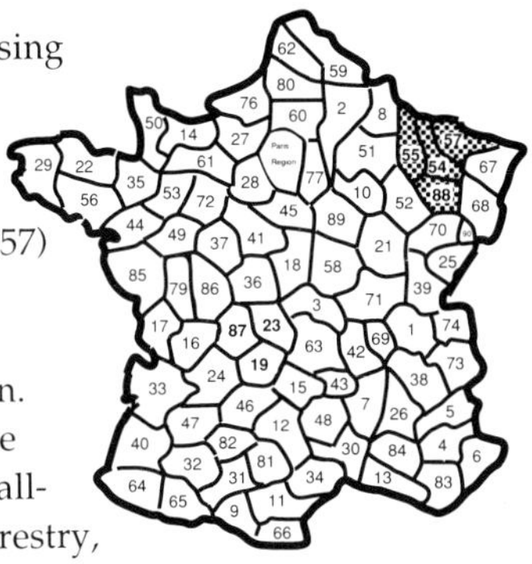

Although much of the region is given to small-scale farming and forestry, Lorraine is essentially reliant on coal and steel, both of which have been in decline over many years. Historically it has swung between Germany and France and its current borders date only from the Second World War. Although in this it is frequently bracketed with Alsace, the two regions are very different. The inhabitants of Lorraine never cease to talk of the role of the Maquis in the mountains and scornfully refer to Alsace as 'full of Germans'. With their fierce patriotism it is fitting that Joan of Arc came from this frontier region and that de Gaulle adopted the Cross of Lorraine as the emblem of the Free French.

Louis XIV (1638-1715)
Known as the *'Roi Soleil'* ('Sun King') on account of his subjects thinking that the sun shone out of his fundament. Consequently if you wanted to see the sun rise you had to be present at his *petit lever*. His reign marked the highwater mark of French influence in poetry, philosophy and science. Louis XIV reigned for longer than any other French king (72 years). A Trivial Pursuits question which will defeat most French people is by which relative, in direct line, he was succeeded. The answer is his great grand-son, so long was his reign and so accident-prone his (legitimate) children. So plenteous were his illegitimate children that half the latter-day population of Versailles is said to resemble him in stature. Among his many mistresses were Madame de Montespan who was believed to poison people that crossed her and Madame de Maintenon, an austere religious woman, who brought up many of his illegitimate children and whom he married at the end of his life.
When Louis XIV proclaimed *'L'Etat, c'est moi'*, he meant it. He built Versailles to his own greater glory and a statue of him on horseback guards its entrance. Similar statues can be seen in Paris at the *Place des Victoires* and in Lyon, *Place BelleCour*.

Louis XVI (1754-1793)
The king - with only 1 part in 128 French blood - who had the misfortune to be on the throne when the *merde* hit the *ventilateur*. Having Marie Antoinette for a wife did not help, particularly in view of the attempts by her family to subvert the Revolution. Had he been content to become a constitutional monarch he might have saved his head, but he wasn't, so he didn't.

Louis-Philippe (1773-1850)
France's only serious attempt at a constitutional monarch. He came to the throne in 1830 and was given to walking around Paris and other democratic gestures. *Hélas!* these were not enough to save him from the 1848 revolution and he abdicated and lived happily for a short while after in Esher.

Lourdes
Town in the *Hautes-Pyrénées* visited by 5 million people annually of whom over half a million come seeking a miraculous cure.

The town has 18,000 inhabitants and 17,000 hotel rooms, second only to Paris. It owes its status as one of the major pilgrimage sites in the word to the visions of the fourteen-year-old Bernadette Soubirous in the 19th century. In all she experienced eighteen apparitions of the Virgin Mary during one of which she was instructed to scrape the ground by the side of the grotto where the visions occurred. A gentle trickle of water turned into a stream of 27,000 gallons a day in which pilgrims seeking cures bathe themselves.

The first miraculous cures took place at Lourdes immediately after the discovery of this spring. To be declared 'miraculous' cures have to be stringently scrutinised to ensure that the cure lies beyond all medical explanation. Since the beginning about five thousand cures have passed medical scrutiny but only sixty-four of these have been officially recognised as miracles.

Bernadette spent her last years in a convent at Nevers where her body remains incorrupt. She was canonised in 1933.

Louvre, Musée de

A large glass pyramid in the centre of Paris surrounded by a museum. The former was commissioned by President Mitterrand from a Chinese American, Mr Pei, and thus became the subject of both political and aesthetic controversy. It also furnished another nickname for the President - MitterRamses.

The museum was begun by François 1er and was opened to the public in 1793. The greatest leaders, Francois 1er, Louis XIV, Napoleon, were also the greatest collectors (i.e. robbers of other country's treasures) and the musuem now contains a volume of works of art sufficient, at one minute's study of each, to keep you busy for over a year.

Lyon

The old capital of Gaul and administrative centre for the Romans, Lyon is now the second largest city in France with 1.2 million inhabitants. It was once the silk *(magnanerie de soie)* capital of France. It is now better known as the gastronomic centre of France and its environs boast four of her greatest restaurants - Bocuse, Chapel, Blanc and *Les Trois Gros.* It is superbly situated between the vineyards of Bourgogne and *Côtes du Rhône,* one hour from the Alps, two hours from Paris (by TGV) and two and a half from the Mediterranean. For many years its tunnel at Fourvière has been a bottle-neck for drivers going on, or back from, holidays in July and August. However, work to by-pass the city completely is well-advanced and they will have *sauté le bouchon* by the end of 1992.

M

Madame Bovary
Famous book by Flaubert in which Jane Austen-style romantic heroine Emma marries stolid middle-class bore, Charles Bovary. He fails to live up to her romantic ideal and she takes up with the local squire (in a most un-Jane Austin way). He abandons her, and her next liaison is with an impecunious lawyer's clerk who finds her too hot to handle. Her extravagance runs her into debt and she resorts to arsenic.

La Mairie
Big towns have a *Hôtel de Ville;* smaller towns and villages have a *Mairie*. It is the place where the *maire* hangs out i.e. the Town Hall.

Mayors, of which there are over 36,000, are more important people in France than in England. They are elected for a period of six years and are chairman and leader of the council. Reflecting the nature of the electorate at this level of government, almost one in three is an *agriculteur*. Becoming a *maire* is often a stepping stone to a national political career. Chirac is mayor of Paris and Mme Cresson of Châtellerault. The latter is one of the 5% of mayors who are female. Of these, one, Catherine Trautmann, is mayor of a town of over 100,000 inhabitants (Strasbourg). There are two black mayors, Kofi Yamgnane, in Brittany, and Berton Demea, in Alpes-Maritimes.

Malle, Louis (b. 1932)
Film producer, married to Candice Bergen, who has worked with many great stars, including making films with Jacques Cousteau. After spending ten years working in the States he returned to France to make the film, *Au Revoir les Enfants*, a story of three Jewish children taken from their school by the Gestapo. It won him the *Lion d'Or* prize at the Venice film festival in 1987.

Malraux, Andre (1901-1976)
Novelist, man of letters and visionary, another in the line of writer turned politician. Originally a socialist, his most famous book, *La Condition Humaine*, is about the communist uprising in Shanghai in 1927. Over three million copies were sold. He led a squadron on the Republican side in the Spanish Civil War, giving rise to his book *L'Espoir*. During the war he was active in the Resistance and was caught and imprisoned by the Gestapo.
After the war he was appointed Minister of Culture by De Gaulle. He became an ardent Gaullist and worked energetically on a succession of grandiose projects, including a massive face-lift for Paris. Outside the capital the most notable of his projects were the *Maisons de Culture*, a network of multi-purpose arts centres jointly funded by the State and the local municipality meant to enable France 'to become again the world's foremost cultural nation'.

Manet, Edouard (1832-1883)
Generally recognised as the founder of the Impressionist school of painting, whose philosophy he described in the following words:

> *'One doesn't paint a landscape, a seascape, a person; one conveys the impression of an hour spent in a landscape, seascape or with a person'.*

He had hoped to sell his famous *'Déjeuner sur l'herbe'* (following page) for 25,000 francs. In the end, after keeping it in his studio for six years, he accepted a tenth of that sum from the composer Fauré. It can now be seen in the magnificent Musée d'Orsay on the Left Bank in Paris.
Although he denied that he was a revolutionary, his technique caused an outcry among conservative artists. He also offended more generally with his painting *l'Olympia*. People were used to seeing nudes but of goddesses, not non-idealised paintings of ordinary people.

Le Mans

24-hour race at Le Mans in the *département* of Sarthe in Normandy. When it started in 1923 it was a demonstration of technological progress in car design to the public at large. Since then many improvements to family cars, such as better lights and windscreen-washers, have originated from this test of endurance. It remains a race for standard cars which have been *améliorées* (souped-up).

It attracts a quarter of a million spectators each year, including 1800 reporters, and a television audience of 375 million in 26 countries.

One unfortunate record is that for the greatest number of fatalities in a car accident when 82 people were killed in 1955 when a Mercedes left the track. Since then vast amounts have been spent, and continue to be spent, on improvements to spectator comfort and safety.

Marchais, Georges (b. 1920)

Antediluvian, Stalinist Communist Party leader who has presided over the accelerating decline of his Party since becoming its Secretary in 1972. His sole political talent has consisted in warding off successive challenges to his disastrous leadership.

Le Déjeuner sur l'herbe, 1863 Musée d'Orsay, Paris

Marianne

The bare-breasted symbol of the Republic seen on bank-notes, coins and posters and as statues in the *Mairie*. She embodies all the virtues of the Republic and is shown on coins strewing money from the cornucopia. Among models for representations of Marianne have been Brigitte Bardot, Catherine Deneuve, the Chanel model, Inès de la Fressange and, most recently, Vanessa Paradis.

Marie-Antoinette (1755-1793)

Whilst on the subject of bare breasts a totally useless piece of information - courtesy of *le Trivial Pursuits* - is that Marie-Antoinette's bust measurement was exactly the same size as that of Jayne Mansfield. This - to quote an Australian expression - should have made her a great help to her husband, Louis XVI. Instead she was a complete hindrance. When she was not playing at shepherdesses in her dolls' house, *le Petit Trianon*, in the Park of Versailles, she was inciting Louis to get rid of people who were trying to help, such as Mirabeau, and generally to adopt the sort of unbending line that got him where he finished up. The famous quote 'Let them eat cake' attributed to her at the time of the bread riots, is unknown to most French people and almost certainly apocryphal.

She came from Austria and was contemptuously referred to as *l'Autrichienne*. Because Austria was antagonistic to the ideals of the Revolution and was suspected of planning to invade France, she became a focal point for opposition to the monarchy. All problems were attributed to her and numerous scurrilous pamphlets circulated one of which claimed that she serviced a complete regiment of Guards in one night. Ultimately power went to her head and she lost it.

Marriages

An opportunity to go to a French wedding must not be passed up. Not least because it is likely to be a gastronomic delight. The French have two totally separate ceremonies - a civil marriage at the *Mairie* followed, if desired, by a religious ceremony at the *église*. There is still insufficient trust between Church and State for them to recognise the other's contracts. The civil ceremony may take place the day before the religious one. It is this that gives you your *livret de famille* i.e. confers the legal status.

Either way, on the day of the wedding, all guests tie white ribbons onto their cars and follow the bride and groom to the church or *mairie* in cars, making as much noise as possible. The ribbons are left on the cars for a week afterwards.

After the ceremony the reception is likely to be lengthy and occasionally spills over into a second day. Ostensibly this is to eat up the 'left-overs' but actually it is an excuse to continue the party.

French weddings are in general more fun than English and will normally include games. Among the latter *la jarretière* is very common. This consists of an auction wherein the bride bares her leg, to reveal a strategically-placed garter. The auction consists of guests putting money into a bucket. Every time a man puts in money, the garter is raised, every time a woman does, it is lowered. The money thus collected goes towards the happy couple's honeymoon. The male guest adjudged as having contributed the largest sum of money *enlève* the garter with his teeth.

Regrettably, given the excellence of the celebrations, the number of marriages has declined over the last two decades. France in fact has the lowest number of marriages per capita in Europe. In 1987 there were 4.7 marriages per thousand population compared with 7.0 in England. The number has risen *légèrement* in the last couple of years. Nevertheless 89% of men, and 72% of women in the age range 20-24 are *célibatairs*. In central Paris one in two people lives alone, of which two-thirds are women.

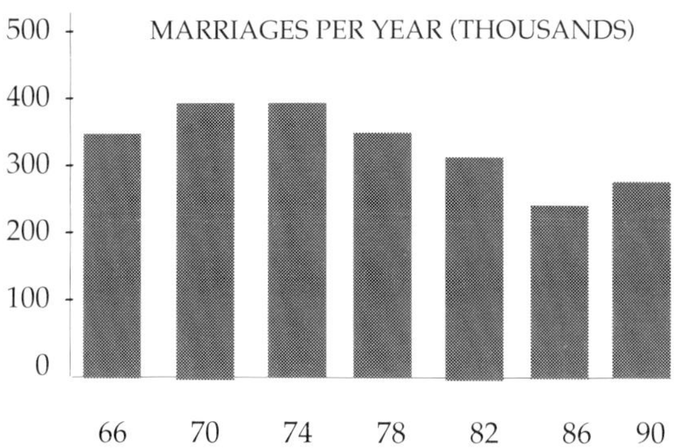

On the other side of the coin, divorce continues to increase, almost tripling in the last two decades to the point where almost one in three marriages is ending in divorce. You are more likely to get divorced if you live in the east of France than the west, in a *grande ville* rather than in the country where religion and tradition are stronger. The main reason given is *'indifference'* (47%) followed by *infidelité* (45%).

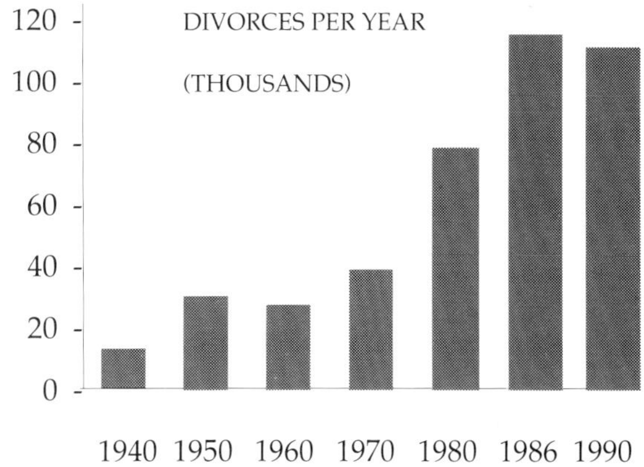

Marseille

Regional capital with population of over a million, it was the first city to be founded in France - by the Phoenicians in the 6th century BC. It is the principal seaport accounting for almost a third of all movements of sea-freight. Famous for its football team, drugs, gangsterism, Arabs (some 200,000 in the *quartiers nords* of whom 60% are unemployed), National Front and *bouillabaisse*.

La Marseillaise

If there were a Eurovision Song contest, nay a World contest, for the best National Anthem France would win it hands down. They are justly proud of *La Marseillaise* and play it whenever possible. As befits a country with a Minister for Culture, the speed at which it is played is a legitimate area of political debate. Almost the first act of Mitterrand when he became President was to order that it be played faster than under the regime of his predecessor, Giscard d'Estaing. The song was composed in one night in 1792, complete with twelve verses, by Rouget de Lisle, who composed nothing of note before or after. Most Frenchmen have difficulty with everything except the first two lines and the last two. But for an aspirant honorary Frenchman it is *de rigueur*. Think how proudly you can stand at the *Parc des Princes* as England yet again beat the French at rugby, singing all the words of this marvellous anthem:

Allons, enfants de la patrie
Le jour de gloire est arrivé.
Contre nous de la tyrannie
L'étendard sanglant est levé,
L'étendard sanglant est levé!
Entendez-vous dans les campagnes
Mugir ces féroces soldats.
Ils viennent jusque dans nos bras
Egorger nos fils, nos compagnons
Aux armes, citoyens!
Formez vos bataillons!
Marchons! Marchons!
Qu'un sang impur
Abreuve nos sillons.

A reasonably free translation is as follows. The literal meanings of words such as *'abreuve'* are given in the Glossary.

Let's go, children of the homeland
The day of glory has come.
Against us the bloody flag
Of tyranny is raised.
Do you hear in the fields,
These fierce soldiers bellowing.
They are coming right among us,
To cut the throats of our children and our friends.
To arms, citizens! Form your batallions!
Let us march! Let us march!
So that their impure blood
Shall water our fields.

Martin, Jacques (b. 1933)
A *téléstar* who has a long-running variety programme on *Antenne 2* on Sunday afternoons called *'Dimanche Martin'*, consisting of a mixture of 'Opportunity Knocks', games, song and dance and satire. He is also a frequent panellist on RTL's *Grosses-Têtes* programme.

Massif Central
Big granite plateau in the middle of France, contained mainly in the *régions* of Auvergne and Limousin. Its main feature is a series of extinct volcanic crests, known as *puys*. The highest of these is the Puy de Sancy at 1886m. Its volcanic origins are preserved in many hot springs and the area has the most spas, such as Vichy, of anywhere in France. It suffered greatly from *l'exode rural* during the last century to the point where, although it covers more than a seventh of the total area of France, it accounts for less than 7% of her population.

Matisse, Henri (1869-1954)
With Derain he was one of the two main *Fauve* (wild beast) artists, a name applied to their paintings at the 1905 *Salon d'Automne* and derived from their disregard for the forms of nature and from their enjoyment of violent colours.

The *Fauves* concentrated on landscapes particularly of the Seine, Midi and Riviera and acted as a bridge between post-impressionism and cubism and surrealism. Shown above is a detail from his *Luxe, Calme et Volupté, 1904* showing the influence of the *Pointillistes* in his earlier paintings.

The Sunday Times' '1000 Makers of the 20th Century' described him as a 'radical painter of half-dressed women in rooms shuttered against the Midi sun'. Is there an analogy with people who see a glass 'half full' as opposed to those who see it 'half-empty'?

Maupassant, Guy de (1850-1893)
Writer of brilliant short stories, which genre he did much to establish as a commercial success. Maupassant was fond of depicting small-time life in his native Normandy and tradesmen and petty officials in Paris. In common with most writers of his generation, he was profoundly influenced by the Franco-Prussian war. His story *Boule de Suif*, telling of the flight of citizens from Rouen to Le Havre and their problems with the Prussians along the way, was one of a collection of war stories which won him overnight fame.
Respectable French writers go into politics, dissolute ones go mad. Maupassant did the latter.

Mauriac, Francois (1885-1970)
Fervent Roman Catholic novelist whose stories are set around Bordeaux and deal with the conflict between sensuality, religion and family loyalties. He won the Nobel Literature Prize in 1952. Among his best-known novels is Thérèse Desqueyroux. Set in the heat and pine forests of the Landes region, it is the story of a woman who was pressurised by her family into an unfulfilling marriage which she attempts to escape from by poisoning her husband.
Mauriac suffered from cancer of the vocal chords which made the sound of his voice very distinctive. The *Académie Française* thinking he was about to die from this granted him a special *Election de Maréchal* to the *Académie* in 1933. He went on to live for another thirty seven years and became an outspoken supporter of the Fifth Republic under de Gaulle.

Mauroy, Pierre (b. 1928)
Mayor of Lille from 1973 and Prime Minister, from 1981 to 1984, in the first Socialist government of the 5th Republic. Influential in initiating the reforms of that government that gave greater devolution of power to the regions. He was displaced by Fabius when his reflationary policies failed to cure unemployment. He became Secretary of the Socialist Party only to be displaced for a second time by Fabius in early 1992.

May 1968
In Britain the 'sixties' is seen retrospectively as the decade of the 'permissive society' when flower-power mixed with anti-Vietnam protest to bring about many liberal reforms and change the consciousness of a generation. In France it was as if the political and educational aspects of this movement were pent up and released in one explosion.
Not quite a revolution but considerably more than a protest, the events of May 1968 are simply referred to as *les événements*. It was started by students as a protest against conditions in the education system. Lead by Daniel Cohn-Bendit 'Danny le Roux' (encouraged by Sartre), they occupied, not the strategic places such as radio and TV stations but the *Opéra* and other cultural centres. After a few days the workers joined them and the whole country was involved in a *grève générale*. Paris, and many other parts of the country, came to a standstill for several days, barricades were erected and cobble-stones thrown. Families were divided with parents and children on opposing sides. De Gaulle disappeared (actually he flew to Germany to make sure of the support of the army) and the riot police (CRS) were left to have a go at any demonstrators which they did with their customary relish.
Ultimately students and workers had very different fish to fry. The former were more interested in over-throwing De Gaulle and the Fifth Republic, the latter more in higher wages for shorting working hours. Nevertheless the workers were caught up in the heady atmosphere much to the consternation of their union leaders who were not quite sure how to react. The events articulated a long suppressed hostility to the educational system and to the *dirigisme* of the de Gaulle government.
As the danger to the regime became more real there was an inevitable reaction from supporters of the government. A counter-demonstration involving a million people, mostly of the older generation but joined by some *jeunes*, marched down the *Champs-Elysées*. De Gaulle made some concessions and won a subsequent referendum supporting the measures and an increased majority at the elections that he called. But it was not long before he decided once more that *la vie politique* was not for him and for the second time in his career walked out.
As with the revolution of 1789, its influence long outlasted the immediate reaction. In many ways the events of May 1968 marked a watershed in French politics and education and led indirectly to loosening the tight hand of the State in many areas of life.

Mazarin, Jules (1602-1661)
Italian protégé of Richelieu and probably lover, even husband, of Anne of Austria, regent during the reign of Louis XIII. Both denied that they were married, Mazarin because he had half an eye on becoming Pope. He wielded enormous power and conducted a highly successful foreign policy notably with the Treaty of Westphalia which ended the Thirty Years War

Medécins sans Frontière
Philanthropic organisation of doctors formally set up in 1972 but with its roots in the idealism of May '68. It is Europe's largest non-governmental humanitarian agency with an annual budget of £15 million. Its president is the outspoken Rony Brauman. Since 1982 the group has sent 5000 doctors to treat victims of war, famine and natural disasters in 80 countries. In 1990 it had 2000 volunteers in 66 countries with a budget of £50 million of which 60% is from private donations and 35% from the EEC. It played a major role in the Gulf War.

Mediterranean
Large expanse of dirty water on southern shore of France. Useful to anthropologists wishing to study the congregating habits of *homo sapiens vacanciensis.*

Merovingians
The first dynasty of kings of all the Franks founded by Clovis in the fifth century. The kings were brutal and barbarous and the history of the dynasty is one of inter-family feuds and assassinations. The other well-known king of this dynasty is Dagobert who, according to a children's song, wore his trousers *à l'envers* (inside out). The dynasty ended when Childéric III was deposed by Pépin le Bref in 751.

Métro

Underground railway system in Paris, Lyon and Marseille. The Paris version has 293 stations and 94 miles of track. It is famous for mice, pickpockets, illegal hawkers, travelling musicians, drugs (Line Nine is known as the 'crack track'), *correspondances* (interchanges) a mile long and cheapness - for 35 francs you get a *carnet* of ten tickets each of which allows you to travel anywhere in the system. Despite this excellent value there are an estimated 450,000 unpaid journeys made each day costing the network £30 million a year. Another source of unwanted cost is the graffitists who cause another £8 million damage each year.

Michelin
Fanatically secretive, right-wing family empire based in Clermont-Ferrand. Inventors of the radial tyre, it has expanded to become one of the world's leading tyre producers. Recently it has suffered from the worldwide drop in new car sales and has had to lay off a substantial part of its workforce. However it has maintained its tradition of investing in Research & Development and has come up with a *'pneu vert'* which is claimed to give 10% better fuel consumption and is therefore environmentally approved. It is hoped that this will restore its fortunes particularly in the US where it has a 40% market share.
The organisation is now almost as well-known for its restaurant guide and maps.

Midi
The name given to the southern region of France roughly starting at Valence in the Rhône Valley. The locals will tell you that *'les gens sont plus sympathiques dans le Midi'* (people are kinder in the South). To agree with the *'plus'* would be to disavow the friendliness that one finds throughout France, particularly once you are away from the big cities, but the author's experience of the Ardèche provides ample evidence that people there are *très sympas.*

Midi-Pyrénées
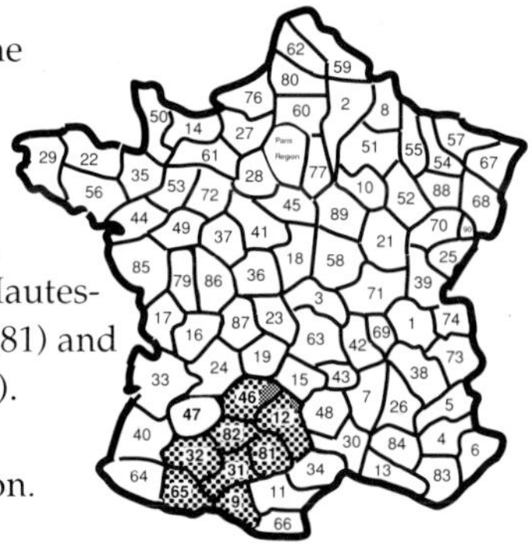
Région comprising the *départements* of Ariège (09), Aveyron (12), Haute-Garonne (31), Gers (32), Lot (46), Hautes-Pyrénées (65), Tarn (81) and Tarn-et-Garonne (82). *Chef-lieu:* Toulouse; population 2.4 million.

The region shares with Aquitaine the ancient province of Gascony whose inhabitants are famous for their bravery and tall stories as well as for producing armagnac.

Minitel

System, launched in 1985, whereby *France Télécom* loans you a home computer terminal free of charge (although for most of its services you pay for the cost of the call). A much more successful version than Prestel and CEEFAX or Oracle combined, it currently has almost six million terminals installed on which, in 1990, over eight hundred million calls were made. It saves the PTT the expense of distributing telephone directories besides bringing in revenues of over £150 million. Looking up a telephone number through Minitel is much more reliable and up-to-date than consulting an *annuaire.*

In addition it provides over 10,000 different services from home banking to travel information, news, stock market, weather, access to 13,000 different companies, all reached by dialling 36 15 followed by the relevant code.

More controversial is the *'messagerie rose'* a computerised contact service, through which you can reach other subscribers and, if desired, arrange assignations. There have been various cases where people have suffered sexual abuse or even death as a result of rendez-vous set up through this service. According to protesters against the service, the number of calls to sex lines rose on Wednesday afternoons when schoolchildren have a half-day off. The FFF *(Fédération des Familles de France* - a sort of Mary Whitehouse association) has accused the PTT of *proxénétisme* (living off immoral earnings) and pursued the company through the law courts for acting as a hi-tech pimp. *Télécom* has now implemented a password system to prevent one's children running up huge bills through accessing the sex lines or playing computer games.

Mirabeau, Comte de (1749-1791)

As a rebellious youth he was incarcerated in his father's Chateau de Vincennes from 1777 to 1781. Although a nobleman, his fellow aristocrats distrusted him and he was elected to the *Etats Généraux* in 1789 as a representative of the *tiers Etat* (commoners) for Aix-en-Provence. A moderate constitutionalist, he was highly influential, though never in office, in the period of the Revolution between the Storming of the Bastille and the Reign of Terror. His aim was to bring in a constitutional monarchy. Unfortunately Marie-Antoinette did not take to him and reduced his influence with Louis XVI whom he may otherwise have saved.

His death - one of a small minority of his contemporaries to die of natural causes - widened the gulf between the king and the National Assembly. After his death he fell from grace and his remains were removed from the *Panthéon.* He has a fine street named after him in Aix-en-Provence.

Mitterrand, François (b. 1916 a.k.a. Ton-ton)

President, 1981- (potentially) 1995. An intellectual and subtle politician mixing the wiliness of Harold Wilson with a smattering of the economics and defence policies of Margaret Thatcher. Consequently he is never to be under-estimated although in recent months he appears to have lost his touch. He is the only President to have been elected twice by direct suffrage and has been in office longer than any ruler in history elected in that way.

Wounded and captured in the war, he escaped and fought with distinction in the Resistance. Following the war he entered politics and served as Minister in various regimes in the 4th Republic. In 1965 he was the Socialist opponent to De Gaulle in the Presidential elections. In 1971 he became secretary of the virtually moribund *Parti Socialiste* and undertook the difficult job of making it capable of gaining power and of government. In 1972 he stood again for President, this time losing to Giscard. He succeeded at the third attempt in 1981 and was renewed in office in 1988.

When first elected his government followed the classic path of socialist parties that have been long out of power and attempted to usher in the millenium without delay. His first government, under Pierre Mauroy, set about nationalising the commanding heights of the economy and reflating its way out of unemployment (at a time when all other countries were deflating). Neither did anything for the economy and by 1983 power had engendered realism. A *politique de rigueur* was introduced.

One advantage of being President under the constitution of the Fifth Republic is that you can change your Prime Minister when you, or the public, tire of him (or her). Mauroy gave way to the social-democratic technocrat Fabius in 1984 and the communists left the government. One problem is that under the constitution of the Fifth Republic, Presidential elections are every seven years, and elections to the *Assemblée* every five. In this way, in 1986 the Socialists lost control of the Assembly to the joint conservative parties and Mitterrand found himself saddled with a right-wing majority. He called upon Chirac to be Prime Minister and form a government. This turned out to be highly useful in the run-up to the Presidential elections two years later as the unpopularity of this government worked in favour of the Opposition. Thus Mitterrand was able to win again. This time he appointed Michel Rocard as his Prime Minister. Three years later the latter either jumped or was pushed, and was replaced by Edith Cresson.

The nature of the Presidency under the 5th Republic reflects the Olympian nature of its creator, De Gaulle. Thus the President is largely above day-to-day internal politics but very much in control of foreign policy. This suits Mitterrand's aloof quasi-monarchical style well. However, if Louis XVIII was correct to say that 'Punctuality is the politeness of kings', then he still has some way to go.

As he enters the eleventh year of power, with the intractable problems of low growth, unemployment and immigration still besetting the country, his popularity has waned. But history will probably see in him the man who first demonstrated that the Socialists could be entrusted with power without the western world coming to an end and as the architect of the first step on the road to devolution of power from the centre and an important contributor to the demise of the Communist Party. It remains to be seen whether he is also credited with the demise of the Socialist Party which he did so much to build up.

Molière, Jean-Baptiste (1622-1673)

Seventeenth-century satirist, favourite of Louis XIV. Since television sit-coms had not then been invented he had to write for the stage. His plays, which are the most-performed of any in France, are called comedies but *comédie* is a *'faux-ami'*. It is not a comedy in the English sense of the word; it is just a play with a happy ending - as opposed to *une tragédie* which his contemporaries Racine and Corneille wrote.

Molière brilliantly satirised the manners of the day - forced marriages, the place of women, religion, medicine, the conflict of generations and pretensions to nobility. He described his intention as *instruire and plaire* - to instruct and please. You should at least recognise *L'Avare* (the Miser) and *Le Misanthrope* among his plays. His best-known work is *'Le Bourgeois Gentilhomme'* in which he satirises a self-made businessman, M. Jourdain, who wants to be accepted as a gentleman - one of the enduring French ambitions. At one stage, having learned to dance, to fence and to sing, he turns his attention to writing poetry. Having mastered that he asks to be taught prose. His teacher replies that anything that is not verse is prose. To which discovery he exclaims with delight that for all these years he has been speaking prose without knowing.

M. Jourdain: Quoi? Quand je dis: 'Nicole, apportez-moi mes pantoufles, et me donnez mon bonnet de nuit', c'est de la prose?
Maître de philosophie: Oui, Monsieur.
M. Jourdain: Par ma foi! il y a plus de quarante ans que je dis de la prose sans que j'en susse rien.

M. Jourdain: What? When I say: 'Nicole, bring me my slippers and give me my night cap', that is prose?
Teacher: Yes, Monsieur
M. Jourdain: Good God! I've been speaking prose for forty years without ever realising.

Monet, Claude (1840-1926)
Impressionist painter born in Le Havre who moved to Argenteuil on the outskirts of Paris. He deserted the artist's studio in favour of the open air. To this end he fitted out a boat as a studio allowing him to paint on the river. Manet visited him and painted him at work.

Monet by Manet

His idea that nature should be captured 'on the spot' left little time for subtle mixing of colours or to apply numerous layers. The image had to be fixed straight onto the canvas in bold strokes, the general effect being more important than the detail. It was this apparently slapdash approach that enraged his critics.

Monnet, Jean (1888-1979)
Main architect of post-war economic recovery through a series of Plans bringing together government and industry. They were similar to those of the 1964 Labour Government except that by and large they worked. Subsequently he became the most influential figure in the founding of the European Community.

Montaigne, Michel Eyquem de (1533-1592)
Erudite and worldly-wise author famous for his *Essais* which, drawing on his own experience and travels, extol a *façon de vivre* based on commonsense and tolerance. The essays, written in the library to which he retreated after giving up travelling, exhibit the profoundest knowledge of humanity. They conclude with the down-to-earth thought that:

Au plus élevé trône du monde...(nous) ne sommes assis que sur notre cul. (Upon the highest throne in the world, we are still only sitting on our arse.)

Montand, Yves (1921-1991)
Singer, actor, film star. Born in Italy his family fled the fascists, a fact that made him a long-term supporter of left-wing politics. Finding success as a singer, in 1944 he met Edith Piaf and lived with her for two years. As a singer his best-known song was *Les Feuilles Mortes.* In 1951 he married Simone Signoret and, given certain ups and downs, this long relationship remained a meeting of minds. One of the 'downs' (for her) was his affair with Marilyn Monroe with whom he starred in *'Let's Make Love'*, an injunction which they pursued off-screen. Monroe described him as 'the most exciting man I've ever met'.

He and Signoret were committed to left-wing and radical causes and they were often at the forefront of anti-war protests and in favour of disarmament.
He broke with communism after the invasion of Czechoslovakia and criticised Mitterrand for inviting communists into his first government. At one time his popularity was so great that eight million people watched his midnight broadcast on economics and 29% declared they would vote for him if he ran for President. His reply to this was that Reagan stood for President because he was a bad actor; he wouldn't, because he was a good one.
After Signoret's death he lived with the much younger Carole Amiel and late in life became a proud father. He is best-known to British audiences through his role as *Le Papet* in *Jean de Florette* and *Manon des Sources.*
On his death France went into that collective grief that it reserves for its own stars. His obituary in *Libération* was twelve pages; in *Le Nouvel Observateur,* thirty two.

Monte Carlo Rally

Famous car rally in which people converge on Monaco from all corners of Europe in all sorts of weather conditions. When it started in 1913 the average speed was 10 kph. With the greater ability of modern cars to negotiate wintry conditions its place in popular imagination has been taken by the Paris-Cape Town rally.

Montesquieu, Charles de (1689-1755)

Writer and political philosopher whose ideas, notably of the separation of powers of legislature, executive and judiciary, derived from his observation of the English system, formed the basis of the US constitution and served as inspiration for the Revolution.

Montmartre

For centuries Montmartre, in the 18th *arrondissement,* was a village of windmills supplying flour to the city below. Hence the *Moulin* in *Moulin Rouge.* The *'rouge'* recalls the red-lights that now characterise the area.
In the 19th century it became part of Paris and its low rents attracted impecunious artists, writers and musicians. It was here that Picasso and Braque and others created Cubism. Now lesser talents paint your portrait for thirty francs in the *Place du Tertre.*

Montparnasse

As with the *Champs Elysées,* the name is of classical origin, recalling Mount Parnassus, the mountain sacred to Apollo and the Muses. In the early years of the century when Hemingway, Apollinaire, Cocteau, Stravinsky, even Lenin and Trotsky were to be seen there, it merited its name. Now it has only the horrible black tombstone of the *Tour Montparnasse,* the Sheraton Hotel and sex shops. The most evocative part is now, appropriately, the *cimetière* where Serge Gainsbourg recently joined fellow composers César Franck and Saint-Saëns and writers Baudelaire and Maupassant.

Musset, Alfred de (1810-1857)

Writer, romantic by school of writing and by temperament. His stormy on-off liaison with George Sand led him to write poetry about love, pain and fantasy. Another writer whose life was cut short by drink.

N

Napoleon Bonaparte (1769-1821)

As a brigadier in Corsica Napoleon was given command of the French army in Italy as reward for breaking up an anti-government riot. He won a series of stunning victories and went on to conquer Egypt. Alarmed by his popularity the government summoned him to Paris to take him down a peg. Instead he overthrew them at gun point. A plebiscite, that favourite legitimising device of anti-parliamentarians, confirmed him in power. He set up a dictatorship and established the *Code Napoléon* - a body of law which previous parliaments had developed but for which history has given him the credit.

In 1804 he crowned himself Emperor and cast off Josephine in order to marry someone of his own (newfound) station - a Habsburg princess. It was this action that decided Beethoven against dedicating the Eroica to him. His birthday was celebrated as a national holiday, coins bore his portrait, in short he was one of many dictators to encourage the cult of personality. He revised the constitution, reformed tax collection, reinstated slavery in the colonies and left the Church entirely dependent on the State.

Detail from: Le Sacré de Napoléon 1er by David, Louvre, Paris

In mainland Europe his military exploits brought a string of victories - Marengo, Austerlitz, Iena - but Nelson ensured that Britain continued to rule the waves and thereby frustrated his intention to invade England.

Finally, in 1812, he set out to conquer Russia with his *grande armée* . He got as far as Moscow but only Pierre Bezukhov was still there. With winter coming he was forced to retreat. Fewer than one in six of the original 600,000 troops survived. Russia, Spain, Prussia and Britain ganged up against him and in March 1814 the tsar entered Paris. Napoleon abdicated and was sent to Elba whence he uttered his famous palindrome. In February he escaped and returned for his 'hundred days'.

Defeated at Waterloo, this time he was sent well out of harm's way to St Helena. This enabled him, in time-honoured style, to write his memoirs. Although the achievement of Napoleon was to reduce France to a smaller territory than before the Revolution, leaving it in a state of financial and military collapse, his memoirs succeeded in establishing his version of events and creating a legend that lasted most of the century. His remains are buried in *Les Invalides.*

In stature Napoleon was a small man; hence his nickname *le petit caporal.* We have long speculated on the effect on history of Cleopatra's nose being a quarter of an inch longer, but what if Napoleon or Lenin had been six inches taller?

Napoleon III (1808-1873)

Nephew of Bonaparte, he made a number of unsuccessful attempts to oust King Louis-Philippe and make himself emperor. For his pains he was exiled and lived for a while in London. The Revolution of 1848 gave him his chance of a comeback and he succeeded in getting himself elected President. Once there he immediately started scheming to make himself emperor and achieved this in 1852, confirming it by a plebiscite. From 1852 to 1860 his authority was absolute. Thereafter he began to introduce some measures of freedom and democracy.

He was a chip off the old block as regards military conquest and got involved in the Crimean War, sent troops to China and colonised Indo-China. He also gained Nice and Savoy. Latterly, however, his luck changed. He lost prestige through a disastrous war in Mexico and then unwisely declared war on Prussia. He got himself captured in the defeat of Sedan (1870) and was exiled back to England whence he had come.

National Front

Unlike the assorted skinheads of the British party, the *Front National* is a serious - some would say, dangerous - political party. Founded in 1972, it is well-funded, makes most of the running on the vexed question of immigration, and has a leader, Le Pen who is a national figure.

In 1986 under the P. R electoral system introduced by Mitterrand it won 35 seats in the *Assemblée* thereby acquiring credibility, although reversion to the second ballot system reduced their representation to one at the next elections. Of those who voted for the party, 61% were men. It has 14 members in the European Parliament. In the 1992 regional elections they won 12.4%, slightly behind the 'Greens'. The party's natural habitat is in areas where there is a backlash against a large Arab presence, but unemployment, by bringing immigration to the fore as a political issue, is helping more generally. In an opinion poll in late 1991 34% of respondents thought they had the best policies on immigration. These include making visitors from the Third World submit to an AIDS test and deposit a bond of 100,000F, and discrimination against non-nationals in jobs, housing and education. In addition to these policies they wish to reintroduce capital punishment and make abortion illegal.

Although theyreceived over 13% of the vote in the regional elections of March 1992, this was considerably less than they had hoped and many others had feared.

Nationalisation

For a variety of reasons, not all ideological, there are more nationalised industries than in England. It started with Louis XIV on the highly pragmatic grounds that cigarette manufacture was a licence to print money. In 1936-37 the Patriotic Front extended the state sector on ideological grounds or because, like the coal industry in England, the company owners were too stupid. This brought in the railways and the *Banque de France*. But the major shaping of the public sector came with the Provisional Government at the end of the war which nationalised the fuel power industries, leading commercial banks and insurance companies and Air France. Renault was nationalised because their owners had collaborated with the Germans. The 1981 Socialist government added to the list to bring a number of strategic industries - aerospace, chemicals, armaments, electronics - under state control. The succeeding Chirac government set about flogging off as many as it could in its two years of office but despite doing so to the estimated extent of £3 billion, nationalised industries still account for over 40% of the sales of larger companies.

The extent to which France is 'corporatist' in business terms is shown by the fact that of the top ten companies quoted on the Bourse two are state-controlled, three are family-controlled and a further three have a nucleus of friendly shareholders protecting them from predators. Three quarters of senior managers of the top 200 companies are the sons of wealthy families.

Newspapers

The obvious and most accessible way of improving both your grasp ofthe language and your knowledge of what currently interests the average Frenchman is by reading newspapers and magazines. As in England, different newspapers give you a different view on the world and develop different aspects of your familiarity.

Only one household in four buys a daily paper in France compared to one in two in England. Regional papers, such as *le Dauphiné* or *Le Progrès,* account for a high proportion of sales so that the circulation of the major national dailies barely reaches half a million. As such they are outsold by a factor of two by the highest circulation weekly magazine, *Paris Match.*

Whereas in England the 'quality' papers are broadsheet and the popular press, tabloid, in France the reverse is broadly the case.

Le Monde

Tabloid intellectual of the centre-left. Nearest equivalent to the 'Times' with a well-informed coverage of foreign affairs. Just as for many years, the Times maintained a tradition of its front page carrying only classified adverts, so *Le Monde* hangs on tenuously to a tradition that it carries almost no photos, adverts or, for that matter, horoscopes. This, plus the typography, makes reading it a matter of duty rather than pleasure.

Le Figaro

France's equivalent of the 'Daily Telegraph'. A right-wing broadsheet given to supporting Chirac and the RPR and experiencing the greatest difficulty in finding anything complimentary to say about Mitterrand. It is owned, as is *France Soir,* by the publicity-shunning press magnate, Robert Hersand.

l'Humanité
Communist newspaper, which at one time had Jean-Paul Sartre as a contributor, but is now as unreadable as the old Morning Star. Since for years it churned out the standard Soviet line, recent events have left its editorial line somewhat high and dry and its circulation has fallen from 400,000 immediately after the war to well under 100,000 today.

France Soir
The nearest equivalent to the English popular tabloids, this paper will do wonders for your command of anything to do with murder, rape, incest and discoveries of mummified bodies.

Libération
Intellectual tabloid of the left, a cross between the Guardian and Independent. Informative and well-written (it has the best headline writers in the industry), it has a high readership among the younger age groups.

Le Canard Enchainé
A satirical weekly more political but less funny (and less frequently sued) than Private Eye. Good investigative journalism of a type less common in France than in England. It carries no adverts and tends to be a thorn in the flesh of all political parties in a country with a long-standing (but declining) tradition of the media being muzzled.

L'Equipe
A daily paper devoted exclusively to sport. Its circulation matches those of the generalised press.

In addition to the national newspapers, each region has its own paper - *Sud-Ouest, Midi Libre* - which combines rather better coverage of major news stories than English regional papers with extended coverage of local events. Dating from the time of the Vichy government, with the country effectively split in two, the regional press established itself at the expense of Paris-based newspapers and continues to enjoy wide readership. *Ouest France,* published in Rennes, covers all the north-west and has double the circulation of any Paris-based daily.

Most papers do not have the long informative articles characteristic of the quality British press. This role belongs more to the magazine market, among which there is an enormous range. France has the most magazines of any country in Europe. The most important of these are:

Paris Match
First published in 1928, a non-intellectual magazine mingling political, human interest, the celebs in an accessible style. Its motto is *Le poids des mots; le choc des photos* - the power of words; the impact of photos. Clear market leader with a circulation approaching 900,000.

Figaro Magazine
The equivalent of a Saturday colour supplement with Figaro newspaper (for which you pay a considerably higher price) with a circulation around 650,000.

Le Nouvel Observateur
Intellectual magazine of the left with a circulation of almost 400,000.

L'Express
Intellectual right-wing magazine, owned for ten years by James Goldsmith, with circulation of half a million. In style it is almost a carbon-copy of the American 'Time' magazine.

L'Evénement du Jeudi
Up-and-coming intellectual magazine of the centre, founded by Jean-Francois Kahn with the aid of 19,000 shareholder/subscribers. This way of raising capital and gaining a committed readership at the same time was tried again in 1991 to launch a new daily, *La Truffe* but failed.

Noah, Yannick (b. 1960)
Spotted by Arthur Ashe at the age of eleven, Noah justified Ashe's confidence by becoming France's No. 1 tennis star, winner of the 1983 French Open. After

retirement from the players' circuit he was appointed captain of the 1991 French Davis Cup team which he inspired to their memorable triumph over the United States in the final. Anyone who could do that with the British team would be knighted; for Noah public adulation and the continuing attentions of the media will have to suffice, although neither will harm his burgeoning new career as pop-singer.

Noir, Michel (b. 1944)
Cello-playing politician, former member of the RPR who left in frustration with the domination by the old guard and set up a new centrist party. Mayor of Lyon, involved in Watergate-type scandal involving the alleged theft of a political opponent's list of supporters. To complicate matters, the opponent is both a former aide and his current son-in-law. Nevertheless, he has age on his side. France's current politicians have a definite air of 'yesterday's men' about them. Mitterrand was a civil servant under the Vichy government, Rocard first stood for the presidency in 1969 and Chirac, Barre and Giscard all held office in the seventies.

Noiret, Philippe (b. 1930)
Prolific screen star, winner of two *Césars,* who has worked with many leading *cinéastes* such as Louis Malle, Claude Berri and played leading roles in films such as *Thérèse Desqueyroux* and *Uranus.* As a writer he has a book to his credit which includes a preface by another noted *littérateur,* François Mitterrand. A lover of dogs and horses, he cultivates an off-screen image of gentleman farmer complete with tweeds and Burberry.

Nord-Pas-de-Calais
Région comprising the two *départements,* named (59 and 62). *Chef-lieu:* Lille; With four million inhabitants this is the most densely-populated area of France after the Greater Paris region. It is well-placed in relation to the Common Market and with excellent communications (particularly when the Channel Tunnel is open and the TGV extended to Calais). Yet its major industries, coal and textiles, are both in decline and the area is depressed.

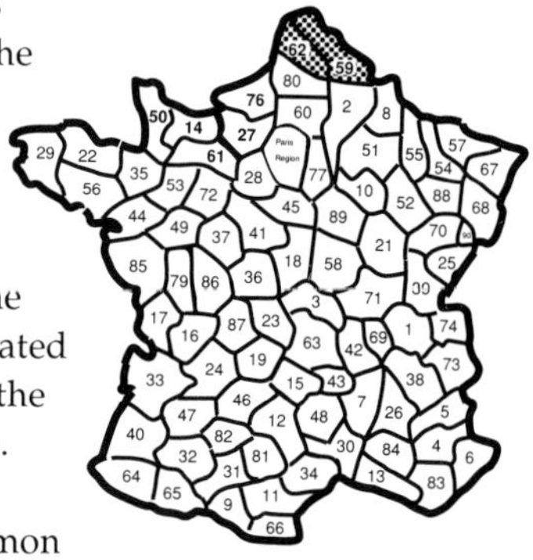

Normandy
Apple-growing (hence cider and calvados-producing) *région* which also gives us camembert. Administratively *Normandie* is split into two *régions, Basse* and *Haute.* The former comprises the *départements* of Manche (50) Calvados (14), and Orne (61); Its *chef-lieu* is Caen. The latter, the *départements* of Eure (27) and Seine-Maritime (76); its *chef-lieu* is Rouen. As a whole Normandy has 1.7 million inhabitants.

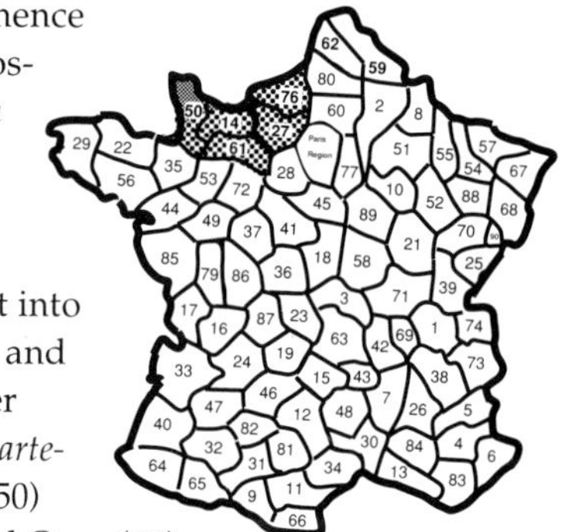

Philippe Noiret

Originally ceded to the viking Rollond in 911, it became closely associated with England from the time of William the Conquerer (previously known as *Guillaume le Bâtard)*. It was taken back into the French fold in 1468 but is currently being bought back by British purchasers of *résidences secondaires*.

It is a region prolific in writers. Corneille, Maurois, Gide, Flaubert and Maupassant all lived there, the latter two writing stories with a strong regional background; Proust spent a lot of time at Cabourg (known as Balbec in *A la Recherche du Temps Perdu)*; Victor Hugo and Sartre both visited.

Notre-Dame de Paris

The site has been a place of worship since pagan times when a temple to Jupiter stood there. The current cathedral was completed in 1330. It survived the Revolution, when it was changed into a Temple of Reason and the Paris Commune when an attempt was made to burn it down.

In front of the main doorway is a plaque marking the point from which all distances from Paris are measured.

Nuclear Power

Having virtually no oil and dwindling reserves of coal and gas, France turned to nuclear power to solve her energy problems. It is second only to the United States in the generation of nuclear power and first in per capita terms. By basing its programme on the uniform pressurised water reactors (PWR), France is the most efficient producer of nuclear energy in the world. It has the lowest industrial electricity prices in Europe, excluding Scandinavia and exports around 10% of its electricity. In percentage terms (with UK figures in parentheses) France's electricity generation is nuclear-powered 73 (20), hydro-electric 19 (2), coal/gas 8 (78).

O

l'Olympique Marseille

France's leading soccer team, home to Chris Waddle and Trevor Stevens, owned by Bernard Tapie. It did the double of cup and league in 1989 and was on course for the treble (double plus European Cup) in 1991. Unfortunately it lost the final of the latter on a penalty shootout to Red Star of Belgrade and subsequently lost to Monaco in the final of the *Coupe de France.*

Opéra

The shortened name of the largest theatre in the world, the *Théatre Nationale de l'Opéra de Paris,* and of its associated Metro station. Not to be confused with the *Opéra-Bastille,* built on the site of the former prison. The latter was planned to be the showpiece of the bicentenary celebrations but was not ready in time. Referred to as *la folie Bastille* by opponents of its construction, it was intended to be the people's opera house - just as Bayreuth was, and with about as much success. The £350 million project, inaugurated in 1989, has been plagued by problems such as the dismissal of Daniel Barenbohm and his replacement by a Korean, Myung Whun Chang. Having overrun its construction costs by a factor of three, it is now showing a £30 million deficit on running costs.

The original *Opéra,* designed by Garnier, dates from the last century. Debussy commented that from the outside the *Opéra* looked like a railway station and inside like a Turkish bath. It has a ceiling painted by Chagall which people either love or loathe. It is an enormous building with seventeen stories of which seven are underground. A scale model can be seen at the *Musée d'Orsay.* During its construction, in the reign of Napoleon III, the builders encountered an underground lake where the 'Phantom of the Opera' is reputed to live.

It employs over a thousand people among whom is Nureyev, director of the Paris Ballet Company which it houses.

Grand opera has enjoyed something of a revival in France in the eighties. In addition to Paris, there are excellent opera houses, or open air amphitheatres in the provinces, notably in Toulouse, Strasbourg, Aix-en-Provence and Orange. The fourteen full-time opera companies invariably play to packed houses.

P

Pagnol, Marcel (1895-1974)

Writer, dramatist and film-maker famous for his stories of bistro life in Marseille as in *Marius, Fanny* and *César.* As with Daudet's letters from his mill, Pagnol's plays about Provence were mostly written in Paris. In 1937 he became the first film-maker to be elected to the *Académie.* To English audiences he is best-known for the wonderfully evocative *Jean de Florette* and *Manon des Sources,* starring Yves Montand, Daniel Anteuil, Gerard Dépardieu and Emmanuelle Béart. The films of his childhood, *La Gloire de mon Pére* and *Le Château de ma Mère* have also been on release in Britain.

Somewhat of an eccentric, he spent years trying to invent a perpetual motion machine and working on a plan to grow square onions.

Panthéon

Aux Grands Hommes la Patrie Reconnaissante

Situated on the left bank of the Seine, and built from the proceeds of the *loterie,* this was originally a church dedicated to St Geneviève, the patron saint of Paris. During the Revolution its use was changed to a secular temple to house the remains of the heroes of the Republic. It reverted to being a church during the Restoration and Second Empire but the Third Republic restored it to its current use as a resting place for the Great and the Good. Among those deemed worthy of this accolade are Voltaire, Rousseau, Gambetta (heart only), Victor Hugo, Louis Braille and Jean Moulin.

It appears, as ever, that *'hommes'* is gender-specific. Only one woman has made it into the *Panthéon* - Mme Berthelot and she only by virtue of being buried with her husband. He was killed in a car crash and she died of a heart attack on hearing the news. Her wish to be buried with her husband was respected, hence the token female. The life of St Geneviève is depicted in a series of paintings as is St Denis picking up his head after his execution.

Papacy

In 1305 Pope Clement V decamped to Avignon in protest against the anarchy that existed in Rome. For the next seventy years this city on the banks of the Rhône was the seat of the Popes. During this period seven Popes reigned, all of them French. In 1377 Gregory was persuaded to return to Rome and the so-called Babylonian Captivity was at an end. A number of cardinals refused to go with him and elected Clement VII, thereby starting the Great Schism. It was during military action to resolve this that the *Pont St Bénézet* lost all but four of its arches.

Paradis, Vanessa (b. 1972)

Young pop-star who achieved overnight fame with *'Jo, le Taxi'* which sold 1.2 million copies. She has since confirmed that she is not a seven-day wonder by winning a *César* for her performance in *Noces Blanches* and being selected as the Chanel girl for 1991.

Paris

> *Whoever looks into the depths of Paris gets dizzy. Nothing so fantastic, nothing so tragic, nothing so superb.*
>
> *Victor Hugo*

One of the most beautiful tourist cities in the world. Although Greater Paris covers 479 sq. km. and has a population of ten million, having doubled since the war, the part that matters, encircled by the *Péripherique* and bisected by the Seine, covers only 106 sq. km and has only just over 2.5 million inhabitants. It is divided into numbered *arrondissements* in a spiral pattern starting at the Place de la Concorde. Parisians drop the word *arrondissement* and refer to themselves as living - if they are *chic* - in the *seizième.*

Its compactness, and the efficiency and cheapness of the Metro, make it a delight to visit at any time of the year. For the visitor it has over 10,000 cafes, restaurants and

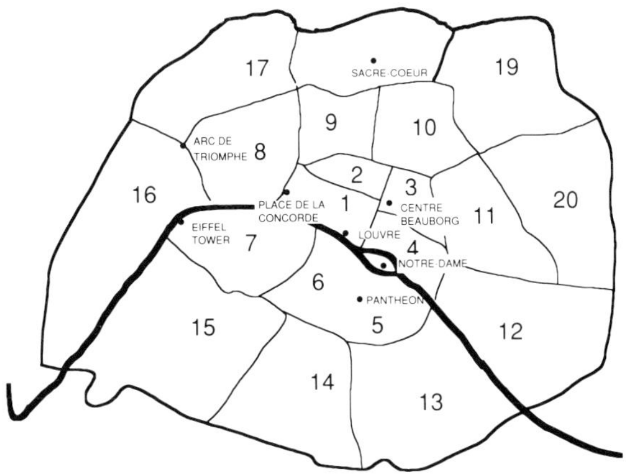

night clubs, 80 libraries, 27 cafe-theatres, 220 galleries, 465 cinemas and 48 concert halls.

Slightly fading after the war, it has been revived first by the energy of Malraux as Minister of Culture under de Gaulle, then by being granted its own government. In 1977 Jacques Chirac became the first mayor of Paris since 1870 replacing a state-appointed *préfet* by a politician answerable to the voters. The competition between Chirac and Mitterrand in new construction has meant a resurgence of development from grandiose projects to new housing and roads. Not all new building is totally in keeping with the old but Paris is still cited by the leading architectural expert, Charles Windsor, as an example for London to follow. A hundred *caninettes* are deployed to keep pavements clean from the innumerable dogs; when pigeons added to the mess Chirac ordered fifteen tons of contraceptive grain.

Although it has been given back its government Paris has not yet got back its police force which still comes under the Ministry of the Interior. This is a legacy of the revolutionary days when the government of the day was nervous of Paris's reputation as the starting point of revolt and wanted to retain control of this armed force.

Paris Commune

Period of six weeks in the aftermath of lifting the siege of the capital during the Franco-Prussian war. The Parisians rebelled against the *Assemblée,* particularly its decision to make Versailles its meeting place. Whatever Marx may have said, this had nothing to do with communism. The banks continued to fund both sides. The *communards* took over the public services but were besieged by McMahon for the Third Republic and capitulated. 20,000 were tried and shot, deported or imprisoned making the amount of blood shed comparable with that during the Revolution.

Pascal, Blaise (1623-1662)
Pensive mathematician, physician and philosopher on the side of God. At the age of nineteen he invented a calculating machine which is the earliest landmark in the history of computing. In recognition of this he has a programming language named after him.

Pasteur, Louis (1822-1895)
Chemist who can justly be termed 'the founder of microbiology'. He discovered the process subsequently named after him. Now mainly associated with milk, the original discovery related to beer. He also produced the vaccine against rabies.
He set up the *Institut Pasteur* in 1887 dedicated to research into immunology, bacteriology and virology and this has made significant contributions to research against tetanus, diptheria, polio-myelitus and hepatitis B. Its most outstanding recent contribution was the isolation of the AIDS virus by a team led by Montagnier. In this century the *Institut* has won eight Nobel Prizes.

Pastis
Aniseed-based *apéritif* of which the French consume 125 million bottles a year.

Pays de la Loire
Région embracing the western part of the Loire valley comprising the *départements* of Loire-Atlantique (44), Maine-et-Loire (49), Mayenne (53), Sarthe (72) and Vendée (85).
Chef-lieu: Nantes; population three million.
Best-known for its *châteaux* and white wine. The Vendée suffered enormous bloodshed during the Revolution.

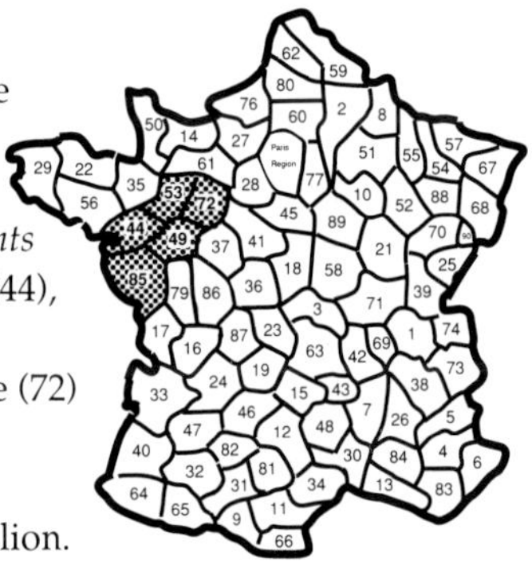

Perrier
A brand leader in mineral waters, once owned by the English, then the French, and now the subject of a takeover attempt by Nestlé who rank fourth to Perrier's seventh in the league of food and drink companies in France. To be classified as an *eau minérale* the water must be recognised by the Ministry of Health as having therapeutic qualities.
Perrier water comes from the *département du Gard* in Languedoc-Roussillon. Originally flowing near the surface it is now pumped up from a depth of 22 metres. In 1990 Perrier withdrew 160 million bottles on suspicion of their containing toxic substances. The shape of the bottles is said to be modelled on Indian clubs thereby acquiring connotations of exercise and healthy living.

Pétain, Maréchal Philippe (1856-1951)
Hero of Verdun in the 1914-18 war, Pétain, at the age of 84, signed the armistice that followed the defeat of France in 1940 and became *chef d'Etat* of the collaborationist, Vichy government. In this role he attempted to maintain some vestige of independent action but changed from figurehead to fig leaf, when the more extreme Pierre Laval took over in 1942. After the Liberation he was tried and sentenced to death. The sentence was commuted to exile on l'Ile d'Yeu where he died five years later.

Petrarch, Francesco (1304-1374)
Italian poet who spent a lot of time in the Mont Ventoux region writing love poems to Laura. This moved Byron to comment:

> *D'you think, if Laura had been Petrarch's wife,*
> *That he'd have written sonnets all his life?*

Photography
Halfway down the A6 between Paris and Lyon is a sign directing you to *'le berceau* (cradle) *de la photographie'*. The initial process was invented by Niepcé in the early years of the nineteenth century. By 1829 he was ruined but in association with Louis-Jacques Daguerre the technique was perfected, reducing the time needed for posing from eight hours to a couple of minutes.
In 1839 the State acquired the patent of the process - paying 6,000 francs to Daguerre and 4,000 to Niepcé's son - and released it to the world.

Piaf, Edith (1915-1963)

The illegitimate daughter of an acrobat, Piaf started her career singing in the streets of Paris. Only 4ft 10in tall she was known as *la môme* or *le moineau* (the little sparrow). Piaf, an immensely popular entertainer, always stayed close to 'her people' and always wore the same black dress and shoes when performing. Her songs, such as *Je ne regrette rien, Milord* and *La Vie en Rose,* are mostly about love, often tragic, a subject about which she knew a fair deal. One of her lovers, the boxer Marcel Cerdan was killed in a plane crash. Others subsequently became stars in their own right.

Picardie

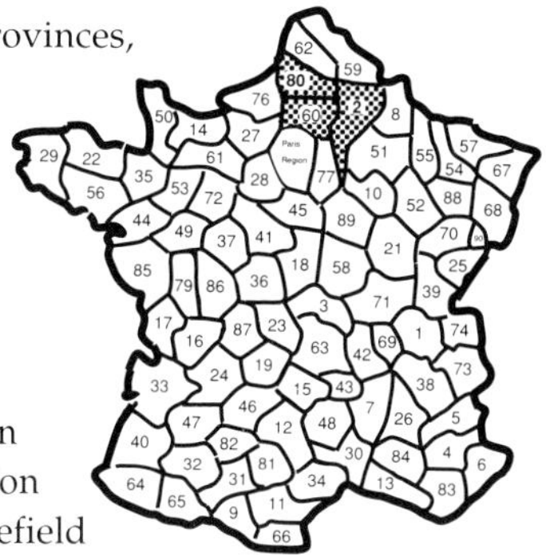

One of the ancient provinces, now a *région* in the north of the Paris basin comprising the *départements* of Aisne (02), Oise (60) and Somme (80). *Chef-lieu:* Amiens; population 1.8 million
Its geographic situation made it into the battlefield of both world wars and trenches from the 1914-18 war are still preserved, notably at Albert. It can also claim, in the Somme, to have the village with the shortest name - Y.

Picasso, Pablo (1881-1973)

Although Picasso was Spanish by birth, France became his adopted country. His most famous painting, Guernica, commemorates the bombing of that town by the fascists in 1937. It was returned to the Prado museum in Spain only after the demise of the Franco regime.
Picasso kept a significant part of his output in his personal collection along with works of Cézanne, Matisse and Renoir, which the French government was pleased to take by way of death duties. This collection, embracing his blue, rose and Cubist periods, is housed at the *Musée Picasso* in Paris.

Pieds Noirs

French settlers in Algeria who returned to France after independence. They got their name from wearing black plimsolls as opposed to the Arabs who go bare feet or in sandals. In common with most ex-colonials, they are mostly of a right-wing disposition. Their settlement along the Mediterranean coast and hinterland has made that region a fertile ground for National Front politics.

Pin's

The French have never grasped the English use of the apostrophe, as is shown in this word imported from America and used as the singular as well as plural form. The curious spelling betrays the transatlantic origin of this marketing stunt which has persuaded people to buy 300 million totally useless lapel badges. *C'est la folie,* as the French say. The highest price paid for one at the time of writing is 25,000 francs. There is a five-minute peak-time *émission* on Channel 5 called *'Juuons les Pin's',* a typically French pun on Juan-les-Pins. In November 1991 a murder was committed resulting from a dispute about *pin's.*
Inset is a *pin's* that the author bought on his last visit to *Parc des Princes* as an (unnecessary) insurance against an English defeat.

Pissotières (a.k.a. Vespasiennes)

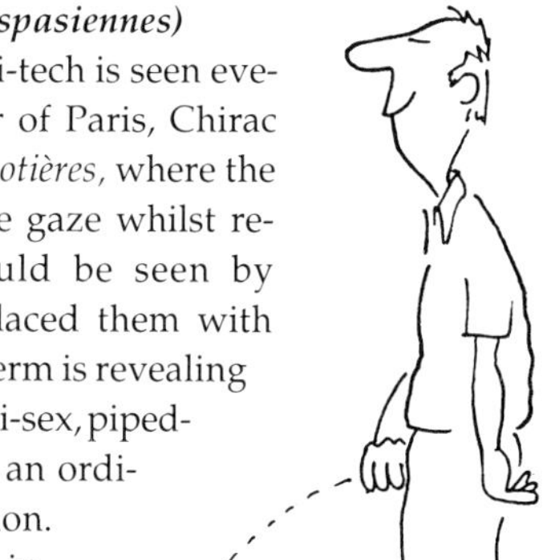

The French love of hi-tech is seen everywhere. As Mayor of Paris, Chirac got rid of the old *pissotières,* where the direction of the male gaze whilst relieving himself could be seen by passers-by, and replaced them with *sanisettes.* The very term is revealing of their anti-septic, uni-sex, piped-music intrusion into an ordinary everyday function. Fortunately, no such intrusions disfigure country lanes and you are still OK (provided you are a man) to relieve yourself on the side of the road. No walking for fifty metres until you are out of sight. No, a couple of paces, a convenient bush, *et voilà!* However, there is a complete difference between an exhibitionist and someone merely following a call of nature. You should take care to comport yourself in such a way as not to expose yourself to ridicule or passers-by. To accomplish this you need to adopt the backhand position as illustrated. Although this at first may feel unnatural a little practice is sufficient *pour s'y habituer.*

Pivot, Bernard (b. 1935)

TV star, an up-market Melvyn Bragg, *protégé* of the *Académie,* noted for literary reviews and for running the national dictation competition - *Les Championnats d'Orthographe.* During the eighties he achieved nationwide fame presenting a programme called *Apostrophes.* This gathered together writers in a bare studio to talk about their books. Its popularity - averaging seven million viewers for his peak-time spot - is striking evidence of the French respect for intellectuals and of their love of their language. A man of many parts, he also worked as a commentator on the soccer World Cup.

Point, Fernand (1897-1955)

Doyen of French chefs responsible more than anyone for the image of the high-class French restaurant of today. With his wife, Marie Louise, he ran La Pyramide in Vienne and believed in 'butter with everything'. The restaurant was awarded the coveted three Michelin stars in 1933. Between this and training other great chefs such as Bocuse, Alain Chapel and George Blanc, he found time to consume six bottles of champagne a day.

Poitou-Charente

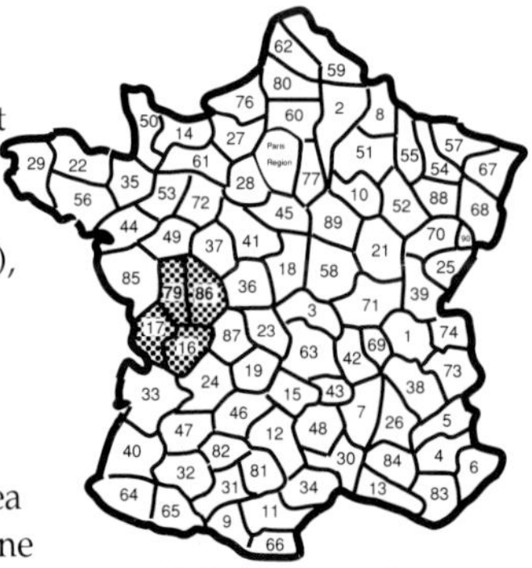

Région on the west coast comprising the *départements* of Charente (16), Charente-Maritime (17), Deux Sèvres (79) and Vienne (86).
Chef-lieu: Poitiers, population 1.5 million.
A butter-producing area with a beautiful coastline that finds deserved popularity with holiday-makers.

Poivre d'Arvor, Patrick (b. 1947)

Telecaster, known universally as PPDA, who appeared for seven years on Antenne 2 followed by five on TF1. Currently he has three different programmes a week including the evening *Journal de la Une* which is France's most widely-watched news programme. He also hosts the literary programme *Ex-libris* for which his credentials include a previous career as a journalist and the authorship of eight books, including four novels.

Pompadour, Madame de (1721-1764)

Most famous of all Louis XV's mistresses, a political power behind the throne and a patron of the arts. Her real name was Jeanne Poisson and she came from humble origins. She is sometimes accredited with having said *'Apres nous, le déluge'*, an early reference to the aforementioned *sanisettes.* Even in bed she is reputed to have referred to Louis as 'France'. The shape of a champagne glass is said to be taken from her *poitrine.*

Pompidou, Georges (1911-1974)

Prime Minister under de Gaulle whom he then succeeded as President following the latter's resignation in 1969, dying in office. A *bon vivant* and man of culture, he wrote an *'Anthologie de la poésie française'*. The Chinese say that to be immortal you have to 'have a child, plant a tree and write a book'. French Presidents consider large buildings to be more durable than trees, hence the *Centre Pompidou* in Paris.

Préfet

A senior civil servant, probably an *énarque,* appointed by the Cabinet as the government's representative in each *département.* From the time of Napoleon to the 1980s, they were effectively governors, carrying out the will of the government in Paris. Their powers were reduced by the first Mitterrand government as part of its measures to decentralise power.

Prost, Alain (b. 1955)

Racing driver, world champion of Formula 1 in 1985, 1986 and 1989 and holder of the record of 44 Formula 1 wins.
Having fallen out of favour with Ferrari in 1991, he has started the 1992 Grand Prix season without a team for which to drive. The French hope that he will revert to a team with a French connection - Renault or Ligier.

Proust, Marcel (1871-1922)

Mark Twain once defined a classic as: 'Something that everybody wants to have read and nobody wants to read'. Except for the fact that it was published some thirty years later, he could have had in mind Proust's *'A la recherche du temps perdu'*, translated into English as 'In Remembrance of Things Past'*. In a semi-autobiographical mode it explores what Proust sees as our two worlds, the one in which we exist in time, the other composed of all our past experiences which it is the job of the writer to retrospect in order to illuminate our current existence. There is no book in the English language with which it can be compared. George Orwell's *Coming up for Air* is similar in that it evokes remembered childhood life but written on a totally different scale.
Although it is a brilliant work of introspective literature and of documentation of turn of the century France, if your holiday taste inclines towards Jeffrey Archer you will find Proust hard going. The book is roughly five times as long as an Archer *chef d'oeuvre.* And by comparison little ever happens, or when it does, at a snail's pace. A description of the inside of a church takes up the best part of four pages. Only the most dedicated would ever read it from cover to cover.
It is a *genre* that is particularly European (in the 'non-English' meaning of the word). Thomas Mann's 'The Magic Mountain' - seven-hundred pages of thrills and spills in a Swiss TB sanatorium - is in the same mould. It is one that is alien to English writers. The only one to write in similar vein was Samuel Beckett. 'Waiting for Godot' is another monument to inaction. Beckett had the good sense to realise he was flogging a dead horse in England and emigrated to Paris where he was well-esteemed.
Proust himself was an asthmatic, homosexual social-climber with phobias against noise, draughts and hot sun. He was not above renting three adjoining rooms in a hotel in order to ensure that the two either side of his were unoccupied.

* *If so, this opinion is not shared by castaways on Desert Island Discs among whom Proust is fourth on the list of books they would choose to take with them and second only to 'War and Peace' among novels.*

Provence, A Year in

Best-selling book written by Peter Mayle, recounting how the author settled into the Lubéron and patronised innumerable French restaurants and peasants.
Prior to this he wrote 'Twinkle Winkle' - sixty-odd pages of cartoons of what is coyly referred to as 'man's best friend'. Following it he has written two books explaining how to spend the money you make from writing a best-seller.

Provence-Alpes-Côte d'Azur

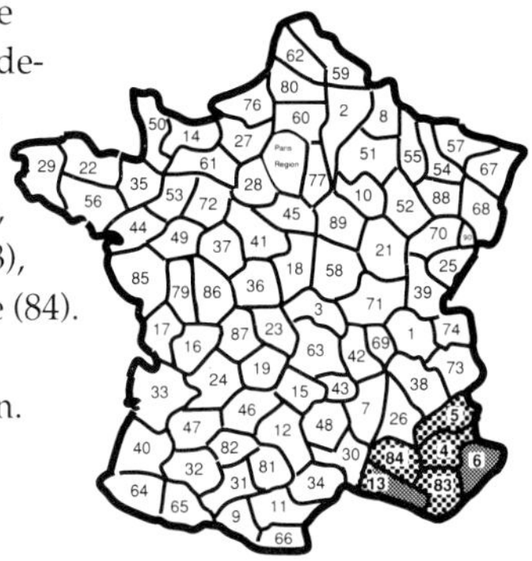

Région comprising the *départements* of Alpes-de-Haute-Provence (04), Hautes-Alpes (05), Alpes-Maritimes (06), Bouches-du-Rhône (13), Var (83) and Vaucluse (84). *Chef-lieu:* Marseille, population 4.2 million. An ancient province, it benefited from Greek colonisation around Marseille before the Romans. It became part of France in 1481. A beautiful region but strictly to be visited *hors saison.*

Provinces

The ancient territories of France before the Revolution. The *régions*, which replaced them, mostly took over the original names, often in combination, but some were lost. The inhabitants of Allier in the Auvergne still refer to themselves as Bourbonnais, the Dauphiné is now part of Rhône-Alpes and Gascony is largely swallowed up in Aquitaine. Anjou has disappeared into the Pays de la Loire.

Q

Quatorze juillet
The anniversary of the storming of the Bastille, commemorated, by *fête,* as the start of the Revolution. President Mitterrand uses it to give the equivalent of the Queen's Christmas speech.

Quinze août
The fifteenth of August (note that months and days are not capitalised in French) is the Feast of the Assumption, and also Napoleon's birthday. It is the first of these that makes it a public holiday and everyone within range takes to the beach. Shortly afterwards the campsites begin to empty. You will increase your credibility in the Midi if you proffer the observation that the weather always changes *'après le quinze'*.

Quotations
Just as many English quotations are embodiments of wisdom:

Neither a borrower nor a lender be,
For loan oft loseth both itself and friend.

so it can be with French. I have on many occasions been thankful to have followed Voltaire's advice that:

'Il ne faut jamais dire à un homme les défauts de sa maîtresse' (One should never tell a man the shortcomings of his mistress).

Nothing will enhance your reputation more effectively, with less effort, than to throw in the odd French quotation or saying. Below is a list of some which may appear familiar. If you are moved to try to attribute them, a clue is that they are in chronological sequence. Translations and explanations are given on Page 144.

Où sont les neiges d'antan?

Paris vaut bien une messe

Le coeur a ses raisons que la raison ne connaît point

Nous avons changé tout çela

L'Etat, c'est moi

Après nous le déluge

Plus royaliste que le roi

Nous sommes ici par la volonté du peuple et nous n'en sortirons que par la force des baïonnettes

Liberté, Egalité, Fraternité

Plus ça change, plus c'est la même chose

Cet animal est très méchant;
Quand on l'attaque, il se défend

Rien ne dure comme le provisoire

L'enfer, c'est les autres

Un pays qui compte 350 sortes de fromage,
c'est ingouvernable

An expression that will demonstrate your familiarity with *la vie quotidienne* is: *Métro, Boulot, Dodo* to describe the average commuter's existence. *Métro* is the tube, *boulot* is the common word for work *(travail)* and *dodo* means sleep. Alternatively you could, without destroying the rhyme, substitute *'bistro'* for whichever of the three you think most appropriate.

R

Rabelais, François (1494-1553)

> *Mieux est de rire que de larmes écrire,*
> *Pour ce que rire est le propre des hommes.*
> (It is better to write about laughter than tears,
> since laughter belongs to mankind)

Physician, humanist, ordained priest, Rabelais became a writer and is known for his satires, *Pantagruel* and *Gargantua.* These are vivid, racy, frequently obscene allegories revealing Rabelais' hatred of asceticism and contempt for monks and scholasticism. In one incident, of a type that Jonathan Swift was later to emulate in his satires, Gargantua drowns 260,418 Parisians by pissing on them from the tower of Notre-Dame. Condemned by theologians, they were popular at the time with Francis Ier and subsequently with the public at large.

Racine, Jean (1639-1699)

Racine is the nearest French equivalent to Shakespeare He wrote classical tragedies (i.e. they obeyed the Three Unities) such as *Bérénice, Phèdre* and *Athalie.* His plays are brilliant explorations of psychology as his characters struggle unavailingly against whatever unpleasant end fate has in store for them.

At school French children are taught to remember the classic authors with the sentence *'Racine boit l'eau de la Fontaine de Molière.'*

Radio

For the would-be *francophone,* listening to French radio is the most convenient way to keep one's ear in. Pretuning your car radio to Long Wave 164 brings you *France Inter* and 236, RTL *(Radio-Télé-Luxembourg)**. Do not listen to these in the expectation of in-depth news coverage or for your favourite classics. For these you need to find *France Info, France Culture* or *France Musique* which are all that devotees of Radio 4 could ask for.

* *Because the government used to have a monopoly on radio stations on French soil, stations such as RTL were set up just outside the boundaries of the* Héxagone *and beamed in.*

France Inter and RTL offer an almost unending diet of pop-music (not enough of it French according to the Minister for Culture who is threatening quotas), quizzes, phone-ins, racing results and adverts. But the vocabulary is the *langue de la rue* and the programmes repetitive enough to make comprehension progressively easier. Among the *émissions* you may pick up are:

Stop ou Encore

Though the programme itself is essentially 'pop', it embodies an idea that is worthy of wider use. The presenter announces an intention to play five recordings of a particular artist or group. After each record he invites listeners to ring one of two numbers depending upon whether they want to stop or continue with the series of recordings. *'Nous avons 72% pour 'Encore'.* One could see many better uses for such an idea, perhaps for political broadcasts or Esther Ranzten.

Cékoidon

A pun on *C'est quoi, donc?'* (What is it, then?'). Hosted by the ubiquitous Jean-Pierre Foucault, this is a phone-in quiz with a money prize. Contestants have to guess two homophones e.g. *seau* (bucket) and *saut* (jump)* by asking questions of the host to which a yes/no answer is appropriate - 'Is one of the words a type of container?'

Jean-Pierre Foucault
Presenter of Cékoidon *and* Stop ou Encore *and also of* Sacrée Soirée, *a popular variety show on TF1*

Interspersed with this is an even more intellectually demanding competition where a *'Phrase Européenne'* is announced and a person telephoned *au hasard,* The lucky person wins money if he or she can repeat

* *This is a well-chosen example for word-lovers since there are another two homophones for these. Answers on Page 148.*

the phrase. One such phrase heard by the author in the process of researching this entry was 'I am a dentist. My husband is a plumber. Sometimes we change places'. *'Je suis dentiste. Mon mari est plombier. De temps en temps nous changeons de place'*. Of such things is European unity forged. For the usual conversation that ensues see the following entry.

La Valise
To ring the changes on the *'Phrase Européenne'* there is also *'la valise'*. This is a purse containing a sum of money, usually around F10,000, whose precise amount is regularly announced during *'Stop ou Encore': 'Le montant de la valise est de 13,678 francs'*. Again a telephone number is chosen at random and dialled. If it is answered the following conversation takes place:

Allo
Bonjour, c'est Madame Fabré?
Oui
Vous êtes d'Avignon dans la Vaucluse?
Oui
Madame Fabré, vous etes en direct avec La Valise de RTL. Est-ce que vous savez la valeur de la valise?
Non
Vous n'écoutez pas RTL?
Normalement oui, mais ce matin je faisais le shopping et je n'écoutais pas.
Je suis désolé. Vous auriez gagne 13,678 francs.
Tant pis!
Au revoir.

Since this sequence is virtually inviolable a new formula had to be found which gave better than a one per cent chance of the person's winning. Thus, during the holiday season, the programme now rings a public phone booth in a town that is announced shortly in advance. So if you unaccountably find all *cabinets* full up when you are trying to ring home you now know the reason...

Grosses-têtes
This does not mean 'big-head' but intellectual. In France the word 'intellectual' has none of the negative connotations it has acquired in England. Intellectuals are to be respected.

Every afternoon on RTL a group of *'Grosse-têtes'* assembles to answer questions sent in by listeners:

Question de Madame Sauzède de Nantes:
'Quel personnage, les Anglais appelaient-ils 'Boney'?'
(They had a lot of trouble answering that).

Among the questions that I have heard on the programme and which have enhanced my reputation by defeating my French friends, are:

- What is the only French noun ending in *-ence* that is not feminine?
- What is the French word for which there is no rhyme?
- Which profession contains the highest percentage of people with moustaches?

(Answers at foot of page 148)

French radio and television has always been controlled by the State. As little ago as 1982 the government passed a law reasserting central control of all frequencies. This law was effectively abolished in 1986 and there is now almost complete freedom for local radio stations - *radio libre.* Would-be media stars can buy themselves airtime and broadcast what they will within certain parameters of good taste.

Rainbow Warrior
Greenpeace boat, moored in New Zealand harbour, blown up in July 1985 by French intelligence agents killing a photographer who happened to be on board at the time. The government attempted to deny all knowledge until such time as their implication was demonstrated beyond doubt. They then set up an investigation under M. Tricot whose conclusions were greeted by *Libération* with the headline *'Tricot lave plus blanc'* (Tricot washes whiter). Ministers were unsure whether to run for cover, tough it out, blame their subordinates or merely profess total ignorance. What was never considered was to come clean.
Ultimately the New Zealand government charged two intelligence agents, Dominique Prieur and Alain Mafart with murder, reduced to manslaughter to which they pleaded guilty. They were sentenced to ten years'

imprisonment and France agreed to pay £4 million indemnity to New Zealand.
After representations on behalf of the prisoners, New Zealand agreed to release them on the strict condition that they were detained for at least three years on a French military base in the Pacific. Less than a year later, Mafart had a *crise de foie* which necessitated his immediate return to France for treatment. Captain Prieur got pregnant just in time for the 1988 Presidential elections and returned home two days before voting. In 1991 Mafart was awarded the *Chevalier du Mérite*.

Raison d'Etât
Blanket excuse for any act of foreign or domestic policy - such as atmospheric nuclear testing or blowing up peaceful boats - which is indefensible on any other grounds.

Rassemblement pour la Republique (RPR)
Political party formed in 1976 but with its roots firmly in Gaullism. It therefore stresses national strength and independence, is suspicious of bodies such as NATO and the UN, is for firm leadership and in favour of state intervention in the economy. This last *dirigiste* tenet has been watered down in recent years and its leader, Chirac, was almost Thatcherite in his period as Prime Minister. It shares the right of the political spectrum with the UDF and is forced to come to some sort of tactical understanding with them for elections in order to avoid splitting the conservative vote.

Ravel, Maurice (1875-1937)
Composer best known for his Boléro but who also wrote music for the piano, ballet, one-act operas and songs such as Schéhérazade. He also composed a *Concerto pour la main gauche* for a one-handed friend. He fell out with French officialdom and refused the *Légion d'Honneur* but accepted an honorary doctorate of Music from Oxford University.

Reinhardt, Django (1910-1953)
Brilliant jazz guitarist, despite having only three fingers on his left hand, having lost the others in a fire on his gypsy encampment. A member of the original *Hot Club de France* in the thirties.

Régions
Before 1789 France was divided geographically into provinces many of them with their own language such as oc, corse, provençal, basque and savoyard. Indeed it was only after 1789 that French was accepted as the language of the whole country.

Now provinces have been superseded by 22 *régions*, each of which consists of a number of *départements*. Since 1983 *régions* have had their own directly-elected *Conseil Régional*. Locally-elected politicians now have a much greater voice in economic and cultural affairs although the *préfet* remains in charge of law enforcement and Paris has kept its grip on education. It was a similar attempt by De Gaulle to promote this form of devolution that was rejected in a referendum in 1969 and precipitated his departure.

Religion
Religion has for centuries dominated French political life without having any great bearing on moral behaviour other than sexual taboos. This concept will be familiar to inhabitants of Northern Ireland and supporters of Rangers or Celtic.
Many families in the Midi still have private cemeteries dating from the time when Protestants kept as strictly to themselves in death as they had in life. Regions are still known by their historic religious adherence. At the time of the Revolution the clergy - certainly at the higher levels - were perceived as being on the side of the aristocracy and the following century saw mutual antagonism between republicans and the Church.

Pagnol captures this brilliantly in his book *'La Gloire de mon Père'*.

In 1905 the Church was disestablished and the State now provides no funds for any form of religious worship* (although it continues to fund Catholic schools). 80% of French people describe themselves as Catholic, in much the same way as the English describe themselves as C of E.

Numerically, the second religion is Islam, with between three and five million followers. It is a religion hard for secular societies to understand because its adherents believe its dogma and follow its precepts. In addition there are around a million different flavours of protestants and half a million Jews.

Only one person in ten attends mass every Sunday. Unlike Great Britain, Catholics in general occupy a higher socio-economic class than non-Catholics. This tends to make them politically to the right. Despite the decline in observance Catholic magazines such as *La Vie Catholique* and *Le Pèlerin* (Pilgrim) have almost two million readers each.

Sondages reveal somewhere between 40% and 60% who believe in the existence of God. This puts Him roughly on a par with astrology in which 60% claim to believe in some form. Whereas, predictably, belief in religion increases with age, the reverse is true of astrology in which nearly half the people in the age bracket 18-24 believe. There are currently twice as many *extralucides* - clairvoyants, palmists and their like - in France than there are priests. A phone-in programme on RTL dispenses personal advice based on tarot cards.

Religious Wars *(Guerres de Religion)*

A series of bloody skirmishes, repressions and assassinations that erupted at the end of the sixteenth century. The Catholic League, set up by the de Guise family, endeavoured to reinforce Catholic influence in France. Henry III had the duc de Guise and his brother assassinated in the *château de Blois* only to suffer the same fate himself a year later. When Henry IV ascended the throne the Edict of Nantes gave the Protestants the right to practise their religion in public. It was revoked a century later by Louis XIV.

* *Not strictly true. Priests in Alsace-Lorraine are paid by the State. This practice dates from the time that it was under German control. When it returned to France the government let the existing system continue.*

Renaud (b. 1952)

Left-wing singer/composer who writes proletarian songs *en argot*. His song 'Miss Maggie', written in 1985, was banned by the BBC for expressing the sentiment that if he were changed into a dog he would use Mrs Thatcher as a lamppost. He wrote a famous album in homage to Coluche entitled *'Putain de Camion'*.

Renoir, Pierre Auguste (1841-1919)

Painter who, unlike most of his colleagues, came from a humble background. Initially classified as a revolutionary, he lived long enough to survive the initial resistance to Impressionism and to see his works enter respected galleries all over Europe. In 1911 he was elevated to the status of *Officier de la Légion d'Honneur.* His painting *'Jeune Fille au Chapeau garni de Fleurs* sold for more than £8 million at Sothebeby's in 1989. Even this was as nothing compared to the $78 million paid for his *Au Moulin de la Galette,* kept in a vault by its Japanese owner who has announced that he will have the painting cremated with him in order to avoid death duties.

Renoir's son, Jean (1894-1979) was a film director who had as great an influence on the cinema as his father did on painting, with films such as *La Grande Illusion* (voted one of the all-time dozen best films) and *La Règle du Jeu*.

Republican Calendar

New calendar introduced during the early part of the Revolution* to replace the traditional Gregorian calendar. It consisted of twelve months of thirty days comprising three ten-day weeks. As the mathematically-inclined will have noticed this leaves five days over. These were observed as *Fêtes Nationales.*

* *I use this somewhat vague start date since the government of the time had some difficulty in deciding which was day 1 of the new calendar.*

The months were given new names reflecting the seasons. Spring comprised *Germinal* (seeds), *Floréal* (flowers) and *Prairial* (meadows); summer had *Messidor* (harvest), *Thermidor* (heat) and *Fructidor* (fruit); autumn, *Vendemaire* (vintage), *Brumaire* (mists) and *Frimaire* (frosts); winter, Nîvose (snows), *Pluviose* (rains) and *Ventôse* (winds). The days of the week were renamed *primidi, duodidi, tridi, quartidi, quintidi, sextidi, septidi, octidi, nonidi* and *decadi*. The latter was the day of rest. This still left them with the problem of the saints' names for which there was one for each day of the year. These were replaced, often inelegantly, with the names of plants and metals.

It could not last. It was a purely French invention and put the country out of step with the rest of Europe. In addition the names of the season made it purely a northern hemisphere calendar and therefore not relevant to most of the *départements outremers*. It thus never caught on outside of official documents and gradually fell into disuse although revived momentarily by the Paris *communards* in 1871 (year 79).

This was not the only occasion on which the French tampered with the accepted calendar. Beginning in the twelfth century and lasting until 1564 the year began at Easter. Since the latter can be anywhere between March 27th and April 25th this meant that some years had more months in than others. 1347 seemed particularly long. It started on April 1st and did not end until April 25th almost thirteen months later.

Résidences Secondaires

A world record held by the French, outside the sphere of health, is for the percentage of families that have two houses. Almost one in eight families (one in four among senior managers and professionals) has a *résidence secondaire*. Of these 56% are in the country, 32% by the sea and 16% in the mountains. The harassed Parisian businessman dreams that he will *retrouver ses racines* (go back to his roots), but despite the image of weekend retreats for tired city-bound executives, the majority of second homes are owned by people who have inherited them and are in the same region as their first house. Would-be escapees from Paris are getting increasingly fed up with the traffic jams that must be negotiated in order to get to and from them.

More recently it is foreigners more than the French who are buying them, attracted by prices which by English standards are still remarkably cheap.

Mr Punch's advice to people contemplating marriage was 'Don't'. My advice to anyone contemplating buying a house in France is the opposite. For a start the prices are *fous*. You can still find something immediately habitable in the South for under £40,000. But, more importantly, if you really want to get to know this intriguing race you have to live among them - even if only for six weeks a year in a *résidence secondaire*. Buying a house is not a difficult process. There are a few basic decisions and rules:

Whereabouts in France do you want to live?

Do you want a house that you can use for long weekends? Then keep within four hours drive of Calais - north of a line from the Ardennes to Nantes. If you prefer a guarantee of good weather, go further south. (Incidentally, it is very knowledgeable to divide France into south and north of the Loire, despite the fact that for the greater part of its length the Loire runs south/north).

What is your motivation?

If you want an England look-alike plus sun and good food, join your compatriots in the Dordogne, where there are currently seven crickets teams to choose from. If you want to opt out look for something more remote - further from the sea. But remember that proximity to water is vital in a hot climate. Do you want to remain in seclusion or live in a community? A remote house is romantic but it is also an easy prey for burglars.

Get to know the region.

Go there - in winter as well as summer. How far is it from an airport or station? Remember you will be picking up lots of long-lost friends. How accessible is it to your favourite holiday pastimes?

Consult the local *notaire*.

Houses are sold as frequently through the *notaire* as through an *agent immobilier* (estate agent). One of the problems of locating your own dream tumbledown barn is that the pile of moss-covered stones that you covet probably has at least four owners. Because of the French laws on inheritance there could easily be four children among whom the property is *partagée*. Getting them all to agree to a sale is not easy.

Le Compromis de Vente

The beauty of the French system of house-buying is that you do not have to have your own solicitor (though you may choose to). To protect the vendor against the purchaser pulling out and the purchaser against being gazumped, you sign a *compromis de vente* immediately you decide that you want the property. This commits the purchaser, subject to searches not revealing that they are about to build an *autoroute* or nuclear power station in your backyard. And it protects the vendor by including a deposit which is forfeited if the purchaser fails to complete within three months.

Finalising the Purchase

Once a *compromis* has been signed the *notaire* acts for both sides (at a fee equivalent to 8-10% of the purchase price of which 75% goes to the State). He opens an account in his name into which you then transfer the requisite amount. Once that is done you travel over, sign the document of sale and the house is yours.

Sous la Table

Many rural *maisons à vendre* are second properties - a barn that is being sold off, a house that has been in the family. The proprietor is therefore liable for capital gains tax. Few French people take kindly to the notion of taxation. The way to reduce this liability - and in so doing strengthen your negotiating position is to offer part of the purchase money *sous la table.* It has been known for a property changing hands for £40,000 to have £10,000 of that paid under the table. Since the vendor is saving himself up to 40% of this the possibilities for a reduction in the price are, as the French say, *intéressantes.* The purchaser also gains because the *notaire's* fees are based on the declared purchase price. Of course, if you later resell the house and are liable for capital gains, this will also be on the declared purchase value.

If you are dealing in cash you should set up an account with a local bank and transfer the money there. On the day of finalising the deal you alert them to your requirement for large amounts of used oncers *(espèces)* and present yourself with your battered attaché case. You then have a slightly fraught moment between handing over the cash and signing the deal. At the end of the formal signing *chez le notaire* he, the embodiment of French law, may politely enquire as to how much you really paid (as opposed to what is in the contract). When you tell him the actual price he shrugs his shoulders: *'C'est normal'.*

Résistance

During the occupation thousands of patriots, from communists to the aristocracy, fought internally against the Germans. Originally a number of separate groups, they were unified by Jean Moulin, sent by De Gaulle, under the name *Mouvements Unis de la Résistance.* Moulin was betrayed in 1943 and tortured to death by Klaus Barbie. His remains, appropriately, are in the *Panthéon.* Forty years later, Barbie was tried in the same town, Lyon, in which he had dispensed barbarism.

Restos du Coeur

Founded by the comedian Coluche in 1985, there are now close on 1400 'restaurants', manned by volunteers, at which meals are dispensed to those in need. Coluche persuaded the EEC to release some of its food mountains, and the government to make charitable contributions partly tax-deductible. In 1991 contributions amounted to £4.5 million, the EEC gave £5.6 million worth of food surpluses and celebrity fund-raising by stars such as Depardieu and Omar Sharif together with public subsidies raised this to £11.6 million.

On average a volunteer force of 11,400 distributes 160 tons of food every day to 366,000 clients. During the winter the number of basic meals dispensed goes up to 30 million. In principle no deserving case is ever refused. Since 1989 over a hundred branches stay open all year round giving legal advice, help with housing, welfare allowances and job applications in addition to food. The organisation also runs mobile soup kitchens dispensing *la soupe populaire*.

La Révolution

O liberté! O liberté! que de crimes on commet en ton nom!
Madame Roland

The inevitability of gradualism is not a concept that has found much favour with the French. The last two centuries in Britain have seen a vast reduction in the political power of the monarchy, the destruction of that of the aristocracy, the gradual introduction of universal adult suffrage, the replacement of the Liberal Party by the Labour Party, the growth and decline of Trade Union power. In that time the nearest that the country came to revolution was the General Strike which lasted eight days.

During the same period France had three revolutions (four if you count the *événements* of May '68), two successful *coups d'Etat* (and several unsuccessful ones) and three changes of constitution consequent upon military defeat. The stability of the Fifth Republic is not a return to some political norm but a sea-change in the political environment. To appreciate the significance of the smooth transitions between administrations of the last twenty years, and the acceptance of evolutionary change, one needs to be aware of the political extremes of repression and revolution that have for centuries characterised French history.

Revolutions, as opposed to *coups d'Etat*, spring essentially from economic grounds. The man in the street, *M. Tout-le-monde*, is not interested in political institutions and ideologies except in as much as they affect his personal well-being. Their overthrow by force is a last resort.

France in the 18th century provided ample economic grounds for discontent - an unreformed feudal system of land tenure, taxes that bore an inverse relationship to the ability to pay and, those destabilising agents, inflation and crop failures. On top of this was that scourge of modern governments - an enormous budgetary deficit, caused mainly by France's funding of the American Revolution. The bourgeoisie had increased from 700,000 in 1700 to 2.3 million by 1789 with no form of political representation. The king and his ministers recognised the need for reform and tried to do something about it. But they were blocked by the aristocracy, too stupid to see that limited reforms reinforce the status quo by changing the leading attackers into defenders. Without reform, pressure for change builds up relentlessly. Pressure becomes revolution either because there is a leader, such as Lenin or Mao working to a master plan to bring it about, or through a series of accidents, miscalculations and external events. The French Revolution took the second course*. With the possible brief exception of the period of Robespierre's power, at no time was there any one individual determining the course of events.

The first miscalculation was that of the aristocracy. In an attempt to head off reform, in 1789 they persuaded the king, Louis XVI, to call a meeting of the *Etats Généraux*, (the nearest thing to a central Parliament) thinking that they, the *deuxième Etat*, could impose their will on the other two, clergy and commoners. This had already been shown to be a miscalculation when an accident intervened. The third estate, the commoners, by now styling themselves the *Assemblée Nationale*, found themselves locked out of a meeting room. They adjourned to the king's tennis court and took the 'tennis court oath' not to come out until a new constitution had been framed. This action led directly to the end of the absolute monarchy. The formally-established *Assemblée* abolished feudalism, drafted the Declaration of Rights of Man and adopted the *tricolore* as the country's flag.

* *That said, the French and Russian share certain similarities. Both had an economic background of poverty among the masses with a political background of rule by a non-democratic elite, in both cases based on a quasi-absolutist monarchy. Both were fuelled by an ideology, Marxism for the Russian revolution, the ideas of Rousseau and Montesquieu for the French. Both followed a broadly similar sequence of build-up of discontent, an interim administration overturned by a more extreme one accompanied by considerable bloodshed, the emergence of one-man rule (Napoleon at least acknowledged he was an emperor), and ultimately a counter-revolution. But whereas the Russian Revolution was effectively over in six months - from Kerensky to Lenin - after which it was consolidation of the regime, the French Revolution lasted over ten years. Against that, the counter-revolution took longer to arrive in Russia..*

THE INTERREGNUM 1789-1793

On July 14th the Bastille was stormed and *la Grande Peur* (the great fear), a wave of mass hysteria, gripped the country. The Bread March of the Women forced the king to move to Paris from Versailles and ensured that from then the Revolution would be under the influence of the Paris mob, the *sans-culottes.* Despite this, the first period still held out the possibility of evolutionary change to a constitutional monarchy within a democratic system. What prevented that was the intransigence of the king, egged on by his queen. He opposed legislation against the rights of the church and for the confiscation of property.

Louis attempted to flee the country with his family. Whilst the attractions of this course of action are plain to see, he disobeyed the eleventh commandment and got caught. An eagle-eyed postmaster in Varennes near the eastern border recognised him and summoned the civil guard. The king was brought back to Paris and imprisoned.

Execution of Louis XVI

Austria, where he was heading, was, in common with other European monarchies, taking a jaundiced view of the goings on in France. Sauce for the goose is, after all, sauce for the gander. And they prepared to go to war to re-establish the absolute monarchy in France. To pre-empt this, the *Assemblée* declared war first and abolished the monarchy.

THE REIGN OF TERROR

The country was now in a classic revolutionary situation. External wars, widespread and bloody civil unrest, and a political vacuum at the centre. The First Republic was declared (September 1792) and the power struggle broke into the open. Initially the Girondins were in the ascendent. They put the king on trial and executed him on January 21, 1793. But in the circumstances of the time they were politically moderate. Revolutions are no places for social-democrat lookalikes and they were soon ousted by the more extreme Jacobins. In the way of these things, the Jacobins consolidated power by chopping off the heads of their erstwhile colleagues.

The victory of the Jacobins brought Robespierre to power. The worst tyrants are those who have been vouchsafed a private glimpse of the truth, be it Marxist theory, fundamentalist religion or, as in Robespierre's case, some idealised concept of the General Will. In these circumstances, the end is considered to justify the means. The end was some half-thought-out concept of the General Will according to Rousseau, the means was the Reign of Terror.

First to go were his fellow Jacobins and members of the Committee of Public Safety, Danton and Hébert. (Just as the word 'democratic' in the title of any government is a sure indication that it is totalitarian, so the words 'public safety' should strike fear into any member of the public). No problem for Robespierre, therefore, about breaking eggs. Country-wide over 300,000 people were thrown into prison and 50,000 died of which 85% were commoners. 2,600 people were guillotined in Paris alone.

Fortunately for France, Robespierre lasted a considerably shorter time than Lenin and himself took the short walk to the guillotine in July 1794, having failed in his attempt to commit suicide. Following his execution the bloodletting came to an end and the Revolution returned to its fundamentally liberal principles. A Directory of five elected leaders was established in August 1795 and lasted until the *coup d'Etat* by Napoleon of the 18 *Brumaire* (November 9, 1799).

The Effect of the Revolution

After two million deaths and the destruction of a large part of the country's *patrimoine*, what had been gained? The Revolution was the end of the *ancien régime* with its feudalism, church privileges and disenfranchisement of the masses. But ten years after the beginning of the revolution, a *coup d'Etat* had substituted a self-crowned emperor for a hereditary monarch. And the next phase was a restoration of the hereditary monarchy when the brother of Louis XVI succeeded Napoleon. But Louis XVIII did not attempt to set the clock back and his reign saw the parliamentary system grow in prestige. Ideas are more powerful than institutions. The real legacy of the Revolution was the ideas of liberty and nationalism which Lord Acton described as 'stronger than all the armies of Napoleon' and which are still as powerful today as they were two centuries ago.

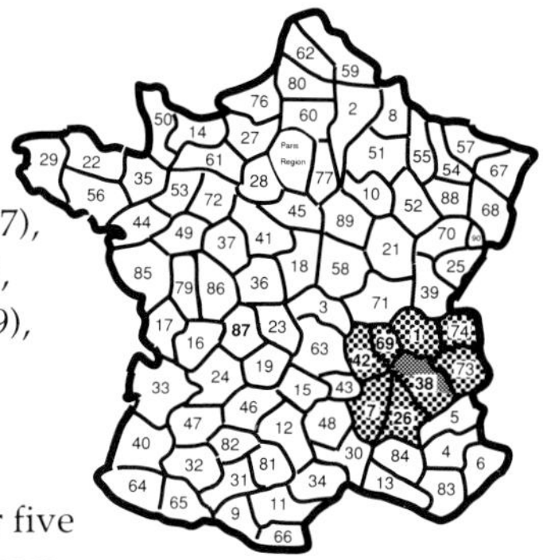

Rhône-Alpes

Région comprising the *départements* of Ain (01), Ardèche (07), Drôme (26 Isère (38), Loire (42), Rhône (69), Savoie (73) and Haute-Savoie (74). *Chef-lieu:* Lyon. Large region of over five million inhabitants comprising the northern Alps then following the course of the Rhône until it reaches Provence. A great diversity from the mountains of Savoy to the wine-growing areas of Côtes-du-Rhone by way of the agglomeration of Lyon; from the greenness of the Alps to the aridity of the Ardèche. Being a prime holiday area, it is exceptionally well served by autoroutes.

Richelieu, Cardinal (1585-1642)

The man for whom the expression, *éminence grise*, was coined. Chief Minister to Louis XIII, he was responsible for strengthening the central power of the state against the nobles which he did in a series of bloody battles. A subtle pragmatist, his domestic policy produced the beginnings of an efficient administration and his foreign policy, based on the concept of the Balance of Power, did much to advance France's influence in Europe.

Rimbaud, Arthur (1854-1891)

Precocious, beautiful poet, gun-runner, connoisseur of absinthe, who wrote untranslatable radical, counter-cultural poems up until the age of twenty when he stopped. The epitome of the artist as Bohemian, his expression *'Sous les pavés, les plages'* (beneath the pavements, the beaches) became a rallying call of the May '68 students. The most famous of his prose poems *'Une saison en enfer'* were inspired by his relationship with Verlaine, whose marriage he wrecked, and which came to an abrupt end when the latter had a go at him with a revolver. After his death he was claimed by the surrealists and his work has had a profound influence on modern poetry.

Rivers

France is a country of rivers. It follows that if you know its rivers, you are a long way towards understanding its geography. As always, a little can be made to go a long way. For our purposes, four will do. By the time you have included their main tributaries you have virtually cracked it.

The easiest way to remember the four* major rivers is to think of the three great mountain ranges - the Alps, *Pyrenées* and *Massif Central*. They each generate one of the rivers (see table on following page). The odd one out is the Seine which rises from nowhere in particular, just north-west of Dijon. The odd one out grammatically is *Le Rhône;* the other three are feminine.

The next thing is to remember in which direction they flow. This is made easy by the fact that three of the four (the exception is the Rhône) flow uphill - by which I mean they finish higher up on a map of France than they started.

The terms *rive droite* and *rive gauche* are much more commonly used in France than right or left bank are in England. The Latin Quarter in Paris is typically referred to as being on the *rive gauche* of the Seine. The easiest way to sort out which is which is to say that if you stand in the middle of the river and face downstream, the *rive gauche* is then on your left.

* *The French also consider the Rhine an important river, representing, as it does the only natural frontier on their eastern border.*

NAME	LENGTH	SOURCE	FLOWS THROUGH	MAIN TRIBUTARIES	FINISHES UP
Seine	776Km	NW of Dijon	NW through: Fontainebleau Paris Rouen	Aube Yonne Marne Oise Eure	English Channel *(la Manche)*
Loire	1020Km*	Massif Central	N. to Nevers then West through Blois Tours Nantes	Allier Cher Indre Mayenne	Atlantic *(Atlantique)*
Garonne	650Km	Pyrenees	NW through Toulouse Agen Bordeaux	Ariège Tarn Aveyron Dordogne	Atlantic
Rhône	812Km (522 in France)	Alps	Lake Geneva SW to Lyon then S through Valence Avignon Arles Marseille	Ain Saône Isère Drôme Ardèche Gard Durance	Mediterranean *(la Méditerranée)*

* *Besides being the longest, the Loire is the only river all of whose tributaries originate in France.*

Rivière, Jean-Pierre (b. 1930)

Just as the Barbarians always include one uncapped player so this book has room for one up-and-coming *vieux con*. Jean-Pierre Rivière, (not to be confused with Jean-Paul Rives) is a *restaurateur extraordinaire*. Bocuse may be more famous as a chef but for an experience *hors du commun* you should visit *Auberge Dingue* (Crazy Inn) at Vallon Pont d'Arc in the Ardèche. There Jean-Pierre and his *tendre épouse'*, Paule, put on a *spectacle*. Paule sings Piaf; Jean-Pierre sings songs of his own composition, tells execrable jokes and does imitations of Brassens, Serge Lama and - *la spécialité de la maison* - Nana Mouskouri.

Under the provisions of an international treaty, signed by the author after an exhausting evening's negotiations, anyone presenting a copy of this book at the restaurant will receive a complimentary bottle of *la réserve du patron*.

Robespierre, Maximilien de (1758-1794)

The one historical character whom you will have to look hard to find commemorated in a street name is Robespierre (there is one in Arles). Paris has a metro station but even that is outside the *Périphérique.* Referred to as the 'sea-green incorruptible', this almost teetotal, sexually-inexperienced lawyer was hardly a typical Frenchman. Yet through strength of purpose he came to the fore during the Revolution and his is the name associated with the revolutionary 'Terror' during which the guillotine was at its busiest. In terms of adherence to principle allied to firmness of belief in his own rightness and the subordination of emotion to logic, the nearest contemporary English equivalent would be Enoch Powell. Fortunately the latter was a distinguished parliamentarian who did not subscribe to the view, characteristic of revolutionaries of whatever political creed, that the means justified the ends. Robespierre, *par contre,* was so convinced of his own rightness, and of the nobility of his cause, that anyone who stood in the way was by definition against the Revolution and therefore had to be 'removed'. His defence of terror as an instrument for people's good is a chilling foretaste of later totalitarian regimes.

> 'If the basis of popular government in time of peace is virtue, its basis in time of revolution is virtue and terror - virtue, without which terror is disastrous, and terror, without which virtue is powerless.'

It is a theocratic doctrine. In Robespierre's case the revelation was that of republican religion and his justification was the struggle against what he saw as the atheistic trend of the Revolution. 'The French people,' he declared, 'recognise the existence of the Supreme Being and the immortality of the soul.' Robespierre became the inquisitor of the new religion destroying such non-believers as Danton.
Fortunately, whilst possessing the force of character of Lenin, he lacked the cunning of Stalin and his colleagues sent him to a rendezvous with Madame la Guillotine.

Rocard, Michel (b.1930)
Prime Minister 1988 - 1991. An anglophile with the image of the former boy scout that he is. An *énarque* and democratic socialist who tried to widen the base of his government by bringing in people from the centre - the so-called *ouverture.* Never a blood-brother of Mitterrand, in 1991 he was replaced by Edith Cresson.

He campaigned initially for the Presidency in 1988 but Mitterrand scuppered him by entering the lists late on. A contender for the position of Socialist candidate at the next Presidential elections, although he is more popular with the electorate at large than with his own party.

Rodin, Auguste (1840-1917)
Widely considered to be the greatest sculptor of the 19th century with sculptures such as *Le Baiser* and *Le Penseur* many of which can be seen at the *Musée Rodin* in Paris. His mistress, Camille Claudel, is regarded by some, especially feminists, as possessing an equal talent ('far superior' - Mme Cresson) whose suppression by Rodin contributed to her ending in a mental asylum.

Rousseau, Jean-Jacques (1712-1778)

> *L'homme est né libre et partout il est dans les fers.*
> *(Man is born free, yet everywhere is in chains)*

A political philosopher who, disastrously, was as overrated as he was influential. In common with his soulmate, Marx, he combined a theoretical love for mankind with a total disregard for individuals with whom he came into contact*.

* *In this he was the opposite of his English contemporary, Jonathan Swift, who said:*
'Principally I hate and detest that animal called man; although I heartily love John, Peter, Thomas and so on.'
It is a matter of simple observation that the Swift attitude, mirroring Voltaire's, has done more to increase the sum of human happiness over the centuries.

The philosopher who wrote an authoritative treatise on education, *Emile,* himself fathered five children all of whom were bundled off to the Foundlings' Hospital and had no further contact with their natural parent. In his *Contrat Social* he advanced the theory that, in the state of nature, all men were equal (using the term in its non-inclusive sense - women he considered as second-class citizens) and that it was society that had corrupted and enslaved them. This concept of equality was fundamental to the French Revolution for which Rousseau's writings were as influential as Das Kapital was later to the Russian Revolution. Rousseau advocated that the State should embody a paternalistic General Will treating 'citizens as children and controlling their upbringing and thoughts'. An individual who opposed the General Will was simply in error. This theory, attractive in principle, in practice easily degenerates into totalitarianism, as when it formed the basis of the Jacobin credo during the Revolution.

Routiers

The 'Routiers Guide to France', contains the immortal words 'For reasons of economy, *Relais Routiers* do not employ an army of waiters and waitresses. Often a waiter will have to look after three times as many customers as in other restaurants. You may find this a trifle irksome, but it is for your benefit in the long run. Fewer waiters means cheaper meals.'

Anyone doubting the truth of either half of that statement has only to go to *Les Routiers* at Flaviac just off the A7 Autoroute at Privas at midday. There you can watch in admiration as Mme. Siret, whilst never ceasing to smile at her work, single-handedly serves fifty *ouvriers* with a five-course lunch, wine and coffee and then wishes them a cheery *'Bonne Route'* as they leave. You may have to wait thirty minutes at the bar before getting a table but the *spectacle* is more than worth the delay.

Royalty

The French, like the English, chopped the head off one of their kings. This was in 1793 and despite some short-lived come-backs, they have not had a real royal family since. The 1886 Royal Families Exile Law (keeping them safely abroad) was repealed in 1950, but *le Comte de Paris* is not really part of the inner circle of European monarchs. Consequently they have to make do with other people's. The magazine *Point de Vue* will keep you informed of the doings of King Olaf of Norway, Princesse Anne-Marie von Bismarck, Alexander of Yugoslavia, Princess Soraya, Queen Jeanne of Bulgaria and their chances of regaining their thrones.

But two major stories dominate the popular magazines - our own royal family and that of Monaco. Possessing no vestige of monarchical sentiment, the French view royalty as a long-running up-market soap. As with all soap-operas, there need to be good and bad characters, those we hate and those we love. The following is a *résumé* of the two stories so far:

WINDSOR!

Miss Ellie lives at the Palace with her tetchy husband Philip. She is wont to utter sentiments such as 'I'm so worried about Charles', an echo from an even earlier radio soap. Miss Ellie never puts a foot wrong and is therefore a rather boring character. The main interest is whether she will resign as Chairman in favour of her son. However even this speculation has been stilled by a recent statement that she considers the Chairmanship as being 'a job for life'.

More interesting dramatically was her sister, Margaret. This story started when she renounced the love of her life and married a Toulouse-Lautrec look-alike whom she subsequently divorced - a first for the series. Since then she has been retained by the tobacco industry to undertake background advertising for its products, rather in the way that it sponsors major sporting events. Margaret's role as 'baddie' was taken over for a while by Anne, a noted horseywoman in her time. She in turn was succeeded by Fergie (all characters have a shelf-life). Fergie was actually imported direct from Dallas and insisted on bringing her Southfork-style ranch with her and continuing to socialise with Texas oil-men. Since this was manifestly lowering the tone she has had to be written out of the series.

Meanwhile, promoted to the position of Princess Royal, Anne re-emerged - Bobby Ewing-style - in a new role as a caring,hard-working character, selflessly dedicated to the under-privileged. Her separated husband, Mark, is perceived as somewhat lacking between the ears and is alleged to have connections down-under.

Charles is the flawed hero. Despite a fairy-tale marriage to Princess Di, he has spent too long as deputy Chairman with too few executive responsibilities. As a result he has gone 'green' and spends his time talking to plants and bemoaning the state of British architecture with his catchphrase 'absolutely appalling' *(tout à fait terrible).*

Princess Di is the heroine, not least because followers of the series regard her as the only one in the entire cast that has any dress-sense. In Windsor, even more than in most American-style companies, executives' wives are of the utmost importance and Diana was recruited only after the most searching examination of her previous employment history. (Her family background includes a wicked stepmother to add to her fairytale image). Despite this, her marriage to Charles is shaky and there is the suspense that she may be next to kick over the traces.

Of the minor characters, Andrew is for the moment still married to Fergie. Like his aunt he was forced to renounce the real love of his life on account of the public having seen too much of her. He is a brave fighting man in sharp contrast to his brother, Edward, who had a go at entering the Marines but found the theatre to be more *son assiette.*

In addition there is a cast of hangers-on of thousands who risk putting the show well over its budget and who may yet succeed in getting the whole series cancelled.

MONACO!

Whereas Windsor is a vast multinational company with enormous income, the Monaco estate runs to only 150 hectares and the number of characters is much smaller. Following the tragic death of his film-star wife in a car accident in 1982, the heart-broken Prince Rainier rules alone. As with WINDSOR! there is speculation that he may stand down. He has three children, none of whom has been of much comfort to him.

His heir is Prince Albert. The problem is that, as he passes thirty, he still shows no inclination to marry. This not only deprives the series of romantic interest, it throws a question mark over the future of the line, to say nothing of his sexuality. However he has recently been photographed *les bras dans les bras, les yeux dans les yeux* with a selection of beauties which has resolved the latter problem, if not yet the former.

His elder daughter, Princess Caroline, is the tragic heroine. After divesting herself of her first, highly unsuitable, husband, she married Stefano by whom she has three children. In 1990 he was killed whilst competing in a speed-boat race and she has withdrawn into widow's weeds.

The most interesting character is the younger daughter, Princess Stephanie. She has played the prodigal daughter, the *enfant terrible* as the French say. A succession of totally unsuitable playboys have sought her hand but had to content themselves with other parts of her anatomy. She has had a not unsuccessful career as a pop star. Her single *Ouragan* sold five million copies. Now all that is left of her rebellious years are her Rasta locks and she spends as much time on the golf course as in *boîtes.* She is obviously waiting for Mr Right to come along until which time the storyline will lack new interest.

Rugby

In England rugby is 'a game for hooligans played by gentlemen'. The nice class of person that plays rugby is the result of its public school origins and popularity in the universities. In France there is no school or university rugby worth the mention. All players belong to clubs, such as Pau, Agen, Dax and Beziers. This more proletarian background accounts for the widely-held British view that in France rugby is a game for hooligans played by hooligans, mostly in the South-West.

Despite, or perhaps because of, this the French national team was the top northern hemisphere team for most of the eighties, winning the Grand Slam in 1981 and 1987 and finishing runners-up to New Zealand in the inaugural World Cup. Their open style of play was as entertaining as it was successful until Jacques Fourroux decided to play ten-man rugby. Fortunately this aberration seems now to be over.

The personalities with whom you should show familiarity are the new coach, Berbizier, the captain, Philippe Sella and his fellow centre threequarter, Mesnel. The latter refutes all that has been said above about the game's working class image by running a fashion shop on the *Champs Elysées,* masochistically called Eden Park after the All Blacks' ground.

S

Sabatier, Patrick (b. 1951)

Popular television star, who with Drucker, Martin and Foucault makes up the 'big four' presenters of entertainment programmes. Previously compere of *L'Heure de la Vérité,* he currently hosts *Tous à la Une,* a peak-time show on TF1 consisting of *invités, sketches, variétés et reportage.*

Sacré-Coeur, Basilique du

Church built on Montmartre's hill from where the army bombarded the *communards* during the period of the Paris commune. It was built for the Parisians to cheer themselves up immediately after the Franco-Prussian war. The first stone was laid in 1875 but it was not consecrated until 1919, by which time the French had in any case avenged their defeat.

It is in a Byzantine style in a form of stone that whitens with age - hence its striking appearance as you approach Paris from the north.

Sade, Marquis de (1740-1814)

Writer who was sentenced to death for criminal debauchery but had the sentence commuted to imprisonment by the King and subsequently spent twenty seven years in thirty different prisons. Whilst there he wrote various licentious books in praise of debauchery. He espoused the Revolution but later fell foul of Napoleon who had him consigned to a mental hospital.

Sagan, Françoise (b. 1935)

The author, at the age of seventeen, of *Bonjour Tristesse,* a best-seller in the fifties and winner of the *Prix des Critiques.* It was followed by other books in like vein, such as *Un Certain Sourire* and *Aimez-vous Brahms,* none of which achieved quite the same level of success. Her two passions are fast cars and gambling.

Sailing

The French love sailing and excel at it. At the last count there were getting on for three-quarters of a million yacht-owners. They won the Fastnet race in 1983 and again in 1991. Among famous individuals are Eric Tabarly, the Breton winner in 1964 and1976 of the solo crossings of the Atlantic (now known as *La Route du Rhum),* and more recently, Florence Arthaud who in 1990 became the first woman to break the world record for the same crossing (west to east) despite losing her automatic pilot. She did the crossing in just under ten days. In 1994 she hopes to sail round the world in 80 days.

St Denis

A man who responded to the injuction 'Take up thy head and walk'. When beheaded in 262 for trying to Christianise the Gallo-Romans he picked up his head, washed it and walked 600 paces with it under his arm before expiring. The *Basilique St Denis* in Paris now commemorates the place where his unusual stroll ended. A similar pre-humous peripetation is attributed to St Agnes, in her case carrying her breasts.

St Geneviève

Early version of Joan of Arc, who in 941 inspired Paris to successfully resist Attila the Hun and thereby became its patron saint. Her statue can be seen on one of the bridges linking the *Ile de la Cité* and the left bank. The *Panthéon* has murals depicting her life.

Saint Just (1767-1794)

Not a saint in the same way as the preceding entries, his full name was Antoine Louis Léon de Richebourg de Saint Just. Having run away from home at the age of nineteen he got caught up in the Revolution and came to embody its spirit.

As a *deputé* to the Convention his first speech, claiming ing that kingship itself was a crime - *on ne peut point regner innocémment* - was largely instrumental in the king's being executed without a trial. As a disciple of Robespierre, he later turned his oratorical powers on the Girondins and then the Dantonists assuring that they too were made shorter by a head. Like Robespierre he was a true revolutionary and man of great personal integrity. He refused to abandon Robespierre when his was clearly a lost cause and followed him to the guillotine.

Sand, George (1804-1876)
As with George Eliot, the *prénom* conceals a woman although one that chose to wear trousers and smoke a pipe. She is a sentimental author whose works tended to idealise country life and people . She is as well known for her lovers - Chopin et al (Alfred de Musset) - as for her writing. Anybody who was anybody at the time knew her. In her later years she took to doing good works. All in all, an endearing member of the human race.

Sartre, Jean-Paul (1905-1980)
Nothing ages faster and more irretrievably than yesterday's cult figure. Sartre himself noted that *'les bananes doivent se consommer sur place'* (bananas need to be eaten at the time) as a comment on fashions in theories and causes.
In many ways he resembles Bertrand Russell in that a distinguished writer and philosopher got mixed up in left-wing political causes. He participated with Russell in the War Crimes Tribunal in Stockholm at which the United States was put in the dock over Vietnam. He also refused the Nobel Prize that he was awarded in 1964. Although interned by the Germans early in the war he was released and led a tolerably comfortable life in Paris during the remainder of the war.
Having collaborated with Camus at the time of the Liberation he fell out with him when the latter renounced Marxism which Sartre described as *'le sommet indépassable de la pensée humaine'*. With the demise of most of the - isms that he espoused his reputation has suffered.
As a philosopher he was the high priest of existentialism. His major philosophical work, *Etre et Néant*, searches for the basis of existence and moral choice in a world that has rejected God. Existentialism as a philosophy is often seen as a reflection of the moral and spiritual disarray caused by two world wars. Every individual has absolute freedom *'condamné à être libre'*. His void, or *néant*, is the complex of circumstances into which an individual is born and in which he creates himself by his choices. Reconciling this highly individualistic view with his regard for Marxism tied him in philosophical knots.
As a writer Sartre was in the French tradition of producing enormous output, writing as much as ten thousand words a day, most of them in Montparnasse cafés. His book *Situations* ran to ten volumes. His reputation was still high enough in 1985 to make his autobiography a best-seller. Over two million copies of his books have been sold in France. All his works are on the Vatican list of banned books. Among his writings were plays such as *Huis Clos,* which brought him instant recognition when it was published in 1944.
Sartre was the life-long partner of Simone de Beauvoir although they were never married, this being too bourgeois a concept. He invented a highly useful distinction between necessary and contingent love - the philosophers' equivalent of having one's cake and eating it. 'Necessary love' was what he had for de Beauvoir and equates to most people's perception of marriage; 'contingent love' is what he felt for any other woman that took his eye and provided a convenient existentialist justification for a succession of mistresses. His necessary love for de Beauvoir did not survive his death at which he disinherited her in favour of a contingent mistress, Arlette Elkaim, who also became his literary executor.

Schools
Education is compulsory up to the age of sixteen and starts earlier than any other European country. 90% of three-year-olds attend nursery school. Control of the education system is still highly centralised compared to England. Teachers in State schools are civil servants and can in theory be posted anywhere in the country that the government chooses.
The so-called 'liberal' approach to education associated with the sixties in England largely passed the French by. Teaching methods are more formalised with greater emphasis on grammar, rote-learning of poetry, philosophy and deductive thinking. Teacher is still presumed to know best. This *dirigiste* attitude was

part of the cause of the '68 uprising and has begun slowly to give way to greater *dialogue* and self-expression. However, after being much scoffed at by English educational reformers the more structured French approach is coming back into fashion. A 1991 HM Inspectors' report on English teaching methods said 'French teachers provide a salutary reminder of a teaching method which many English teachers might reinstate for the benefit of their pupils'. It should, however, be pointed out that at the same time French educationalists are moving towards the British system. We could adopt theirs just as they adopt ours.

Compared to England there is little feeling of attachment between pupil and school. School is a teaching factory - a place to go to to get one's *bac.* There are no assemblies and few sports teams. Teachers are badly-paid, mostly left-wing politically but highly conservative about any changes that affect their own working lives. They have no obligation to be in school outside teaching hours which are typically eighteen to twenty up to *bac* and twelve thereafter.

Private (i.e. English public) schools exist but without the same status *snob* as in England. Almost universally private school means a Catholic school. About 14% of primary school pupils attend these and 21% of secondary. Staff salaries and some running costs are paid by the government. Hence fees are relatively low - around 4000 francs a year. Pupils are perceived as getting a more disciplined education.

In 1984, under pressure from the left-wing teachers' union, the Mitterrand government brought in a measure to bring such schools within the State system. Previously this would have raised all sort of State versus church hackles. Now it was more the prospect of having to pay increased fees that brought two million people onto the streets of Paris. The government was forced to back down and the minister involved to resign. In France it is the Education Ministry that is the 'bed of nails'. France has had 33 different Ministers of Education since the war.

French schools hold one world record - for the longest holidays. French schoolchildren on average go to school for only 158 days a year (compared to 200 in the UK). They partially compensate by working longer hours.

Sébastien, Patrick (b. 1953)

Téléstar who started as an impersonator and graduated to his own peak-time programme on Saturday evenings on TF1 - *Sébastien, c'est Fou* - a variety programme of satiric sketches, impersonations, interviewees baring their souls and dancers baring their breasts. Late in 1991 he became miffed at the success of former weatherman, Laurent Cabrol's *'voyeuristique'* programme on Antenne 2 at the same time spot and announced his intention of giving up regular appearances on TV.

Service National

Every male has to do his national service at some time between the ages of 18 and 26. This universality is more to do with *égalité* than efficiency, character-building than military preparedness. There are different ways in which it can be done and these attract different lengths of time.

The standard option is to go into the armed forces, though one can as an alternative go into the police or the fire brigade. For any of these you stay in for ten months, posted away from your home region.

If you have a skill that allows you to go in as a doctor, dentist or in some other profession, then you stay in twelve months as they can find more use for you.

If you opt for the *aide technique* your period is of sixteen months. If you are a conscientious objector and choose community service the authorities have no objection on their part; they just double the length of time to twenty months.

Sex

This is the most difficult area in which to undertake research. To resolve the question of whether the French are bad drivers one can have recourse to statistics. But what about lovers? Are the stereotypes of better lovers and more sexy women true? Or true in the *grandes villes* but not in the country?

At a time when Paris was renowned for being naughty *la France profonde* was among the stricter societies. In recent years there has been a regression to the norm. Technology, whether in the form of the media encouraging you to do it, or the pill, enabling you to do it, has diminished the gap between permissive Paris and puritanical provinces. So what is the current situation? Perhaps it is easier to start from the stereotypes and examine how accurate they are:

- **French men are more direct.**
  The language can give us a clue here. The verb *draguer* (literally 'to dredge') means to try to pick someone up. In this sense it is very *courant*, as is its equivalent noun, *dragueur**. Thus a linguistic approach would suggest that Frenchmen are more assiduous in their pursuit of the opposite sex. Personal evidence, or to be precise, that of my family, suggests that French men are more direct if they do not know you and, if they do, nurse higher expectations than an Englishman's after an evening out with a girl.

- **Mistresses are an accepted part of life.**
  This may possibly be true among a certain *beau monde* in Paris though even there the acceptance is probably more of the world at large than the wife back home. But an area where there is undoubtedly greater tolerance is in public life. The recurrent sex scandals in Britain involving ministerial resignations, or America necessitating demonstrations of connubial bliss, are a source of mystery and amusement to the French. When Giscard's car bumped into some milk crates on the way back to the Elysée at three in the morning it was widely assumed that he had been discussing Central African affairs with an *experte*. It is no part of this book to speculate on whether the current President has mistresses. If he does then no-one is going to get worked up about it - *c'est normal.* But, with these exceptions, mistresses are as *clandestines* as anywhere else. A survey in *Le Nouvel Observateur* in 1988 showed that 69% of the French had had only one sexual partner in the preceding twelve months. Of those who had strayed at any time 4% regretted having been unfaithful to their spouse. However, the level of regret (at *not* having strayed) was twice as high among those who had stayed *fidèles*.

  To the extent that all such opinions and statements are symptomatic of one rule for men and one for women they are gradually going out of fashion. The move is towards greater sexual equality.

- **Frenchmen are better lovers.**
  Qualitative statements are always the most difficult to verify or disprove. Quantitatively, one survey revealed that 7% had sex every day, also that 43% of men (but only 23% of women) wished they had it more often. Whether any of the 7% were also included in the 43% was not made clear.

What are the implications of these attitudes for readers anxious to take to heart my message of getting to know the natives ?

On this topic a 1991 survey in Paris Match is both illuminating and directive. When men were given a list and asked 'With which of the following would you like to have a holiday romance?', 51% answered 'A young tourist *who cannot speak French* (my italics)' Exactly why the italicised qualification was made remains a mystery - a tourist who could speak French was not on the list of possible responses.

For men, the best bet is to teach windsurfing. 39% of women placed this top of their list. This is slightly difficult to reconcile with a different poll in which women said they were more attracted by a man's library than by his suntan. Perhaps the secret is to be a well-read surfer.

If you are successful as a *dragueur* then you can look forward to a novel experience. In response to 'Where you would most like to make love?' 75% of women chose 'On the beach at night', but an enterprising 14% were unable to wait for the instructor to get off his windsurfer and an even more athletic 17% nominated the *pédalos*.

One final question was based on that posed by George Bernard Shaw to a lady next to him at dinner 'Would you go to bed with me for a million pounds?' The going

* *The female equivalent,* dragueuse, *is not used. Women do not* draguer, *they have to* trainer dans les rues *and hope to be* dragué.

rate for French men and women is (percentages shown are cumulative):

For what amount of money would you be prepared to go to bed with someone for whom you had no attraction?

	Men	Women
10,000F	17	2
50,000F	20	5
100,000F	25	6
1 million F	27	8
5 million F	54	37
Never	42	59
Don't Know	4	4

SIDA
The transposition of letters caused by adjectives following nouns masks the French for AIDS. It was a French virologist, Luc Montagnier, who led a team of researchers at the Pasteur Institute which in 1983 discovered the AIDS virus, although it took eight years for his American counterpart to acknowledge his primacy.
The number of people with AIDS in France, 6 per 100,000 is higher than in most other European countries although this figure could in part be due to an earlier start on screening. There is also a scandal arising from the government's refusal in 1985, on cost grounds, to allow hospitals to boil donated blood prior to transfusions. This led to hundreds of cases in which haemophiliacs were unnecessarily infected with the virus. The massive costs of indemnifying such cases is being controversially met by a levy on all types of private insurance.

Simenon, Georges (1903-1989)
Belgian-born Simenon claimed to have made love to over 10,000 different women in his life. Since most of these were commercial transactions this has failed to earn him a place in the Guinness Book of Records. Nor was David Frost present to verify them. Between times he wrote a lot of non-sex-obsessed novels about Inspector Maigret. If you want to improve your French by reading something that is easy to understand, non-intellectual ('I do not think out my characters, I feel them'), reminds you of French bars and has a good story, these are excellent.

Sinclair, Anne (b. 1948)
Popular *télé-star* of *'Sept sur Sept'*, a weekly programme on Sunday evenings on TF1 in which she interviews international politicians and statesmen and also Prince Charles (the programme was watched by eight million viewers). Her smiling style is more Sue Lawley than Robin Day and she is reputed to be Mitterrand's favourite interviewer. This could be because of her presumed political sympathies an indication of which is her marriage in 1991 to the Minister of External Commerce, Dominique Strauss-Kahn. The ceremony was wedged in between interviews with Gorbachev and Jacques Delors. Born in New York of Jewish parents who had fled Germany, she decided at the age of ten to become a journalist. In a 1989 poll France's mayors chose her as Marianne, the symbol of the Republic.

Ski-ing
16% of all French people are *pratiquants*. Which means that, like hunting, it is not the province of one social class. You cannot consider yourself an all-round Frenchman unless you have made some attempt at ski-ing. If you consider yourself past the age of hurtling down black *pistes*, then

strap on some *skis de fond* and set off across country. Whatever you do, absent yourself from the 'Hooray Henry' brigade - the upper class's answer to lager louts. Unless, that is, you prefer to have your coffee served with milk in it and drink in English-only bars. There are plenty of good, lesser-known resorts where ski-ing is still more important than *après-ski.*
If you are under thirty you should not be ski-ing in any case but snowboarding (or, to give it its French name, surfing). Not least because you get a younger instructor. If you are over thirty be sure to bring your four-year-old child and teach it to whizz between the legs of other skiers queuing at the lifts.

SMIC

The *Salaire Minimum Interprofessionel de Croissance* i.e. minimum wage legislated by the government. Originally called SMIG (G for *'garanti')* it was introduced in the fifties and linked to the retail price index. In the sixties this caused it to fall behind salaries which had risen faster than prices and it was changed to SMIC and tied to both prices and salaries. People earning the SMIC, typically in low-paid professions such as textiles, hotels and cafes, are referred to as *smicards.* In 1990 they numbered two million, with women 2.5 times more numerous than men. The rate for SMIC has just passed the level of 5000 francs a month.

Smoking

Dieu est un fumeur de gitanes, according to a line in a Gainsbourg song. How true this is I have no way of verifying but of His French subjects 45% of men and 28% of women are smokers. Perhaps helped by the fact that cigarettes are half the price that they are in England. Interdiction of smoking in public places is less widespread than in the UK possibly since it goes against the the smokers' view of *liberté* .
The tobacco industry was the first to be nationalised - by Louis XIV. Successive rulers have seen no reason to pass up this easy source of income (200 million francs in 1990). The money thus raised for the government goes some way towards meeting the hospitalisation costs caused by the habit which contributes to the death of 65,000 a year. Lung cancer is statistically the greatest cause of death in men.
'Le smoking' is a well-known *faux ami;* it means a 'dinner jacket'.

Socialist Party

The *Parti Socialiste (PS)* came into being formally in 1905 as the *Section Française de l'International Ouvrière.* In 1920 disagreement over Lenin's policies caused a split whence originated the Communist Party. Ever since, the PS has been bedevilled by the existence of a Communist Party able to gain up to 20% of the popular vote. In the inter-war years this meant that the only way of gaining power was in a disastrous coalition as with the Patriotic Front. One of Mitterrand's greatest services to his party has been to marginalise the Communists.
With the exception of the period of cohabitation - 1986-1988 - the Socialists have been in power since 1981 although for all but the first two years in a minority and relying on Communist support. Despite jettisoning most of their ideological baggage in a manner not unreminiscent of the British Labour party, their disastrous performance in the 1992 regional elections, in which their vote dropped below 20%, suggests that they are heading for defeat in the elections for the *Assemblée* in 1993.

Sondages

With almost 600 opinion polls published every year, not counting statistics from government bodies, the French are compulsive contemplaters of their own navels. Indeed this concept has its own noun, *nombrilism,* from *nombril* meaning 'navel'. Every two years a compilation and analysis of such polls and official statistics, is published in an invaluable book entitled *Francoscopie* - invaluable to writers of books on France, that is.

Sorbonne

Founded in the thirteenth century, the Sorbonne is the oldest and most highly reputed of French universities. Situated on the *rive gauche* in Paris, it has now lost much of its former glory largely through the rival attractions of the *Grandes Ecoles.*

SOS-Racisme

Organisation founded to combat the growth of racist sentiment. Whereas Le Pen would prefer to send all the foreigners - at least the non-Europeans - back whence they came, *SOS-Racisme* wants to integrate them into society. Its leader, Harlem Désir, a West Indian, is a frequent talking head in the media. The organisation adopted an anti-war stance in the Gulf crisis which lost it a lot of support including that of Patrick Bruel.

Space
As we have seen, the French love hi-tech and there is none higher than sending things into space. They are the most dynamic member of the European Space Agency whose satellites are launched using the French-based Ariane rocket, from French Guyana. Its first commercial launch was in 1983 since when there have been another thirty, with thirty more satellites currently waiting in the queue.

Stendhal (1783-1842)
A writer who was not appreciated in his lifetime. Confirming his own opinion that he was before his time, his reputation has increased in recent years with the appearance of his complete works and the publication in English of his private diaries. His best-known works are *Le Rouge et Le Noir,* a torrid tale of sex and religion under the Restoration and *La Chartreuse de Parme.* The latter was written in seven weeks. Both are based on real-life incidents which Stendhal uses to explore human emotions. His theory of falling in love - *la crystallisation,* based on extensive personal research - is set out in *'De l'Amour'.*

Strasbourg
This delightful city of 250,000 inhabitants, famous for its *saucisses,* is the seat of the European Parliament. Since the Commission is in Brussels, it would save a lot of travel and movement of documents if the Parliament were also there. But the chances of the French agreeing to this are not thought to be very high or at least not without some trade-off of monumental proportions.
The city has a magnificent 13th century cathedral with a famous *horloge astronomique* showing the movement of the planets as well as the time. On its completion its builder was blinded so that he would not be able to recreate a similar artefact anywhere else.

Street Names
In England you do not run across many streets named after politicians or dates. The occasional Mandela Crescent or Guevara Close in Southwark but Thatcher Terraces, Callaghan Crescents or Attlee Arcades are not thick on the ground. In France, *par contre,* you everywhere meet streets named after various famous historical personages and events as well as writers. To help you recognise those which have not warranted a separate entry in this book here is a list of the most common:

Apollinaire, Guillaume (1880-1919): Trendy poet and playwright, associate of Picasso and the Cubists. Arrested briefly in 1911 on suspicion of stealing the Mona Lisa.

Briand, Aristide (1862-1932): Socialist Prime Minister eleven separate times during the inter-war period. A strong supporter of the League of Nations he gave his name to the Kellogg-Briand pact which was highly successful in outlawing war.

Fabré d'Eglantine (1750-1794): Revolutionary, supporter of Danton whom he accompanied to the guillotine.

France, Anatole (1844-1924): Writer who gained the Nobel Prize for Literature in 1921. The Dreyfus case politicised him and he became an outspoken opponent of both church and state.

Gay-Lussac, Louis (1778-1850): Physicist and chemist who had sufficient self-belief in his works on gases to break the then world record for ballooning, ascending to 7000m in 1804.

Gautier, Théophile (1811-1872): 19th century poet, novelist and critic.

Joffre, Joseph (1852-1931) : Commander-in-Chief of the French armies at the start of the First World War.

Kléber, Jean-Baptiste (1753-1800)
Commander of Napoleon's army in Egypt and subsequently governer there. Assassinated by a mameluke.

MacMahon, Patrice (1808-1893): Monarchist President of Third Republic who suppressed the Paris Commune.

Mallarmé, Stéphane (1842-1898): Poet, leader of Symbolists. Wrote *L'après-midi d'un faune,* illustrated by Manet, set to music by Débussy.

Merimée, Prosper (1803-1870): Erudite writer of historical fiction, practical joker and friend of Napoleon III. He wrote Carmen which Bizet turned into opera.

Poincaré, Raymond(1860-1934): President 1913-20; He was the first ex-President to become prime minister which he was at various times in the twenties. An ardent nationalist.

Rue du:

8 mai:	VE Day in 1945
18 juin:	De Gaulle's broadcast from London in 1940 calling on Frenchmen to continue fighting.
29 juillet:	Revolution of 1830 which overthrew Charles X
25 août:	Surrender of Paris by the Germans in 1944
4 septembre :	Start of Third Republic in 1870.
11 novembre:	Armistice Day, 1918; the German surrender was signed in a railway carriage at Compiègne, north of Paris.

Saint-Exupéry (1900-1944): Pilot, lost in action, who wrote highly popular novels such as *Vol de Nuit* based on his experiences of flying. His remains were recently found on the battlefield. A delightful non-flying book to read is *Le Petit Prince.*

Stalingrad: One of many names commemorating famous battles and also evidencing the French erstwhile communist sympathies. There are also quite a few *rues Lénin.*

Thiers, Adolphe (1797-1877): First, conservative President of Third Republic turned historian.

Supreme Being

'If God did not exist it would be necessary to invent him'. Thus wrote Voltaire in the early 18th century. Eighty years later he was proved right. Robespierre invented the Supreme Being to replace Christianity without descending into atheism. A *fête* was hurriedly organised in the Tuileries and people sang the 'Hymn to the Supreme Being'. The cult did not outlast its creator.

Syndicat d'Initiative

Extremely useful source of local information for tourists on sights, walks, places to visit, accommodation. For those wishing to locate a particular *Syndicat* for information in advance of going to France, the *Fédération Nationale* is at 2, rue de Linois, 75015 Paris. Between them the 3273 Syndicats publish fifty million documents a year so somewhere in there is something for you.

T

Talleyrand, Charles Maurice de (1754-1838)
An ecclesiast in direct line of the Vicar of Bray as he switched sides with bewildering ease throughout his life. As Bishop of Autun he was elected to the Assembly at the start of the Revolution and sided with the revolutionaries. He sensibly exiled himself to the United States from 1792-96 after the execution of the king returning to become Foreign Minister during the Directory, Consulate and First Empire. He fell out with Napoleon but returned with the Restoration of Louis XVIII to play an important part in the Congress of Vienna in 1815. Having subsequently become disillusioned with the policies of Charles X he gave his support to Louis-Philippe and was rewarded by being appointed Ambassador to England in 1830. He returned to the church on his deathbed.
He was known as *'le Diable Boiteux'* (limping devil) on account of being both a cripple and a skillful politician.

Tapie, Bernard (b. 1943)
Self-made immensely wealthy businessman - at last estimate reckoned to be worth £850 million - owner of Adidas. He combines membership of the Socialist Party (he did well against Le Pen in the 1992 regional elections) with free-market business policies. He has devoted a large part of his personal fortune (unsuccessfully at time of writing) to making his football team, *l'Olympique Marseille*, champions of Europe. Both of these traits may recall a certain deceased publishing tycoon but there is no apparent reason to suspect that he shares others of that person's propensities. Originating from a response to a challenge made on a TV show, *Le Jeu de la Vérité*, he has also set up four schools dedicated to helping the unemployed become salespersons. In April 1992 he became Minister for Urban Affairs in the Bérégovoy government.

Tati, Jacques (1907-1982)
Actor and film-maker best-known for *Mon Oncle* and *Les Vacances de Monsieur Hulot.*

Tax
The tax system places less emphasis on income tax (although the highest marginal rate is 57%) and more on indirect taxes, notably VAT - or TVA as it is in France. A variable rate VAT is levied - the standard rate is 18.6% with a lower rate for some essentials and a higher one for luxury goods. To the extent that indirect taxes predominate, the tax system is more regressive than in the UK.
Secondly, it treats the funding of the social security system - requiring almost as much as all other government expenditure put together - as a separate issue. Employers' contributions fund approximately half of the £ hundred billion raised. With increasing demand for health care, an ageing population and growing unemployment, funding social security is as big a headache to French politicians as to British - as intractable a problem to Socialists as it is to Conservatives. The emphasis on indirect taxes and on company-based taxes may be connected with the Latin sport of tax evasion. Less than 25% of French businessmen and artisans file a tax return. Under the so-called *régime forfaitaire*, they supply information of sales, purchases, inventory and wage costs upon which semi-fictional account the authorities decide what was their likely income and consequently their liability for tax. If, as is extremely seldom the case, the taxpayer thinks that he has been over-taxed, he has the right of appeal.

Telephone
France Télécom is another example of French technological efficiency. Having invested £50 billion between 1975 and 1990, it claims the world's most digitised switching system with 75% of lines now operating in this enhanced style. Following the success of Minitel, *Télécom* plans to begin installing video phones. The first two hundred, costing around £4000 each, will be available for business use in 1993. With economies of scale the price should drop to an estimated £600 and the service will be extended to home users in 1995.
Bills are itemised (essential if you let your *résidence secondaire* or leave it to the kids) and installation and maintenance of equipment leaves British Telecom in its wake.

All French telephone numbers consist of 8 digits, split into four sets of two. Paris is the exception; to dial Paris from outside you have to prefix the number with 16 plus the Paris sub-exchange; to ring out from Paris you prefix numbers with 16 only. The first two digits tell you the subscribers' region.

Television

For a country that so prides itself on its culture, television is the biggest disappointment to a British viewer. Until TF1 was privatised, all the major channels were government-controlled and their documentary and news output reflected this.

The highspot of evening viewing on all channels is the feature film that commences around 8.30 and lasts till after ten. All channels carry advertisements (*'la publicité* or *'pub'* for short).

TF1 is by far the leading channel with almost double the audience (44%) of its nearest rival, Antenne 2. There were fears that privatisation would lead to a decline in standards (perhaps not displaced since Robert Maxwell was one of the original share-holders) but apart from the introduction of mindless game shows and soaps this appears to have been unfounded.

Antenne 2 and FR3 *(France Régional)* are still State-owned - *la chaîne publique* - and are run by the same management. FR3 attempts to be more intellectual (for example, it is there that you can see Benny Hill) and more regional.

La Cinq is third in audience ratings with around 12% of the viewing audience. However this has not been sufficient to keep it free of financial problems and 80% of its seven hundred staff were made redundant late in 1991. It may shortly be rescued in some form of buy-out by a rival chain.

M6, which originated in 1987, mainly offers dubbed American series. It has little sport other than *le sport de la chambre.*

Canal-Plus is the pay channel - currently F160 a month - for which you need a *décodeur.* It has cornered many of the top sporting events, notably in football and shows more recent films than its competitors. It also features late-night movies that would render Mrs Whitehouse apoplectic. As a result it has attracted 3.1 million subscribers.

Thanks to the wonders of satellites, keen francophiles can watch French television in the UK. A satellite dish and converter costs upwards of £350 to install.

Tennis

The French are enthusiastic about tennis as befits the winners of the 1991 Davis Cup in which their *tennismen* defeated the odds-on American team amid scenes of immense patriotic fervour in Lyon. The victory, the first since winning the tournament six times in succession from 1927-32, was a triumph for the captaincy of Yannick Noah, both in motivational terms and in his inspired recall of Henri Leconte (inset) from the dead. The latter had always been firmly in the general British sporting tradition of losing magnificently (as opposed to the specific tennis tradition which is of just losing). On this occasion, ranked 160th in the world and recovering from a back operation five months before, he inspired the French team to unsurpassed heights. Alas, the triumph was as short-lived as it was intense. France was defeated 3-2 by Switzerland in the quarter-finals of the 1992 Cup.

The French Open, held at Roland Garros in Paris, is part of the Grand Slam. Current No 1 male is Guy Forget; Nathalie Tauziat, the leading woman player also achieves seeding status at Wimbledon.

At the level of a pastime, tennis has lost its place as purely a rich person's sport to golf and with almost 1.5 million *pratiquants* in 10,000 clubs it has grown twenty-fold in the last two decades. France lays claim to having invented the game. It was, after all, tennis balls that the Dauphin offered Henry V as an alternative to his claims on various French dukedoms.

Terrorism

France has a highly creditable tradition of political asylum arising out of its historical commitment to the rights of man. It shelters an estimated 200,000 refugees from political oppression. The most famous of these was Ayatollah Khomeini who lived in Paris before returning to head the Iranian Revolution. Far from this earning any protection against Arab terrorism, a bombing campaign by suspected Islamic groups in

1986 caused thirteen deaths. Exiles from the Iran regime, such as the former Prime Minister, Chapour Baktiar, have been relentlessly pursued and assassinated.
French hostages were also taken in the Middle East although these usually seemed to obtain their release just before elections. After one particularly blatant swap the *Association des Juges d'Instruction* issued a statement condemning it as 'spitting in the face of their victims and the rule of law'.

TGV
Le Train à Grande Vitesse - a magnificent train by which, under normal circumstances, you can set your watch. It is a classic example of French engineering genius backed up by centralised state planning. The first line between Paris and Lyon was opened in 1981 reducing the 500 Km trip to a mere two hours. It is now the established method of transport between the two cities, to the detriment of airlines flying the route.
In service the TGV achieves speeds in excess of 250kph although the sensation of speed is only noticeable if you can talk your way into the cockpit. In August 1990 it set the world record of 515 kph. A totally new line was constructed between Paris and Lyon for the TGV. In order not to have to construct too many tunnels, cuttings and embankments, the train had to be capable of tackling slopes of 35:1000. The effect of this is that when a *TGV Double* with a length of 400m is taking the highest incline, the front of the train is 14 metres higher than the back.

In 1990 a new line joined Paris to Bordeaux. Between them the two lines carried 22 million pasengers in 1990 with a load factor of 75%. The link between Paris and the Tunnel, in marked contrast to British Rail, will be ready in time for the opening. In another contrast, towns in Northern France were begging to have the line routed through them in view of the economic benefits it will bring to one of France's economically depressed areas.
However it is a different story when it comes to extending the line through Provence in order to cut the Paris-Marseille journey time to three hours. Now the local farmers put up the sort of opposition with which English importers of lamb are familiar. *Ça reste à voir* whether centralised planning will overcome local barricades. Normally in France the planners win this sort of confrontation but *agriculteurs* are not the easiest opposition with which to tangle.
The TGV is also a commercial success with a profit of 20 million francs a year. It has been sold abroad, most notably for the Houston-Dallas-San Antonio line in the States. In 1991 the TGV network was of 700 km; the plan is to extend this to 4,700. As a country France invests 0.66% of its GNP in its railways, compared to only 0.14% in the UK.
As a footnote, do not be fooled by the terminology of trains in France which exhibits the normal tendency towards exaggeration. Although *un express* is faster than *un omnibus* which stops at all stations, it is still not as fast as its name suggests. A fast train is *un rapide,* which in turn is slower than the TGV.

Tintin
Weekly comic strip founded in 1929. Tintin is a reporter on *'Le Petit Vingtième',* always accompanied by his fox-terrier, Milou (Snowy). The cast includes characters such as Captain Haddock and Professor Tournesol ('Calculus' in the English version).

© Hergé/Casterman

It has been translated into more than forty languages. Created by M. Hergé, a Belgian, it has total annual sales of 130 million of which 85 million are published in French.

Tocqueville, Alexis-Henri-Charles-Maurice Clérel, Comte de (1805-1859)
Historian of high reputation. He is the author of *La Démocratie en Amérique* in which his study of the American political system led him to the belief in democratic principles and equality as the best safeguard against tyranny. Yet another in the line of writer turned politician he was Foreign Minister for four months in 1849 but disliking the authoritarianism of

Napoleon III he retired to his estates where he wrote his classic book *'L'Ancien Régime et la Révolution'*.

Toulouse

Chef-lieu of the *région*, Midi-Pyrénées, on the Garonne river 679 Km south of Paris, with 350,000 inhabitants. Capital of the Visigoth empire, then of Aquitaine it suffered during the crusades against the Cathars. It became part of France in 1271. Now it is known for its beauty - it is referred to as *la ville rose* - and as the home of Aerospace Industries, the European consortium which produces the Airbus.

Toulouse-Lautrec (1864-1901)

Stumpy, bearded artist, *habitué* and artistic chronicler of the Moulin Rouge and other bars, cafés and brothels in Montmartre, which he did with both paintings and posters.

His stature was partially the result of centuries of in-breeding in the aristocratic milieu from which he came. Unlike many painters he had commercial success during his life as he was able to pay for meals by a quick sketch of barmaids, prostitutes or their clients. It is uncertain whether the drink or syphilis got to him first. He originated from Albi where a museum displays many of his paintings.

Tour de France

Cycle race round France usually staged in July. Originating in 1903, the route of some 4000 Km changes each year but always encompasses lung-bursting mountain climbs through the Pyrenees and Alps and finishes on the *Champs Elysées*. In recent years a tradition has grown up of including one stage in an adjoining country. In 1992, in recognition of the abolition of barriers within the EEC, seven countries will be visited. The effect of this on the route through France has been to reduce the mountain climbs drastically. In 1967 Tommy Simpson, a British competitor, died during such a stage. Greg Le Mond, winner in 1989 and 1990, virtually forfeited the 1991 tour in one *étape* in the Pyrenees where he lost 15 minutes.

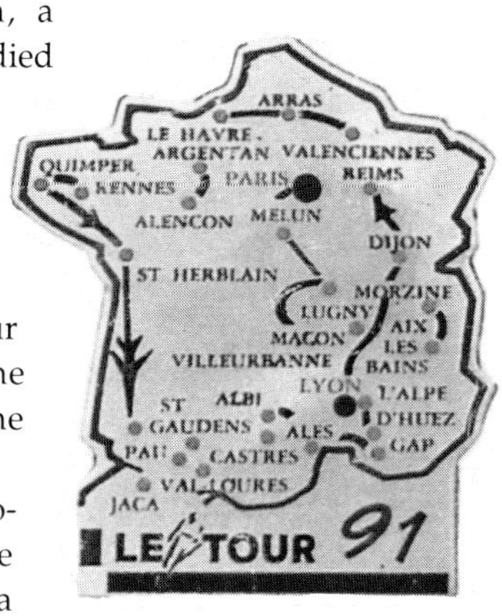

Twenty million people stop work to line the route (causing a blip in the GDP) and world-wide coverage makes it one of the top three international sporting events in terms of audience. Everything happens 'on the run' including eating, drinking and calls of nature (which must be taken outside of town limits).

Three people have won the race on five occasions, Jacques Anquetil (one of those people to whose name the adjective 'legendary' is always attached), Eddy Merckx and Bernard Hinault. Merckx holds the record for most stages won (34) and for wearing the leader's *maillot jaune* the most times (96 days). In the past the winner tended to be a Frenchman but latterly Americans, Belgians (of whom Merckx is one) and Spaniards are beating the French on their own ground.

Tourisme

France is the first country in Europe, second in the world, for tourism. Income from tourism during the bicentenary year exceeded F40,000 million. Having been overtaken in 1984 by Spain as the main overseas destination for British holidaymakers it reasserted its premier position in 1989 and has pulled further ahead since then. 28% of British people have at some time visited France. At the same time only 13% of the French went abroad for their holidays, a much lower percentage than most other countries. But then if you have the good fortune to live in France who needs to go elsewhere?

Trades Unions

Fortunately for the size of the national economic cake, but possibly not its division, unions are weak. Between 1981 and 1989 union membership dropped from 28% to 14% (the 1987 figure for UK was 43%). Only 15% of men now belong to unions and 7% of women.

There are three main unions: the CGT *(Confédération Général du Travail)* is controlled by the Communist Party and has just under a million members. Slightly behind it in membership is the CFDT *(Confédération Française Démocratique du Travail)* which is the most radical. *Force Ouvrière* (FO) has about half a million members, mostly among white-collar workers. It is more moderate.

Historically unions are organised by industry rather than trade, thereby reducing demarcation disputes. Apart from air-traffic controllers and other public sector groups, they are virtually quiescent. Every so often they will remember their heritage and stage an enormous one-day stoppage.

Troisième Age

The expression for people of retirement age. Before that you are not of the *'deuxième âge'*, but *'d'un certain âge'*. Retirement at sixty is the same for both sexes and the retired currently account for 20% of the population. Pensions are more generous than in the UK and are financed by both the person's own contributions during his or her lifetime and from the contributions of the current workforce. As in the UK increased longevity, allied to a declining workforce, will, in future years, mean a shrinking number of contributors supporting an ever larger number of beneficiaries.

Pensions are earnings-related and calculated by applying a figure - varying from 50% to 70% - to the best ten years' gross earnings before retirement, subject to a minimum of 37.5 years of contributions. This is frequently supplemented by private schemes so that many pensioners are better off than when they were working. Statistically, the income of retired people is higher than the national average.

Truffles

Truffles are one of the world's great culinary delicacies. That is to say that if you persevere long enough you will finally develop a taste for something that you cannot then afford. The current wholesale price is around 2300F a kilo. The romantic notion is that they are found in the Dordogne by trained pigs searching at random. The more prosaic probability is that they are either imported from Central Europe or farmed commercially in the Rhône Valley and Cévennes using dogs.

'Tu'* or *'vous'?

One of the areas for which your school French will only theoretically have equipped you is the vexed question of when to call someone *'tu' ('tutoyer')* or when to stick with *'vous' ('vousvoyer')*. At school you will have learned that all animals, including children, are *'tu'*. Also your superiors, in age or rank, are *'vous'*. *'Vous'* shows respect; *'tu'* shows familiarity. But there is a vast grey area in between. The first thing to realise is that the use of *'vous'* is in no way unfriendly. Nor is it automatically reciprocal. You should not necessarily switch to *'tu'* just because that is how someone is addressing you. At work you may *tutoie* someone when you are alone but *vousvoie* him in front of clients.

It is something about which it is almost impossible to generalise. One can say that young people *'tutoie'* much more readily than old; that country people are more formal than town; that French-speakers outside *l'héxagone* use *'tu'* more. But essentially it comes down to each individual. Quite close acquaintances may still address each other by surnames and use the *vous* form. Simone de Beauvoir addressed Sartre as *'vous'* throughout their relationship; Serge Gainsbourg *par contre, 'tutoie'd'* everyone.

U

Unemployment

Le chômage is as intractable a problem in France as elsewhere within the European Community. The government, as in the UK, occasionally changes the basis on which it is calculated (such that the total decreases) so that exact figures are difficult to compare. Nevertheless the increase in the last two decades is unarguable. In 1985 it breached the 10% mark and has remained around that figure since (approximately two and a half million). INSEE, the government statistics agency forecast three million by mid-1992 prompting Mme Cresson to introduce a series of measures remarkably akin to YTS.

A figure of 10% puts France among the highest rates in the European Community. Unemployment is worst among young people, women and immigrants. In 1990 18.9% of the under-25 age group were unemployed in France compared with 9.2% in the UK.

Union pour la Démocratie Française (UDF)

Non-gaullist political party of the centre right founded by Giscard d'Estaing in 1978. In British terms they would equate roughly with the left-wing of the Conservative party with a touch of liberal sentiment on personal freedom and responsibility, proportional representation and support for Europe. Not a mass party like the RPR, its members are mostly locally-established *notables.*

Universities

Noel Coward advised Mrs Worthington not to put her daughter on the stage. In France he may have changed that to university. The university system is by far the weakest part of the educational system. There are good reasons for making this statement:

- The *grandes écoles* cream off the top 10% of students.

- Universities do not offer their own degrees. All *diplômes* are (inevitably) centralised with the university merely being the issuing body.

- A university degree, with the possible exception of law and medecine, carries little weight. For it to become in any way comparable with the degree issued by a *grande école,* the student needs to stay on and complete a Masters.

- There is no selection. Anyone who has passed the *bac* has the automatic right to entry to university. Intake operates on a 'first come, first served' basis. The effect is that the selection process is postponed until the end of the first year when over 40% of students drop out. At a university such as Nanterre this figure rises to close to 70%. When the Chirac government attempted to give universities greater independence - to issue their own degrees, to select entrants - thousands of students poured onto the street in a knee-jerk reaction in favour of *égalite'* and the proposal had to be withdrawn. The French can be revolutionary even in defence of the status quo. A later opinion poll among students found a majority in favour of some form of selection similar to the English system.

- Only one in eight students receives a grant and then only a few thousand francs. In consequence most have to find work in order to finance themselves and live with their parents in order to reduce accommodation costs. This means that the vast majority of students attend the university nearest them.

- As with schools, there are few sports teams and little social activity. With the increasingly harsh economic climate, the pursuit of knowledge as an academic exercise, however laudable, has taken second place to the need to get a job. This has lead to an increase in popularity of another competitor to the conventional universities, the *Instituts Universitaires de Technologie,* set up in 1966. These *instituts,* with their emphasis on business courses, provide a popular recourse for students who have failed to get into the *Grandes Ecoles* and prefer a more vocational course to those offered by most universities. Alternatively the BTS *(Brevet de Technician Supérieur)* is a popular post-bac two-year vocational course in subjects such as marketing or tourism.

A world record held by French universities is for the number of foreign students. These, mostly from the Maghreb but with a sizeable minority from other EEC countries, South America and China, number over 120,000 or one in eight of the university population.

V

Valois
Dynasty of kings starting with Philippe VI in 1328 and coming to an end with the assassination of Henry III in 1589. It was followed by the Bourbons.

Van Gogh (1853-1890)
Depressive Dutchman who took up painting after being sacked as a an evangelist for an excess of religious zeal. He emigrated to Paris in 1885 and met up with the Impressionists and literary set. From there he went to Arles in Provence. Pissarro said of him 'I knew he would either go mad or surpass us all. But I did not know he would do both'.

In Provence his paintings showed the emphasis on colour that made him a precursor of the Fauves. His invitation to Gauguin to live with him turned into a disaster and he cut off his ear, as depicted above. Shortly before committing suicide he painted 'Portrait of Dr Gachet'. In 1990 the painting was sold in three minutes for the world record sum of $82.5 million.

Veil, Simone (b. 1927)
The first successful female politician, a liberal lawyer, appointed Minister of Health by Giscard. She quickly became his most popular minister mainly on account of having introduced legalised abortion (IVG) in 1975. She was subsequently President of the European Parliament from 1979-1981 and remains a *député*.

Vendanges
The season of grape-picking normally late September, early October. As with hop-picking in Kent technology has taken over so that groups of pickers from the Cevennes, or latterly from Spain, have given way to machines. Only the *petits viticulteurs* now pick their own grapes, taking them to the local *coopératif* for pressing, bottling and marketing.

Verdun
Historic ten-month siege during the First World War in which almost half a million Frenchmen and 400,000 Germans were killed. With Passchendaele and the Somme, it remains a monument to the disregard for casualties that infected military thinking in the war. At one stage the French troops mutinied and the experience of Verdun was partly responsible for the construction of the Maginot Line, meant to protect France from future invasion from the East.

Verlaine, Paul (1844-1896)
Poet who had unfortunate encounters with drink, Baudelaire and Rimbaud which lead him to becoming a mystic and writing decadent verse. In 1884 he had a success with the appropriately named *Poètes Maudits* (cursed). He was imprisoned twice, once for shooting at Rimbaud, once for beating up his mother, and died of alcoholism.

Verlan
Type of slang language, popular among the young, wherein the word is pronounced backwards or the syllables are reversed. *'Bouteille'* becomes *'teille-bout'*, *'moi'* sounds like *'wham'*, *'femme'* turns into *'meuf'*. An example which has passed into common use (and has been accepted by Larousse) is *'ripoux'* to mean corrupt police. It comes from a film entitled *'Les Ripoux'* which is *verlan* for *'pourris'*. *'Verlan'* is itself *'l'envers'* (meaning 'reverse') with its syllables transposed.

Verne, Jules (1828-1905)
Prolific author of adventure stories about imaginary trips starting with 'Five Weeks in a Balloon' and continuing with 'Round the World in 80 Days' and '20,000 Leagues under the Sea'. He is the appropriate hero of a travel film to be seen at Euro Disney.

Vercingétorix (72-46 BC)

The first French hero of the resistance - against Julius Caesar in the first century before Christ. France's answer to Boadicea, he defeated Caesar once but capitulated at Alésia in 52 B. C. and was carried back to Rome in triumph and executed after six years' captivity. His exploits form the inspiration for the Asterix comics.

Versailles, Château de

Egomaniacal edifice, devoid of both taste and utility, built to the glory of Louis XIV. Nevertheless *il faut le voir* and four million visitors take the trouble every year. At the height of its construction 36,000 men and 6,000 horses were employed and there was a plan to change the course of the river Eure to make it run through the gardens.

It was the capital of France for the hundred years preceding the Revolution. Symbolising, as it did, *la gloire,* it was chosen by Bismarck for the signing of the treaty ending the Franco-Prussian war. France's revenge came some years later with the punitive peace terms of the Treaty of Versailles at the end of the First World War.

Vichy

Chef-lieu of the *département* of Allier in the Auvergne. It was the seat of the collaborationist government during the Second World War. Now it is a Bath-like spa where retired people take the waters.

Villon, François (1431- c. 1463)

Mediaeval poet regarded by no less a critic than Bernard Levin as second only to Shakespeare as a poet. A close brush with the hangman led him to write the *Ballade des Pendus* and his total output amounts to little over 3,000 lines, written in less than seven years.

Voltaire (1694-1778)

A true Anglophile, resulting from his appreciation of our democratic institutions (by contemporary French standards) and religious tolerance. Having been thrown into the Bastille for writing lampoons against the aristocracy, he exiled himself and spent three years in England in the early seventeenth century from where he wrote his *'Lettres Philosophiques sur les Anglais'*. They have been called 'The first bomb thrown at the *ançien régime*' and had an explosive effect on the Paris of the 1730s. The book was proscribed and publicly burnt by the executioner in Paris.

When he came back to Paris he enjoyed the patronage of Madame de Pompadour. This saved him from further aggravation and was instrumental in his entry into the *Académie Française* to which he remains the only person to have been elected unanimously in a full ballot. He became immensely rich with a retinue of some sixty servants and twelve horses. His most famous work, *Candide,* was published after his return from a stay at the court of Frederick II of Prussia.

Voltaire is a sharp, witty and perceptive writer. An iconoclast whose war-cry *'Ecrasons l'infâme!'* was directed against any form of bigotry and intolerance but most particularly against the Catholic church and its priests. His contempt for authority and institutions paved the way for the Revolution. He remains one of the outstanding geniuses of European thought and literature.

Vosges

Very old chain of mountains in Alsace-Lorraine with distinctive tops worn away and rounded. Only one mountain is over 1400m, they are distinctive for their heavily-wooded slopes with pine trees up to 40m high and for the profusion of their lakes.

W

War Memorials

Every commune in France has its monument to those *'Morts pour la Patrie'*. On November 11th, the mayor and other dignitaries conduct a Cenotaph-style ceremony. Dotted around the hills of Savoy, Dauphiné and other areas of southern France are reminders of the Resistance. France lost a million and a half people killed in the first World War (compared with 900,000 British casualties). In the Second World War they lost 211,000, slightly less than the equivalent British figure.

Wealth

In the late eighties the top 1% of people accounted for 20% of private wealth; the bottom 10% for 0.1%. Senior managers spend 40% more than workers on food and drink and 200% more on leisure activities. The children of a senior manager will inherit on average £29,000 as against £500 for those of the working class. Not only that, they will grow more. On average a senior manager will be 5cm taller than a workman and 7cm taller than those stunted peasants you see in the Midi.

Despite having had a Socialist government for almost all the eighties and the early part of the nineties, inequalities of wealth and income are still high compared with most European countries. Wage differentials, roughly 7:1 between managing director and unskilled worker, are among the highest in Europe and lower taxes on property, and income advantage the better-off. The Socialists government introduced a Wealth Tax *(Impôt sur les Grandes Fortunes)* and then reintroduced it after its abolition by Chirac. This starts at quite a low level - £500,000 including the value of property - but with an initial rate of 0.5% rising to a top rate of 1.5% it is only for the seriously rich that the pips squeak. In 1989 it brought in £454 million.

Weather

English people are not unique in talking about the weather. It is a topic of universal interest and therefore one that you should bone up on. Your school French will hopefully get you as far as *'Il fait beau, aujourd'hui'* but you should use such a common topic as an area in which you can work to become fluent. There is, after all, only a relatively small number of things one can say about it. To master the vocabulary you have only to read a French newspaper. Words like *'maussade'* (literally, 'surly') will become familiar. If you have access to a television you should watch *la Météo* in order to accustom yourself to hearing the words as well as reading them. Use the *météo*, whether on radio, TV or in the paper, as a quick-returns way of improving your French. Do not, however, make the mistake of basing any plans on them. The connection between forecast and actual weather (except when *beau temps* is forecast) is often tenuous. *La météo* on television is not part of the news but part of the entertainment. Forecasts are illustrated with cartoons, children, frogs and other animals and weathermen become *téléstars*. The weather forecast typically gets a million more viewers than the news which it precedes or follows. France won the first International Meteorology Festival, a competition involving 25 presenters from 17 countries. The leading weatherman, Laurent Cabriol (inset), now has his own entertainment programme at peak time on Saturday evenings.

If your goal is to impress the natives you should make yourself familiar with local wisdom. *Le Mistral chasse les nuages* is the appropriate comment in the Rhône Valley to the arrival of the wind from the North (which, incidentally, is supposed never to blow for more than three days at a time). Another Rhône Valley view is that the weather changes at Valence. To espouse these views is to show yourself *dans le coup*. A common expression in the Midi is:

Noël au balcon; Pâques aux tisons
('Christmas on the balcony; Easter in front of the fire'; i.e if it is warm at Christmas you pay for it at Easter).

Wine

Le vin est la France, l'eau est la souffrance

France is second only to Italy in wine production and equal first in consumption. The first point to grasp is that French wine is superior to all other. It is perfectly safe to opine that 'Some Australian wines are very good these days', provided that it is said with that faint air of surprise that they come anywhere near the real stuff. Few Englishmen, reared on the produce of hops and barley rather than the grape, can really aspire to appreciate wine properly . But, given that, you need to be seen to have made monumental attempts to overcome the handicap of birth and to have acquired some appreciation of the real things in life. The French can do as they will - put their red wine in the refrigerator as my neighbours do (admittedly it is *pinard* - plonk - rather than a 1981 claret which is to be treated with greater respect), but you have to be like Caesar's wife, above suspicion.

It is essential to establish at the outset that you have the right attitude - a mixture of enthusiasm and discernment. Enthusiasm is easy; what is difficult is to cultivate the correct level of discernment. Particularly if, like me, you were shortchanged at birth on the tastebuds. In this situation you may have to resort to bluffing in order not to let the side down.

- Remember the saying : 'A glance at the label is worth a lifetime's experience'. If your host has served you a 1981 Nuits St George it's a pretty safe bet to praise it highly. Likewise if the local vineyard's *Vin de Pays* has won a prix at the *Mâcon Concours.*

- When in doubt, agree with your host. If he says, 'I was lucky enough to be given this by a *vigneron* in St Emilion as a present after buying four cases of wine' you are on safe ground in praising it to the skies. If he modestly says that the wine comes from a local *vignoble* but is worthy of regard, you should describe it as *'pas mal'.*

- If you are put on the spot and asked for your opinion of a wine, err on the side of praise, but not so far that you cannot modify it later (it may, unbeknown to you, be the first in a comparison exercise).

- If you are asked to compare two or more wines:

  - taste each wine at least twice, taking great care to go through the obligatory swirling and sniffing exercises for each and assuming an air of intense concentration. Whilst doing this, see if your host's body language gives you a clue. He may well, consciously or unconsciously, indicate a preference. In which case, choose that one.

  - take a long time to come to a conclusion. Pyschotherapists and salesmen both know the value of silence. If you can outlast your host he may give you the desired answer.

  - if all else fails, describe one of the wines as *'intéressant'.* This sounds discerning whilst being totally non-committal. You can upgrade this judgement to fulsome praise or downgrade it to a polite rejection depending on your host's reaction.

  - if your host fails to fall for any of these ploys and is still eagerly awaiting your opinion, then fall back on the 'My French is not up to it' ploy or use the half-sentence ploy, *'Je trouve que.....'* , trailing off and leaving him to finish it.

  - if everything fails, and you speak fluent French, choose both.

Footnote: If you go on a wine-tasting tour of *vignobles* be sure to carry a little *saucisson* with you. Popping a thin *tranche* in your mouth immediately before tasting will mark you out as someone not to be trifled with.

XYZ

Xs'

Entries for 'X' are hard to come by. But to ensure that each letter is represented I include an illustration of the badge of crossed canons that gives the *Ecole Polytechnique* its nickname of 'l'X'.

Archives de l'Ecole polytechnique

Yamgnane, Kofi (b. 1948)

Originally from Togoland, Yamgnane became mayor of Saint-Coulitz in Finistère, where he was so popular that he was voted Breton of the Year. A chance meeting with Mitterrand whilst out walking in the pine forests in the Landes (all 2300 sq Km of them) led to his becoming France's first black minister with responsibility for promoting better race relations.

Yves St Laurent (b. 1936)

Former head designer at Dior, then his successor. Since 1962 he has been head of his own fashion empire worth over £400 million on the Paris Bourse. Although in 1964 he posed nude in order to publicise his perfume 'Y', he is now largely reclusive and manages to be depressive and gay *en même temps*.

Yourcenar, Marguerite (1903-1987)

A writer of plays, novels and poems, she had the distinction of being the first woman to be admitted to the *Académie* (in 1980). Born in Brussels, she had become a naturalised American but had to change yet again as only people of French nationality can become *académiciens*.

Zola, Emile (1840-1902)

Another great help to compilers of dictionaries. A friend of Cézanne and Manet, he wrote a series of passionate books, such as *Germinal*, collected together as the Rougon-Macquart series, about the history of a family under the Second Empire which, as a socialist, he disapproved of. It was his famous newspaper article, *'J'accuse!'*, about the Dreyfus case which was influential in ultimately remedying this blatant miscarriage of justice. It earned Zola a prison sentence which he avoided by fleeing to England.

1. Abbreviations

2. Crossword Solution

3 Quotations

4. Glossary of French Words

5. Solutions to Word Games

6. *Et Avec Ça* (Further Reading)

7. Index

Abbreviations

RER	Réseau Express Régionale	Paris Rapid Transit System
RPR	Rassemblement pour la République	Rightist political party
HLM	Habitation à loyer modéré	Cheap rental housing
TGV	Train à Grande Vitesse	High-speed train
IVG	Interruption Volontaire de Grossesse	Legalised abortion
PC	Parti Communiste	Old-style communist party
IGF	Impôt sur les Grandes Fortunes	Wealth Tax
l'OM	l'Olympique de Marseille	Leading soccer club
VDQS	Vin Délimité de Qualité Supérieure	Wine classification between *Vin de Pays* and *Appellation Controlée*
MLF	Mouvement pour la Libération des Femmes	Women's Lib
ONU	Organisation des Nations Unies	United Nations Organisation
ENA	Ecole Nationale d'Administration	Finishing school for aspiring politicians and civil servants
PCV	PerCeVoir	Transfer-charge telephone call
EV	En Ville	By hand (letters not sent through the post)
CRS	Compagnie Républicaine de Sécurité	Riot police *(a. k. a. Cons Racistes et Salauds)*
EDF	Electricité de France	State-owned electricity company
CGT	Confédération Générale du Travail	Left-wing trade union
PPDA	Patrick, Poivre d'Arvor	Television celebrity
BCBG	Bon chic, bon genre	Sloane Ranger
BNP	Banque Nationale de Paris	Nationalised bank
SIDA	Syndrome d'Immunité Déficitaire Acquise	AIDS (Alternative interpretation given by the National Front to describe the Socialist Party - *Socialisme, Immigration, Drogues, Affairisme)*
TVA	Taxe sur la Valeur Ajoutée	VAT
SMIC	Salaire Minimum Interprofessional de Croissance	Statutory Minimum wage
PMU	Paris Mutuel Urbain	TOTE
SGDG	Sans Garanti de Gouvernement	An item whose quality is not assured by the government
VSOP	*Versez Sans Oublier Personne*	Pour without leaving anyone out

How French-wise are you?
Count 10 points for each correct answer from column 1 and 5 for each correct answer from Column 2. VSOP scores a bonus of 50.

Less than 40	There is life beyond Dover..
40-60	At least you've made a start..
60-80	*Pas mal....*
80-100	*Ça commence à venir...*
100-120	*Ça y est presque...*
120-140	You are a great French lover
140+	You have a great French lover

Crossword Solution

Sport Cérébral comes in various levels of difficulty indicated by stars. The one given below is *'3 Etoiles'* i.e. medium difficulty. As explained earlier, the advantage of this magazine over a crossword in a paper is that it gives you a complete list of all words used in the fifty or so crosswords in each issue. If you are solving crosswords in a foreign language you need all the help you can get! Let us work through the crossword employing:

- our knowledge of French endings
- our list of commonly-used words
- the list of words at the back of the magazine
- and a dash of logic...

If this is the first time you have attempted a French crossword you have probably already decided that it is impossible. You have no idea what *'Airelle canadienne'* (2 across) means, and if you did, you probably still would not know the answer. And you are not hot on Spanish poets either...

But stick with it. Don't be intimidated by the language. Let's look at the clues in order and see whether there are any words or letters that we can fill in.

Our first piece of luck is with 1 across. You don't need to be a *grosse-tête* to get that. All you need to know is that Liza Minelli starred in 'CABARET'. Incidentally this can give us another rule; the obvious answer is the right one 99% of the time. So we can fill in the top line.

Let us continue *horizontalement.*

'Airelle canadienne' means nothing to us.

'Marquera' is a third-person singular plural. Its synonym is almost certain to end with either *-era* or *-ira.* We can fill in the last two letters.

'Initiales du premier couple' It looks as though the compiler has been saddled with finding a clue for 'AE' and has had recourse to Adam and Eve to get him out of his difficulty.

'Paradis' (4) is always EDEN.

The rest of the across clues are a mystery, although *'Signal de départ'* could presumably be 'GO'.

So far the crossword looks like this:

Horizontalement
1 Film avec Liza Minelli.
2 Airelle canadienne.
3 Marquera.
4 Initiales du premier couple. Paradis.
5 Pensées.
6. Arbuste à fleurs blanches.
7. Signal de départ.
8. Relatif à l'os cubital.
9. Poète et romancier espagnol.

Verticalement
1. Répertoire.
2 Foyer. Récipients.
3. Pièce vestimentaire féminine. Romain. Neptunium.
4. Parviendrai à
5. Amiral allemand. Branché.
6. Brame. Monnaie scandinave.
7. Refroidi. Particule étrangère.

	1	2	3	4	5	6	7
1	*C*	*A*	*B*	*A*	*R*	*E*	*T*
2						■	
3						*R*	*A*
4	*A*	*E*	■	*E*	*D*	*E*	*N*
5		■					
6						■	
7			■		■		■
8							
9							

Now let's examine the vertical clues:

Répertoire' is a reverse *franglais* word. Given the C and A already filled in, it is obviously CATALOGUE. This also agrees with 'GO' for 7 across.

'Foyer' is a clue beloved of compilers as the solution has the type of letters they always need: ATRE.

Pièce vestimentaire feminine (3) could be 'BAS' (stocking) but this would make 3 across start with three consonants.

'Romain' indicates that the compiler has had to resort to Roman numerals to find a two-letter word. Usually it will be found to be 'II'. Trying this make 5 across *'Pensées'* begin with an 'I' - which sounds like IDEES. Put it in.

'Neptunium', according to our table of elements (following page), is NP.

'Parviendrai' is a first person singular future so that its synonym must end with *'rai'* - usually *'erai'* or *'irai'*. The latter makes 6 across impossible so we can fill in ERAI.

'Brame', from the list of common words (following page) is REE.

Our crossword now looks like this:

	1	2	3	4	5	6	7
1	C	A	B	A	R	E	T
2	A	T				■	
3	T	R				R	A
4	A	E	■	E	D	E	N
5	L	■	I	D	E	E	S
6	O			E		■	
7	G	O	■	R	■		■
8	U		N	A			
9	E		P	I			

Go back to words of which we now have some letters:

6 across must be OSIER. If necessary, we can check this against the list of words at the back of the book.

7 down can only have an 'r' as its second letter. The dictionary gives us *'transir'* as 'to pierce with cold' which looks to match with *'froid'*. *'Refroidi'* is a past participle, therefore the answer must be 'TRANSI'.

Now we are down to clues that we do not recognise. However we have sufficient letters of most of them to be able to consult the word list. For 2 across we find three five-letter words beginning with AT: ATELE, ATOCO, ATOLL. It cannot be 'atoll' because of 5 down. Our 'Micro Robert' dictionary does not list either of the other two. Let us have a look at 3 across - *'Marquera'*. When we consult the word list we find only TRACERA that fits with the existing letters. In English 'to mark' and 'to trace' have roughly the same meaning so we assume this is correct.

3 down has now to be either BEA or BOA. We recognise the latter as the feathery thing that women put round their necks. This reveals ATOCA to be the answer to 2 across (we are still none the wiser as to what it means). The 'German admiral' is now RAEDER which again we can verify in the word list.

The same word list gives us ULNAIRE and EXPINEL. The Scandinavian currency is ORE and Bob's your uncle.

	1	2	3	4	5	6	7
1	C	A	B	A	R	E	T
2	A	T	O	C	A	■	R
3	T	R	A	C	E	R	A
4	A	E	■	E	D	E	N
5	L	■	I	D	E	E	S
6	O	S	I	E	R	■	I
7	G	O	■	R	■	O	■
8	U	L	N	A	I	R	E
9	E	S	P	I	N	E	L

Common Clues

The following is a list of the most frequently found short answers with their most usual clues. In all cases where it applies, the singular masculine, or infinitive version is given. If an adjective is feminine, plural or both, you will need to add the appropriate 'Es' and/or 'Ss'. Thus *'choisi'* is given as *'élu'*; *'choisies'* would become 'élues'.

With verbs any of the persons or tenses could appear. Thus the list gives *'risquer'* but the actual clue could be third person plural conditional tense and the appropriate ending would have to be supplied by the solver.

Some entries are representative of a general class of clues. Thus *'Fin de journée'* is given as 'EE' but there is a number of semi-cryptic constructions which invite you to take a couple of letters from the beginning, middle or end of a word.

SGDG: *This list is advisory only and the author disclaims all liability for errors resulting from over-hasty inking-in of solutions.*

A la mode	IN
Article	LE/LA/LES
Auroch	URE
Baie de Japon	ISE
Bière	ALE
Champion	AS
Cheville de golf	TEE
Choisi	ELU
Chose Latine	RES
Cité Biblique	UR
Condition	SI
Conjonction	ET/OR
Connu	SU
Cours en Bulgare/Japon*	LEV/YEN
Coutumes	US
Cube	DE
Démonstratif	CA
Divinité Egyptienne	ISIS
Eclos/venu au monde	NE/ISSU
Ecole Supérieure	ENA
Existe/existes	EST/ES
Fin d'infinitif	ER/IR
Fin de Journée	EE
Fleuve de Russie	OB
Fleuve du Nord	AA
Groupe Nazi	SS
Lentille	ERS
Métal	OR
Negation	NE/NI
Note /Dans la gamme	UT
Paradis	EDEN
Paresseux	OI
Période	ERE
Possessif	** See footnote
Préfixe	ISO
Préposition	EN/ES
Prince de Troie	ENEE
Pronom	ME/TU/TE/IL
Réfléchi	SE
Rigolé	RI
Risquer	OSER
Roi d'Israel	ELI
Saison	ETE
Sur-Tille	IS
Troublé	EMU
Un étranger	EIN
Volcane	ETNA

* 'Cours en..' *signifies the currency of the country in question.*

** *If two-letters: ma/ta/sa*
If three-letters: mon/ton/son/mes/tes/ses
If four-letters: leur, mien, tien, sien

List of elements

Actinium	Ac	Molybdène	Mo
Aluminium	Al	Néon	Ne
Antimoine	Sb	Nickel	Ni
Argent	Ag	Niobium	Nb
Argon	Ar	Or	Au
Arsenic	As	Osmium	Os
Astate	At	Palladium	Pd
Baryum	Ba	Platine	Pt
Beryllium	Be	Plomb	Pb
Bismuth	Bi	Plutonium	Pu
Brome	Br	Polonium	Po
Cadmium	Cd	Radium	Ra
Calcium	Ca	Radon	Rn
Cérium	Ce	Rhénium	Re
Cesium	Cs	Rhodium	Rh
Chlore	Cl	Rubidium	Rb
Cobalt	Co	Ruthénium	Ru
Cuivre	Cu	Scandium	Sc
Erbium	Er	Sélénium	Se
Etain	Sn	Silicium	Si
Fer	Fe	Sodium	Na
Francium	Fr	Strontium	Sr
Gallium	Ga	Tantale	Ta
Germanium	Ge	Tellure	Te
Hafnium	Hf	Thallium	Tl
Hélium	He	Thulium	Tm
Indium	In	Titane	Ti
Iridium	Ir	Xénon	Xe
Lanthane	La	Ytterbium	Yb
Lithium	Li	Zinc	Zn
Magnésium	Mg	Zirconium	Zr
Manganèse	Mn		
Mercure	Hg		

Quotations
(from page 104)

Où sont les neiges d'antan? - Where are the snows of yesteryear?
Lament of hoteliers in ski resorts suffering from the greenhouse effect. Originally from Villon.

Paris vaut bien une messe - It's worth saying a Mass to get Paris.
Henry IV's comment on his politic second conversion to Catholicism in order to gain the acceptance of Paris and control of the throne. The actual words were more probably spoken by his Minister, Sully.

Le coeur a ses raisons que la raison ne connaît point
The heart has its reason that the heart does not know
One of Pascal's *Pensées*

Nous avons changé tout çela.
From Molière,'s *'Le Médecin Malgré Lui,'*, in which someone is accidentally taken to be a doctor. When, in the course of examining a patient, he looks for the heart and other vital organs in all the wrong places, he excuses himself by saying that 'All that's been changed'.

L'Etat, c'est moi - I am the State.
Louis XIV's definition of himself as the ultimate source of power and authority.

Après nous le déluge - After us all hell will break loose.
Attributed either to Madame de Pompadour or to Louis XV. Depending upon who is chosen it is quoted either as *'après nous'* or *'après moi'*.

Plus royaliste que le roi - more a royalist than the King himself
Quoted by Chateaubriand as originating under the reign of Louis XIV. Its full form starts with *'Il ne faut pas être ...'* i.e. it is a warning against the dangers of being too partisan in someone's cause.

Nous sommes ici par la volonté du peuple et nous n'en sortirons que par la force des baïonnettes
We are here by the will of the people and we shall come out only at the point of a bayonette
Mirabeau challenging the king's authority when the *tiers état* had holed themselves up in a tennis court and were in the process of forming the first democratic *Assemblée.*

Liberté, Egalité, Fraternité - Liberty, Equality, Fraternity
The rallying call of the Revolution. From the *Journal de Paris* in which everyone was invited to paint these words on his house. The original version had *'ou la mort'*, at the end but this was later dropped.

Plus ça change, plus c'est la même chose - the more things chamge, the more they stay the same.
Alphonse Karr

Cet animal est très méchant,
Quand on l'attaque il se défend
This animal is very dangerous; when you attack it, it defends itself.
P K Théodore, La Ménagerie, 1828

Rien ne dure comme le provisoire - nothing lasts as long as the temporary.
Anon, although Victor Hugo did say *'En France, le provisoire est éternel.*

L'enfer, c'est les autres - Hell is other people
Jean-Paul Sartre in misanthropic mood in *Huis Clos.*

Un pays qui compte 350 sortes de fromage, c'est ingouvernable
A country with 350 different varieties of cheese is ungovernable
General de Gaulle lamenting the problems of office.

Glossary of French Words used in Text

abreuver	to water, to feed
à part	except for
agrégation: nf	exam to become a teacher - at school or university
agriculteur	farmworker
allez-y!	Go! Imperative form of - er verb
ancien	adj. - 'former' if preceding the noun, 'old' if it follows
apéritif: nm	preprandial social drink
apprendre	learn or teach (whereas 'I learned him' is incorrect in English, 'Je l'ai appris' is OK; 'enseigner' is used for formal teaching)
arbitre: nm	referee
argot: nm	slang
arrêter	stop, arrest
arriver	arrive, happen
arrondissement nm	administrative subdivision of Paris
assez	quite, as in 'assez bien'; enough, as in 'assez de...'
assiette: nf	literally 'plate' - dans son assiette = feeling good
attendant	waiting for; present participle of -er verb
au contraire	on the contrary
auditeur: nm	listener (fem: auditrice)
aujourd'hui	today
aventure nf	adventure, often with sexual connotation
baguette nf	literally 'wand'; small loaf
baiser	as noun, a kiss. as verb, the 'f' word (N.B. not 'federal')
bandes déssinées	cartoon strips
beau monde	high society
beaucoup	much, a lot
bientôt	soon
bière: nf	beer
bis	twice; 'biscuit' = (twice cooked'), '12bis' = 12A (street number)
bises/bisous	kisses
bizarre	odd, curious
blague: nf	joke
boîte: nf	box (boîte de nuit - nightclub)
bordel: nm	brothel, mess
bouchon: nm	cork, hence also bottleneck or traffic jam
bouffer	eat (vulg)
bouger	move
bouillabaisse: nf	fish soup (originally a cheap peasants' dish made from fish left-overs, now including prawns so as to sell to tourists at an inflated price)
boulangerie: nf	baker's
boulot: nm	work (colloq)
branché	with it, street-wise, expert, switched on
bras dans les bras	arm in arm
ça reste à voir	that remains to be seen
ça y est!	that's it! You're there!
cahier: nm	notebook
camion: nm	lorry; suffix 'ette' is diminutive as in camionette, fillette
carreau: nm	diamond-shape. Also one of the suits in a pack of cards
carte bancaire: nf	cheque card
ceinture: nf	belt, as in safety belt
cela dit	that said
célibataire	unmarried person.
chef-lieu	county town
chevalier: nm	member of honorific order
chez	at the house of: widely used - go to the doctor: aller chez le médecin
chiffre: nm	number
cinéaste: nm	film-maker
clandestin	secret: used to describe illegal immigrants
clochard: nm	tramp
coeur: nm	heart
colon: nm	settler
compris	understood (past participle of comprendre)
concours: nm	competition
conseiller	advise (déconseiller = advise against)
copain, copine (f)	friend, sometimes more than...
coup, dans le	in the action
courant	literally 'running'; fluent when applied to languages
crise: nf	crisis
croissant	crescent-shaped, calorie-filled breakfast pastry
dame de fer	Iron Lady a.k.a. Mrs T
de rigueur	necessary by convention;
politique de r.	deflation, belt-tightening

débarrasser, se (de)	get rid of
débrouiller (se)	sort out
débutant(e)	beginner
dégager	disengage, go away (vulg)
dégeler	melt, unfreeze
délation: nf	denounciation
démerder	stronger version of 'débrouiller' for when you are really 'dans le merde'
dépanner	get out of trouble (en panne: out of order)
dépassé	overtaken, out of date
député	member of Assemblée Nationale
déranger	disturb
deuch	2CV
digestif	post-prandial drink
dirigisme	direction from the centre
disponible	available
dormi	slept - past participle of -ir verb
doucement	gently, slowly
draguer	chase women
droit	right
économe	careful with money
église: nf	church (always Catholic - Protestant is 'temple')
embêter	annoy
émission: nf	radio or TV programme
en même temps	at the same time
énarque: nm	graduate of ENA (see Grandes Ecoles)
engagé	(politically) committed
enlever	take off (clothes), kidnap
époux: nm	husband: wife = épouse
étape	stage in journey, stop-over
étranger: nm/adj	stranger, foreigner
évident	obvious
exceptionnel	same as English but more used
exprès	on purpose
extralucide	paranormal
façon de vivre	life-style
faut - as in 'il faut':	it is necessary to; one must..
faute de	lacking in
faute de mieux	having nothing better to offer
ferié (jour)	non-working day, holiday
fermé	closed, both of doors and of (introverted) people
feuille: nf	leaf, document
ficelle nf	literally string, therefore a loaf even thinner than a baguette
fichez-moi le camp!	piss-off!
fléchissez	bend: imperative form of -ir verb (see also 'ralentissez')
fleur: nf	flower
flippers	pin-ball machine
flûte: nf	loaf of bread, next up from baguette
foie nm	liver
folie: nf	madness, craze
formidable	tremendous
fou	mad (e.g. conduire comme un fou)
francophone	French-speaker
fuite: nf	flight (de la campagne);
fuite d'eau	leak
fumeur de gitanes	smoker of revolting black cigarettes
gagner	win
galère: nf	galley; hard work
gauche	left
géler	freeze
genre: nm	kind, type
glisser	slide, slip
grandi	grown bigger - past part of -ir verb (c.f. dormi)
gratuit	free, as in 'Dégustation Gratuite' (which normally turns out to be costly)
grève: nf	strike
grossesse: nf	pregnancy
guerre: nf	war
habituer, (s') à	to get used to
habiter	to live
haut	high, tall
hors (saison)	out of (season); c.f. 'hors du commun'
impeccable	literally 'spotless' - perfect
infiniment	infinitely
invariable	unchanging
jarretière: nf	garter
jeu de mots	pun
largement	widely
légèrement	slightly
légion d'honneur	decoration, civil or military, originally created by Napoleon

lever: nm	getting up in the morning
libre	free, in sense of non-captive
ligue: nf	league
lire	to read
loin	distant; 'pas loin' = 'near'
à louer	to rent; corresponding noun = 'location'
maillot: nm	sweater, swimsuit
maillot jaune	jersey worn by person leading in the *Tour de France*
mal	adv. badly, or noun as in: 'il ne ferait pas de mal à une mouche'
maison d'édition	publishing house
marc: nm	residue of pressed grapes - made into eau-de-vie
marché: nm	market
marre	enough of as in 'j'en ai marre' (I'm fed up with...)
meilleur	better
merveilleux	marvellous
messe: nf	Catholic mass
midi: nm	1. middle of day 2. south of France
midi moins le quart	quarter to twelve - used as a play on words for the part of France that is almost the 'midi'
mignon	sweet, charming
moeurs: nfpl	customs
monter	climb
montant: nm	amount (of cheque)
morceau: nm	bit, part, morsel
mouche: nf	fly
moulin: nm	mill
nègre: nm	literally 'negro'; petit nègre = ungrammatical French
nommer	name, appoint
nord: nm	north; J'ai perdu le nord' 'I've lost my bearings'
nuage: nf	cloud
obligatoire	obligatory
oreiller: nm	pillow
outre	beyond; 'outre-tombe' = 'beyond the grave'
ouvert	open (see fermé)
ouverture nf	opening as: 'heures d'ouverture'
ouvrier: nm	workman
par contre	on the other hand
parler	to speak
parti	left, gone (past part. of -ir verb)
parti: nm	political party
partie: nf	part, duration of a game
partout	everywhere; 'trois partout' = 'three all'
passé	past, out-of-date
patrie: nf	homeland, native country
patrimoine: nm	heritage
péage nm	toll booth
peine: nf	literally 'pain'; trouble, bother. 'à peine' = hardly'
pendu	hanged (p.p. of -re verb)
péniche: nf	barge
peste: nf	plague
pieds noirs	French-Algerian settlers, (from their black plimsolls)
piste: nf	track, ski-slope
plein	full, pregnant (of animals)
plume: nf	pen, feather
poire: nf	pear
poitrine: nf	chest, bust
poubelle: nf	dustbin
pouce: nm	thumb
pouce, (manger sur le)	to eat standing up
poulet: nm	young chicken
pourri	bad, rotten, corrupt
pratiquant	practising, adherent
prélèvement: nm	direct debit
prendre	take
prénom: nm	first name
prévu	foreseen, anticipated
prier	to pray. commonly used as polite form of request: 'prier de ne pas fumer'
prochain	next
profond	deep (la France profonde - rural France)
putain merde!	rude expression of annoyance
quotidien	daily
ralentissez!	slow down!
rechercher	to research, find
reçu	received (past part. of 'recevoir); as noun, a receipt
remercier (de)	thank (for)
rentrée: nf	return (to school)
réseau: nm	network
résidence secondaire: nf	second home
revanche: nf	revenge, return match
rien	nothing
sang: nm	blood
sanglier: nm	wild boar
sauter	jump, explode
sans culottes	Paris mob unable to afford decent trousers

sauvage	wild
savoir	know - facts as opposed to people (connaître)
serrer	grasp, hold tight
service: nm	favour
si	1. if; 2. so, as in 'si riche' ('tellement' is more courant)
siècle: nm	century
sien, le	his/hers
soleil: nm	sun
son et lumière	sound and light spectacular
sondage: nm	opinion poll
sortie: nf	exit
spectacle: nm	show, entertainment
succès fou	triumph
suif: nm	tallow
sympathique:	friendly
tant mieux	so much (tant) the better (mieux)
tant pis	so much the worse, too bad
tellement	see 'si'
tiers: nm	third
tire-bouchon: nm	corkscrew; lit. 'draw-cork'
tirer	draw, pull, fire
tourner	turn
tout à fait	completely
tout, tous	all
toute à l'heure	in a little while, a little while ago (i.e. it can refer to the future or the past)
tranche: nf	slice
tricoteuse: nf	knitter-woman
truc: nm	thingymujig
truffe: nf	truffle
tutoyer	to address someone as 'tu'
vacances: nfpl	holidays
valise: nf	bag, suitcase
vaut	is worth; e.g. il vaut la peine - it's worth the trouble...
vendre	sell (à vendre - for sale)
veuillez	polite form of request - 'Please would you...'
vie: nf	life
vieux con	old has-been, dirty old man
vigneron: nm	wine-grower
vignoble: nm	vineyard
vignette: nf	label (on medicine bottle)
ville: nf	town
volcan: nm	volcano (all French ones are extinct)
voudrais, je	I would like...
vousvoyer	to address someone as 'vous'
vrai, c'est pas:	literally 'it's not true' i.e. 'I can't believe it!'
vulgaire	common, pertaining to the crowd

Answers to Questions:

Page 61:

1. anticonstitutionellement

2. hétérogénéité

Page 105

sot	silly, foolish
sceau: nm	seal, stamp

Page 106:

1. *Silence.*
   Only the French would dare attribute this to silence not being a feminine virtue.

2. *Triomphe*
   The equivalent word in English is 'orange'.

3. Ventriloquists.
   An even better answer is 'Presidents of the Third Republic' - every one of whom had a moustache. For the Fifth Republic the Presidential fashion has moved in favour of big noses.

Et avec ça?

In the introduction to the main part of this book I stated that my intention was to motivate you to find out more for yourself about France. If I have succeeded then you will want to know what to read next. I have long harboured a sneaking suspicion when I read bibliographies listing hundreds of references that they are intended more to emphasise the depth of the author's research than as an aid to further study. The following list is meant to serve the latter purpose. The most important fact about a book is not what it is about but whom it is by. I have therefore started by listing three authors whose writing about France is unreservedly recommended.

Thereafter I have listed books under different subject categories. Most of them, however, cut across such arbitrary divisions.

Ardagh, John

The doyen of all writers about France. His *France Today* (Penguin, 1990) is the standard work for any serious student of France - within the education system or just an amateur. It was my starting point and I am trusting to this effusive tribute to turn aside any litigation on account of plagiarism.

'France Today' is 600-odd pages packed with information and not an illustration in sight. As if to compensate for this, Ardagh has produced two books which, were they not so beautifully written, would be worth buying for the pictures alone. *Cultural Atlas of France* (with Colin Jones, published by Facts on File) is a guide, region by region, to French culture. Using the same structure he has written *Writers'France* (Hamish Hamilton) which is *obligatoire* as corrective reading for the scant justice done to France's literature in this book.

Richard Binns

A kindred spirit both in his love of France and in publishing his own books. Richard threw up his career in computers and management training to concentrate exclusively on writing. His first book, *French Leave,* was published in 1980 and was an immediate best-seller. Since then he has continued with his delightful series of guides to where to stay, eat and visit in France. They are more useful to the English traveller than Michelin and Gault-Millau together and many of us have benefited from his excellent advice. His next book, *French Leave Encore,* will be published in Autumn 1992. He promises that this will be one of the most controversial travel books ever published.
We self-publishers occasionally have problems with would-be readers having difficulty in finding our books. Should you have any such problem with Richard Binns' books you can write to him at Honeywood House, Avon Dassett, Leamington Spa CV33 0AH.

John Harris

John Harris has lived in the Languedoc region for some twenty years. He has written two books based on his experience of living among the French. The first, *Understanding France* (Papermac, third edition, 1991) is packed with relevant up-to-date information about day-to-day France - shopping, the language, *loisirs,* motoring and so on. It is the book if you are contemplating living in France or spending long enough there to want to really *se débrouiller.*
His second book, *An Englishman in the Midi* (BBC Books), is a charmingly self-deprecating account of his every-day life among French people concentrating on his neighbours rather than on himself.

Personal Accounts

In addition to John Harris's books, there are various personal accounts written by people who have lived in France for some time, often journalists. Of these there are three that I recommend:

Fragile Glory (Bodley Head, 1991) is by Richard Bernstein, formerly Paris correspondent of the New York Times. Easy to read and well-informed, it succeeds in conveying the 'feel' of the country.

Portraits of France (Hutchinson, 1991) illuminates French history and culture through a series of portraits which are rooted either in the study of an individual, such as de Gaulle or Jacques Anquetil, or of a place. Its anecdotal approach makes it easy to read.

Hannibal's Footsteps by Bernard Levin recounts how he preceded Ian Botham in walking across the Alps (though without the elephants). As with everything from this writer it is a delight to read full of amusing *aperçus.*

Information

If I have whetted you appetite for facts and statistics you can slake this with a variety of reference books. The start and end point of any reference book about France is Larousse. Those who can read French should simply contact Larousse at 17, rue de Montparnasse, 75298 Paris and get a catalogue of their reference books These extend far beyond the standard *Dictionnaire* and are beautifully illustrated. They also publish *Francoscopie,* a compendium of government statistics and opinion polls which does for France what the government publication Social Trends does for the UK only twice as readably.

For value for money it is hard to beat Quid (again in French). This is a better equivalent of Whittaker's Almanac with over two thousand densely-written pages on all aspects of French (and international) life. The index runs to 30,000 entries. Having personally had problems in locating many 'Zs' I idly looked to see their final entry. It was ZYJ (than which it is difficult to think of a later one) which turned out to be short for Zhongtong Yuanbo Jiachao the oldest banknote in the world of which an example remains, issued in 1260.

If it is business that takes you to France then *France - the Economist Guide* - will give you an authoritative overview of the political, industrial and commercial scene with guides to the top sixteen cities thrown in. To come to terms with the infuriatingly different business customs and avoid insulting the PDG with whom you are close to finalising a deal, you should read the Industrial Society's book, *Mind Your Manners*,.

A book referenced in the A-Z is *Faux Amis and Key Words* by Thody and Evans of Leeds University (published by Athlone Press, 1985). For people who speak passable French it is often the words and expressions that are similar to English ones that trip you up. Thus *passer un examen* means to sit an exam, not pass it *(réussir à)*. The book uses such examples to illustrate not just linguistic traps but to illuminate the complete area of differences between French customs and ours - e.g. in law - which are often concealed beneath similar-looking terminology.

Touring

I have already mentioned Richard Binns' books. Travel guides to France is a major industry in its own right so I shall avoid the obvious. A friend of mine once coined the acronym SOSI standing for Same Old Stuff Index. Thus a highly original book might achieve a SOSI of around .2, a rehash of old information could easily score around .99. I shudder to think of the SOSI of all those 'Guides to the Loire Valley' which abound on book stalls.

In an attempt to reduce the SOSI of this book I shall steer clear of these and mention some that are out of the mainstream.

The first is the *Bluffer's Guide to Paris.* The virtue of this series is that the booklets conceal a sizeable pill of good information inside a coating of humour. If your palate is not all it should be you can benefit from their similar version on wine.

Secondly, for those who read French, you can frequently pick up local guides - such as the *Petit Paume* in Lyon - which are goldmines of local information, as well as being free.

Finally, for those who wish to be reminded quarterly of the beauty of France and kept up to date with current affairs, the magazine 'France' is both extremely readable and wonderfully illustrated. It is available from:

France Magazine
Dormer House
Stow-on-the-Wold
Glos GL54 1BN

Index

Some of my best friends are French is not intended as a work of reference. As explained in 'Guide to Entries', many facts and people appear in unexpected places. The following index shows where you can find them.